Studies in Contemporary Metaphysics

Originally published in 1920, this title wrestles with the critical conflict in modern philosophy of whether philosophers should employ
pure reason in a world of abstracts or, rather, should rely upon experience and rationality to examine the actual world. Hoernlé argues for
the latter and emphasises the importance of metaphysics in the intellectual quest for knowing reality. This title is ideal for students of
philosophy and provides insightful background into the diverging
philosophical views of the early 20th century.

I0592980

Studies in Contemporary Metaphysics

R.F. Alfred Hoernlé

Routledge
Taylor & Francis Group

First published in 1920
by Harcourt, Brace and Howe

This edition first published in 2016 by Routledge
2 Park Square, Milton Park, Abingdon, Oxon, OX14 4RN
and by Routledge
711 Third Avenue, New York, NY 10017

Routledge is an imprint of the Taylor & Francis Group, an informa business

© 1920 Harcourt, Brace and Howe

Publisher's Note
The publisher has gone to great lengths to ensure the quality of this reprint but points out that some imperfections in the original copies may be apparent.

Disclaimer
The publisher has made every effort to trace copyright holders and welcomes correspondence from those they have been unable to contact.

A Library of Congress record exists under LC control number: unk83011851

ISBN 13: 978-1-138-18728-3 (hbk)
ISBN 13: 978-1-315-64326-7 (ebk)
ISBN 13: 978-1-138-18729-0 (pbk)

CONTEMPORARY METAPHYSICS

BY

R. F. ALFRED HOERNLÉ

HARVARD UNIVERSITY

NEW YORK
HARCOURT, BRACE AND HOWE
1920

THE QUINN & BODEN COMPANY
RAHWAY, N. J.

TO THE MEMORY OF

MY FATHER

PREFACE

THE *Studies* contained in this volume may be described as chips from a metaphysician's workshop, or perhaps I should rather say blocks hewn out experimentally in the effort after a systematic synthesis; not unlike the painter's sketches, or the sculptor's rough modellings in clay, which precede the finished work. The day for systems, we are constantly told, is passed, but not, let us hope, the day for philosophers to continue the effort to think systematically. Much scorn has been poured on the philosophical systems which sprang into being so abundantly a hundred years ago, fit heralds of a century which has been well called, in retrospect, " the Century of Hope ". We children of an age of disillusionment need to recapture something of the confidence, the speculative daring, of the great thinkers of the past. On the printed page their " systems " are apt to appear as vain attempts to imprison the rich and varied life of the world in a rigid pattern of conceptual pigeon-holes. But of their spirit, their endeavour after wholeness, their effort to think systematically, we cannot have enough. We certainly need more than we have. At any rate, the following *Studies* are inspired by the conviction—itself not an *a priori* assumption, but à conclusion slowly gathered from the business of philosophising—that experience, taken as a whole, gives us clues which, rightly interpreted, lead to the perception of order in the universe, a graded order of varied appearances. The concepts of the " order of the universe " and—in the Platonic phrase—of the " saving of the appearances " define, between them, the ideal which I have had before me. The saving of appearances calls for a theory which enables us to appreciate each appearance for what it really is, and which exhibits each in its place among other appearances in the universe. I should be false to this conviction if I did not add that it does not seem to me alien to the practical task of meeting the varied incidents of human life with steadfast wisdom.

The student surveying the multifarious tendencies and movements of contemporary thought, may well feel as if he stood at the parting of many ways, presented as alternatives for his choice. On the one side he will find himself told that the philosophic spirit is in essence subjective and sentimental, that it allows moods and desires to colour its view of the world, that it rebels against the inevitable limits of human knowledge. He will be advised to turn his back on the chaos of the actual world and seek comfort amidst the eternal verities of pure reason. He will hear it said that only those subjects are fit for the philosopher's attention, in the study of which he can be ethically neutral. He may meet with the view that it has never yet been proved that the universe is not a grand, and in parts rather cruel, joke and that he who enters into the joke and plays with it, is more likely to get real insight than he who takes the universe seriously and stakes reason and happiness on its orderliness and goodness. On the other hand, he will meet with a continuous tradition in philosophy, supported by the greatest thinkers of the past, and vigorous at the present day, not from mere subservience to their authority, but because fresh generations of philosophers find the insight of their predecessors verified by their own thinking. This tradition stands for the " rationality " of the universe, not merely in the formal sense of every detail in it being subject to the law of sufficient reason, but even more in the profounder sense of its being the home of the values which we commonly call spiritual.

Such, briefly, are the alternatives before the student. His choice cannot be settled by tossing. It cannot, like the choice of Buridan's ass, be unmotived. And though it be temperamental, it will not, therefore, be irrational or arbitrary. For the factors which determine a thinker's choice in fundamental matters such as these are " objective "—drawn from his nature which is conditioned by the universe of which he is a part; drawn from his experience which is a function of the age in which he lives, the education he has received and continues receiving, the incidents and accidents of his checkered existence, all he has done and left undone, all he has felt and thought. It is, once more, the universe which communicates itself to him in these miscellaneous ways. From these, and with these, materials he must gather his philosophic vision. He has no other materials to work with. In them he must find his clues, learning to discriminate the thoughts which are superficial from those which yield the deeper knowledge. Having done this honestly, he must stand by the result. It is truth for him, and he has done his part.

From this confession of my philosophical faith, I turn gratefully to record my countless obligations to others. These obligations are not to be judged merely by the quotations in the text or the references in footnotes. The selection of the former is due often to no more than the caprice of memory, or the chance of recent reading. The latter are given mainly where the argument is polemical, or a particular allegation stood in need of support. I know that I owe more than I can in detail set down to discussions with, and to the books of, many friends and colleagues, at Harvard and elsewhere. Like every teacher I know, too, how much my students have helped me to clearer thought and expression. It is a sincere pleasure to record here my gratitude to all who were, in that I learned from them, my teachers, willing or unwilling, nameable or nameless.

But there are two specific obligations which I cannot forbear to single out. One is to the training which I received at Oxford—a training the method and spirit of which still seem to me beyond praise, in that it combined sound historical foundations with keen attention to every living movement of the present day. From the example and practice of my teachers I learned to read the great thinkers of the past as if they were contemporaries—as indeed they are in that realm of speculation where great thoughts do not age—and to feel how, across centuries and generations, the sense of fellowship in the quest of truth and wisdom may bind men together.

And the other obligation is to Dr. Bernard Bosanquet in whose philosophical life-work I find the most vital, and in the best sense empirical, statement of "idealism" or "speculative philosophy" in modern philosophical literature. So far as I can judge, I owe to him, more than to any other single writer, the essential frame-work of my own philosophical thinking.

It is my hope shortly to continue the present series of *Studies* in a second volume which will be devoted especially to problems bearing on the controversy between idealism and realism. It will also give me an opportunity to expand and defend the positions taken up, or implied, in the present volume on such topics as universals, theory of knowledge, and truth.

It remains to add that the sixth essay originally appeared in the *Philosophical Review*, and that a few passages in the second essay formed part of an article in the *Chronicle*. My thanks are due to the editors for their permission to reprint.   R. F. A. H.

CONTENTS

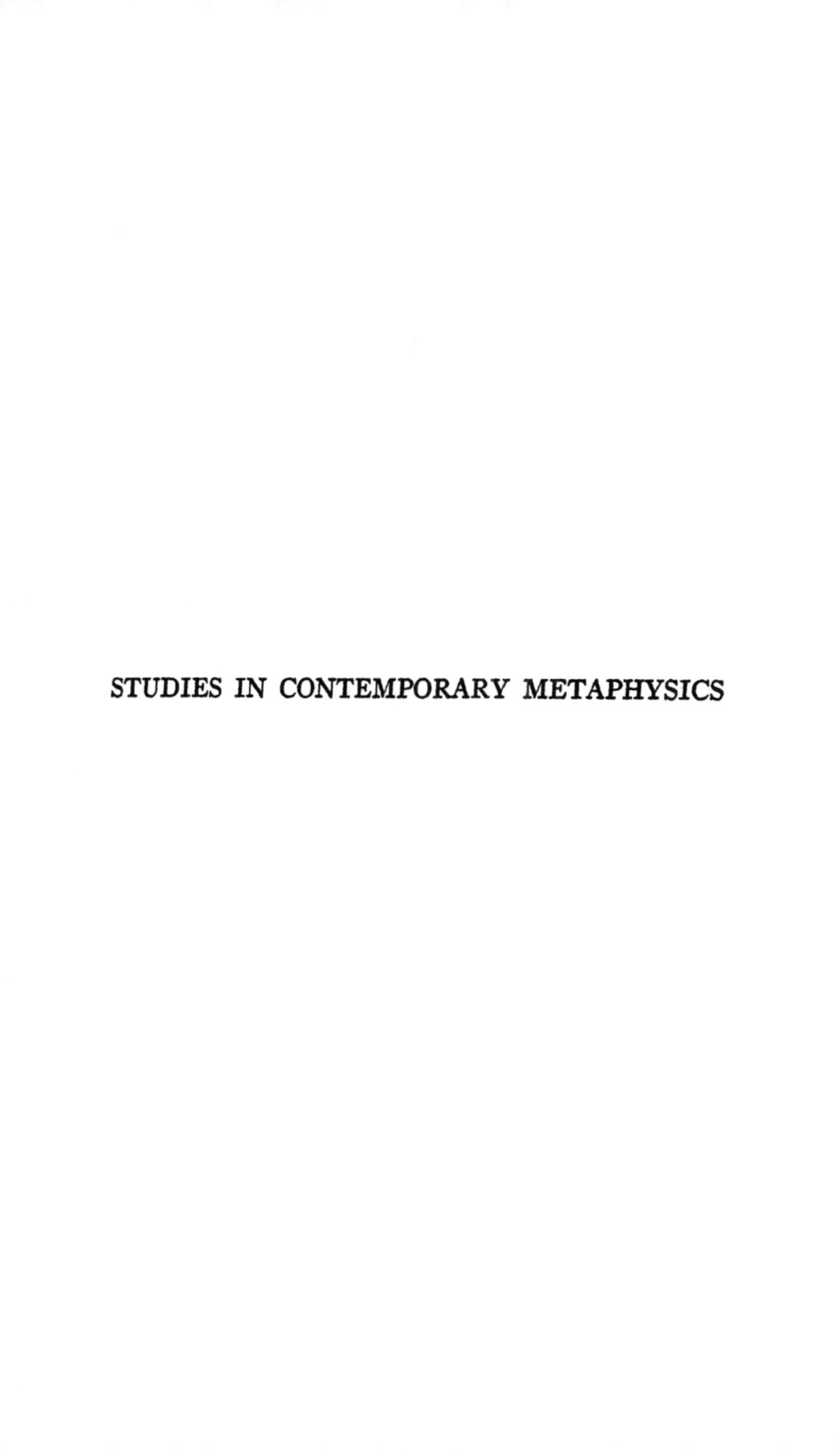

STUDIES IN CONTEMPORARY METAPHYSICS

CHAPTER I

WHAT is Philosophy? Once again this has become a burning question for philosophers. For behind all the current self-criticism of philosophers, behind all the argument about method, subject-matter, function, value; about the alleged lack of progress; about the desirability of greater agreement and the best way of achieving it, there lies the uneasy suspicion that all is not well with philosophy. Philosophy, we are told, especially in its academic form, nay because of its academic form, has become barren; it has lost touch with the vital problems and perplexities of our age.

True, to a kindly eye there are evidences in plenty of vigorous philosophical life. Speculative interest and activity have been of recent years increasingly varied and enterprising. There has been no lack of originality. There has been an abundance of new methods, new insights, new movements, if not new systems. The opening of the century found idealism widely established as the dominant doctrine. Since then the trumpets of pragmatism have blared for the fall of the walls of the idealistic Jericho, and realisms of all sorts, " new " or " critical ", have sought to shake its foundations by many novel forms of intellectual battering-rams. But the defenders have rallied and are rallying, and between the vigorous resistance of old, and the heralding of new, idealisms, the battle is far from having been won by the assailants. In some detachment from the main struggle, vitalism in several forms, from Driesch to Bergson, has attempted philosophical constructions and

3

reconstructions. And there are minor movements and currents too numerous to mention.

To a student content to enter heart and soul into this conflict of theories, the present situation may well seem full of interest and promise. And yet the very variety and ingeniousness of these modern philosophies may beget a disheartening doubt. Is anything, after all, being achieved by all this brilliant thinking and vigorous arguing? Does novelty guarantee progress or truth? Does any question get settled? Is there any gain in insight and wisdom? Is the whole enterprise of philosophy at bottom really worth while?

The mood from which such questions spring is especially prevalent at the present day. Nor is it hard to see why this should be so, why the familiar criticisms and self-criticisms of philosophy should come home to its students just now with peculiar poignancy, and be the source of a singular ferment and unrest. The broad contact of philosophy with all sides of human life and experience has always exposed it to certain criticisms, but these have received fresh point and force alike from the tragic sufferings which humanity has undergone in the recent war and from the rapid changes in the economic, social, and political order which we are now witnessing. Philosophy is being weighed by practical men and by social reformers, by scientists and by theologians. Why is the verdict so frequently, " Found Wanting "?

In the average man's life the pressure of practical needs is constant. In manual labour and in business, at work or at play, there are always things to be done, and done immediately. There is at best little leisure for sustained thought on " first and last things," and even less inclination, for such thinking is at first unsettling, always arduous, and not always crowned by the attainment of certainty. So far as the plain man has a working faith to live by, he has not got it from philosophy. So far as he feels the need of one, it is not through philosophy that he will seek it. For that way is long and difficult, and he wants a short-cut to certainty. Moreover, many philosophical problems do not seem to bear on his troubles and perplexities, his hopes and fears, at all. Hence he is impatient of such speculations, and has little tolerance for enquiries which promise no solution for his pressing difficulties; which cannot be translated forthwith into a plan of action; which have no direct bearing on his comfort, prosperity, happiness. Indeed, inasmuch as philosophy requires leisure, it may seem to him even an improper luxury, a form of pretentious but unproductive idleness.

In an even more formidable form this accusation of uselessness has recently been levelled against much of current philosophy by philosophers and others whose first interest is in social and educational reform. Philosophy, these critics complain, has either lost contact with the urgent problems of present-day society, or else maintains this contact in an unfruitful way. " There is no force so explosive as the force of ideas "—but present-day philosophers have ceased to produce ideas that move the world as ferments of reform. In the past, philosophical theories have more than once shaken the social order to its foundations: to-day the philosopher's tendency is to look upon social phenomena simply as facts to be observed and understood. Divorcing theory from practice, he becomes a mere recording spectator even of social ills, of economic injustice, political tyranny, educational stupidity. His interest even in movements towards reform and revolution, and in the ideals by which these, and the resistance to these, are inspired, is restricted to that of the aloof, dispassionate onlooker. Yet is he not a citizen as well as a philosopher, and should he not put his philosophy in the service of his citizenship? Does not a completer conception of his function demand of him that he be both observer and leader? Especially to-day, when the war has thrown the old order into the melting-pot; when the traditional relationships between classes and nations, and the beliefs by which these relationships were sustained and approved, are rapidly being dissolved; when vast changes are in process the drift of which no man can foresee and none claim to be able to guide assuredly to a wise and happy issue—is it not pre-eminently a time for taking thought, and devoting trained intelligence to the great task of making this a better world for men and women to live in? If the " lover of wisdom " have any wisdom, here surely is his opportunity. To refuse this service to the common weal would be for him the great refusal, the great betrayal. In this spirit many hard things have recently been said about " otiose speculation " and " parasitic professors," about the sheltered irresponsibility of the academic scholar, who either ignores these problems, or else is tempted to defend the established order of which he is one of the beneficiaries, or at best propounds theories which he never submits to the searching test of practical application. And apart from the special need for thought on social and political reform, these critics lay down the principle that the only kind of thinking which is worth while is the thinking which is instrumental to action, and that the only way of determining the truth of a theory is to experiment with it by putting it into practice.

When we turn to the contact of philosophy with science, we pass into a calmer air. Not philosophy's bearing on conduct, but its methods and achievements as pure theory are now the subject of challenge. In part this challenge is still inspired by the old suspicion against " metaphysics "

which we have inherited from Comte's positivism in France
and from the reaction against post-Kantian idealism in Germany. The philosopher is still supposed to want to settle,
in a high-handed *a priori* way, empirical problems which
science unravels by patient observation and ingenious experimentation. Or else he is regarded as indulging in fanciful guesses concerning the " unknowable " reality which lies
behind phenomena—guesses which must remain forever
unverifiable seeing that their object is beyond the reach of
experience. Where these criticisms have gone out of
fashion, they have frequently been replaced by a more
formidable, because more plausible, challenge based on the
proverbial lack of agreement among philosophers. They
are invited to note how complete, by comparison, is the con-
sensus of scientific experts; how steady and cumulative the
progress of scientific theory. On the one side a perpetual
clash of individual opinions and inconclusive arguments, on
the other a solid accumulation of well-observed facts and
experimentally verified theories by the coöperative researches of successive generations—this is how the comparison is apt to appear to a scientist. Nay, he may push
his challenge deeper still. Is philosophy really entitled to
rank above science in the system of knowledge? Does it
deserve the name of " knowledge " in the scientific sense
at all? Is it not rather to be classed with faith and belief,
or again with poetry and imagination? How can its multifarious guesses be valued above the certainties of science?
This, clearly, is to call in question the traditional claim of
philosophy to offer a profounder and more comprehensive
insight into the nature of the universe than any other mode
of thought. No other indictment has found so ready an
echo in the ranks of philosophers as this. Not for the first
time at the present day is the comparison with science being
used by philosophers themselves to point a moral for philos-

ophy and press home a demand for a fresh start by the application of " scientific method."

Lastly, there is the contact of philosophy with religion, of which philosophy appears, now as the rival, now as the critic, now as the sympathetic interpreter and defender. In each rôle, it lays itself open to challenge. It is being criticised either as too religious or as not religious enough. To those who care, above all, for the stability of religious faith, and are accustomed to rest that stability upon authority, most modern philosophy seems little better than the presumptuous emancipation of the individual's reason from the assured truth which church and revelation provide. To others—and they are many—who turn to philosophy in the hope of finding there a ready means of dispelling religious doubts and rebuilding a shattered faith, it seems but too often to bring nothing but deeper doubt and greater perplexity of spirit. Yet when a philosopher defends, not perhaps the details of dogma, but at least the legitimacy of religious faith, or when he characterises reality as God, there are always critics ready to accuse him of disingenuousness, or, at least, of self-deception; of cloaking unorthodox doctrine in orthodox-sounding language; and delaying the inevitable death of a creed outworn. Yet, for all this, no other problem stirs the philosophical thought of the age so profoundly as this problem of religion. For religious need and religious experience are facts too universal to be ignored, and whether he adjust his religion to his theory of the universe, or his theory of the universe to his religion, no philosopher who deals with fundamentals, or tries to get beyond piecemeal problems to an understanding of the whole, can avoid dealing with religion as one of the central experiences.

These criticisms, grave at all times, have recently cut with a sharper edge wherever philosophers have found themselves citizens of countries at war. At a time when all were eager to put their best at the service of their nation, what had they to offer? Other workers in theoretical fields did not lack opportunity to apply their knowledge. There was an obvious call and use for the trained skill and special information of almost every kind of scientist. Chemist and physicist, engineer and geologist, doctor and psychologist—every one had specific contributions to make to the effort of a nation at war. Philosophers, no doubt, on both sides did something to maintain their nations' *morale*, expounding their ideals, exhibiting the falsity of the enemy's philosophies. But, in the main, a philosopher capable of bearing arms, seemed able to serve only with his body, not with his mind. Whatever the value of philosophy in days of peace, much of it was inapplicable in the emergencies of war. The nations at war could make little, if any, use of their philosophers except as propagandists, and propaganda too often proved demoralising to philosophy.

This experience, added to the instability of the existing order, the uncertainty of the future, the perplexing practical problems which beset mankind on every side, has given a sting to that call for self-criticism to which philosophers at no time have been wholly deaf.

Many influences are thus converging upon putting philosophers out of humour with philosophy. What can a philosopher who, in this mood, faces the question of the nature and value of philosophy do to reassure himself? There is, it would seem, only one way. He must recall to himself, he must try to communicate to others, what philosophy is like as an experience dominating his life, as an absorbing occupation, as a concentration in intense activity of his whole being. What is wanted is not some definition of philosophy, not some catalogue of problems, or drawing of boundary-lines around its subject-matter, not comparisons with science, religion, poetry. These touch the fringes, not the heart of the matter. Instead of asking, What is philosophy? we should ask, What is it to philosophise? Call philosophy an enterprise, an experience, an attitude, as you will:—the spirit of philosophy as it is experienced by the thinkers engaged in philosophising is what we have to understand. To render this spirit, we must not set down a philosophical system, or any special doctrines, which have been gained as the results of philosophising. Let systems and results be as different as they may: there is an acknowledged kinship of philosophers in the spirit of their enterprise. This spirit is open to recognition in the writings of philosophers: it forms the common ground in all philosophical discussions. It introduces the individual thinker into a fellowship, a company, a communion of men engaged in the same endeavour though they may disagree about its very scope and method. "Think for yourself"—"Go straight to the facts." These are, indeed, the elementary rules for learning to stand intellectually on one's own feet and not to philosophise with second-hand material. But they would be dangerous fallacies if they were interpreted to mean that the individual has nothing to learn from others, or that his experiences and thoughts do not need to be checked by comparison with those of others. Thinking is always social; its typical form is that of debate, and even the single thinker in his solitary meditations is debating with himself. This is why philosophers so largely argue at and for each other, and why the theories of the great thinkers of the past retain their living interest for later generations. Eschewing *a priori* assumptions about what philosophy ought to be, can we not reflect on what the spirit of philosophising as a spontaneous activity in ourselves and others actually is?

That spirit is the spirit of wholeness. To philosophise is to seek an attitude towards the universe as a whole, or, in so far as the search at all succeeds, to have such an attitude. What does this mean? It cannot mean obviously, that the whole of the universe in any quantitative sense is present to the thinker. Quantitatively, no finite mind can exhaust the universe. No accumulation of experiences would bring us appreciably nearer exhausting the inexhaustible. There is always the future of which no man knows what it may bring. There is always the past of which in the main but a few sketchy, shadowy outlines are revealed even to our most patient and detailed research. There is, in short, the whole immensity of space and time to bring home to the individual thinker the limitations of his range, to make him realise that what he effectively grasps of the universe by detailed exploration is but a fragment, a sample, a cross-section. Wholeness, thus, is not to be understood quantitatively, but qualitatively. It consists, at the very least, in that quality of *organisation* in virtue of which alone we can say that we experience a " universe " or live in a " world." Order, correlation of differences, system, are aspects of it, or forms of it. Without it, belief and conduct, our judgments and our actions, would be equally chaotic, contradictory, mutually destructive. In some degree it is characteristic of the life of every mind. In a greater degree it belongs to the coöperative achievements, like science, or society, in which many minds share. The explicit effort to achieve the maximum possible of such wholeness is philosophising. It is, thus, a continuation, at the level of reflective thought, of a principle the working of which can be traced at every level of experience, in feeling and perceiving, in reasoning and in willing. It rests on the fundamental fact which everyone can verify for himself, that experiences are not isolated and disconnected but expand and modify each other.   Each illuminates others, gives meaning to them, derives meaning from them.

This fact is so familiar and so universal that, for this very reason, its presence tends to pass unnoticed, its importance to remain unappreciated. It is hard to discriminate it and keep attention focused upon it just because of the infinite variety of its illustrations which every moment of conscious life affords.   Whenever we say that one fact throws light on others, that one thing helps us to understand, or do, some other thing better, this principle of organisation is operative.   The development of knowledge, the growth of character are equally instances of it.   When repeated observations of the same object, revealing its different qualities and modes of behaviour under different conditions, yield comprehensive and systematic knowledge of it; when countless diverse facts suggest and verify a theory which explains them; when practice brings skill in the execution of a movement; when habit brings economy of time and thought; when interests and purposes which might conflict, are adjusted to each other on a scale of relative urgency and value, with much discipline of desires and feelings in the process, and careful control of conduct— the quality of wholeness is displayed.   Yet another way of pointing it out is to remind ourselves that experiences do not simply come and go: they live on, they endure, they are retained, mostly not as distinct memories, but fused into what certain psychologists used to call an " apperceptive system ", which is but the technical name for the power which a mind acquires to assimilate fresh experiences, to interpret their meaning, respond with appropriate action, and to learn and grow in this very process.   Indeed, it may fairly be said that the principle of wholeness is most obviously manifest in all learning by experience.   But to say that there is learning by, and from, experience is to say that it contains a lesson to be discovered and elicited; that experience has something to teach or to reveal. To philosophise is nothing but the sustained attempt to elicit this lesson, to focus and concentrate experience systematically—what else but this is reflection and speculation?—and to state its message and its meaning in the form of a coherent theory.

If we want a provisional formula for the topic of this lesson, any one of the many current descriptions of the object of the philosopher's quest will do as well as any other. We can put it, if we please, as the universe and man's place in it; as man, the world, and God; as nature, self, and the reality which includes them both; as the order of appearances in the universe. But if such formulae are to have any value as conveying the spirit of philosophy, they must be interpreted as pointing us, by the mention of certain objects, to the central and dominant types of experience in which these objects reveal themselves, come to be known, and to determine behaviour. And, even so, a catalogue of objects and experiences names rather the data or materials for philosophising, than the effort at synthesis, or synopsis, which acknowledges at bottom but one " object " —call it, as we will, reality, God, the absolute, the universe, the whole.

The spirit of philosophy, then, as exhibited in philosophising, is the highest form of the principle of wholeness which is present throughout the life of mind wherever something is being learnt in, and from, experience. Philosophy thus is continuous with the rest of experience, as, indeed, it must be, if it is the effort to grasp reflectively its quintessence. At the same time, it has its specific character and is distinguished from other forms of experience in that it is the explicit, self-conscious, and therefore completest, form of the operation of the principle of wholeness. For it is at least the aim of philosophical theory to satisfy that principle most fully, alike in comprehensiveness and in systematisation.

The data and materials for philosophical reflection, again, are not the crude and chaotic experiences of immature minds, but the already highly organised systems of experience in which mature minds participate through their feelings, thoughts, and actions. We must have art, science, religion, social and political life, and all these in various degrees and forms, before a situation can arise in which the need for philosophising in the proper sense is felt; before the peculiar problems present themselves whicn supply the persistent occasion and stimulus for philosophising. This situation, these problems, arise from the contradictions and conflicts between these several types of experience, or within each of them, which threaten to defeat the demand for wholeness, consistency, order. The effort of philosophical reflection is then directed in part upon eliciting the essence, or real nature, of each type of experience, by grading the examples of it so as to study those which exhibit the nature of each at its best, most fully, most characteristically. This is what is meant when it is said that philosophy is not content with first appearances but seeks the ultimately real; that it does not stay at the surface, but penetrates to the deeper meaning. Behind these formulae lies the simple fact, once more easily verifiable for the looking, that the examples, instances, cases, of a quality, nature, law (in short of a universal) commonly can be graded according as they exhibit that universal character more or less adequately, and that the standard of interpretation must be taken from the examples which show the character at its best. More particularly, anything which, like mind, is in process of evolution, requires this analysis from the top downwards. But, further, the task of philosophy is to point out by analysis of the bearing upon each other of conflicting types of experience, how their conflict is actually overcome, and how, therefore, in principle it admits of solution. Here is the place to acknowledge that the spirit of wholeness meets, apparently, with its most formidable defeats through its very triumphs. Its successes in organising orders of experience produce the acutest contradictions and antinomies. Life threatens to remain chaotic in a chaotic world so long as the very systems of order which supply its framework, impose incompatible judgments and actions upon us. A unified life is possible only in a unified world; in a cosmos, not in a chaos. To philosophise is, therefore, to seek to translate the implicit conviction of order into explicit insight, to show that the lesson of experience, taken comprehensively in range but with the best of each type as the clue to interpretation, yields and sustains this insight. Perhaps the most fundamental antinomy, we might even say predicament, which runs through modern civilisation and carries conflict and perplexity into the thought and conduct of modern men, is that between science and religion, between facts and values, between the actual and the ideal, between nature and spirit. A closely allied predicament arises from the existence of evil and the divergent attitudes towards it of morality and religion. If the moral life is essentially a fight against evil, an effort to perfect an imperfect world, how is it compatible with religion, *i.e.*, with the worship due only to that which is perfect? Yet another predicament is always present, and always liable to become acute, in the relations of the individual to the community of which he is a member, when, *e.g.*, the individual's conscience condemns the public action which is done in his name and in which he may be called upon to take an active part. All such situations, sometimes for the sake of unified conduct, always for the sake of unified theory, operate as stimuli for discovering by reflection a more comprehensive point of view, in which the divergent ways of thinking and acting may be brought together and adjusted so that unity, consistency, wholeness are recovered, or, rather, are brought to light.

In this sense, then, to repeat it once more, to philosophise is to seek to apprehend the universe as a whole, and to employ all the resources of experience in this task, taking each type of experience at its best, when its lesson is clearest, and learning most from those experiences which in range and organisation emancipate us most from superficial first impressions and lead us deepest into the heart of reality. Finality in this enterprise no philosopher has a right to expect, for fresh developments in experience, new scientific theories, new religious movements, profound social and political changes, will continue to present the familiar antinomies in ever fresh forms. The predicaments to which philosophising is the response, renew themselves in each generation, and the effort to deal with them needs a corresponding renewal. But if there is no finality in the sense of a termination, there is a stability which comes from the possession of an insight which as much enables the philosopher to interpret fresh experiences aright, as it is itself confirmed and sustained by these experiences.

This account of the spirit of philosophy may provoke the contention that wholeness is predicable, not of the universe as a fact, but only of the philosopher's point of view as an aspiration; that it means wholeness of attitude rather than attitude towards a whole; that it is subjective and psychological, not objective and metaphysical; an intellectual demand or ideal, not an actual, or at least not a verifiable, character of the nature of things. The universe, it may be urged, cannot be apprehended by us as a whole, for, not knowing all of it, how can we know that it is a " whole " at all? We have no right to give it that name; at most we may speak of it only *as if* it were a whole. As it comes to us in experience, it is sufficiently chaotic to stamp the suggestion of its all-pervading orderliness as, at best, an hypothesis—a " regulative ideal," in Kant's language—for thought and conduct, not an objective truth. This contention may be variously developed. So far as wholeness is a fact, it consists, it may be said, in the effective organisation by a mind of its experiences so as to achieve and acquire a stable, consistent disposition of thought and action towards nature, fellowmen, and God (if there is a God). To reflect this subjective wholeness upon the universe is illusion and make-believe, conscious or unconscious. It is arbitrary and artificial. It succeeds, so far as it does succeed, by selecting exclusively those features of the universe which lend themselves to being ordered, and shutting one's eyes to the abundance of negative evidence. Bold pragmatists may even glory in this forcible imposition of order on a disorderly world. The world is, or can be made to become, what we would have it be. If we but consistently will to believe in its orderliness, then orderly it is. " Faith in a fact helps create that fact ". Others regard the belief in objective order as an escape from intolerable actualities into the purer world of imagination. Philosophy, like art, is to them an escape from the real. The dreams of metaphysicians offer a vicarious satisfaction for wishes which the actual world cruelly represses and frustrates.

Against this view, in all its variations, it must be urged that it involves an ultimate dualism, a discord in the universe, a discord in our lives. Actual chaos confronts imaginary order. And whether we regard the universe as plastic or as hostile to human desires and ideals, whether we deal with it in robust pragmatic aggressiveness, or in self-pity console ourselves with metaphysical fancies, in either case a dualism remains. No unity of mental attitude which is not supported by the facts, which is not rooted in the nature of things, will do. Unless the universe is a whole, it is meaningless to talk of seeking an attitude towards it as a whole. The "point of view of the whole" is not an idle phrase. It means that the conviction of the wholeness of the universe is a lesson of experience, is taught us by the logic of the facts. It claims that experiences, drawn together by reflection, focused so as to interpret each other and thus reveal their common and total meaning, supply the evidence which justifies the conviction of unity and order. Successful organisation of experiences means that the order inherent in them is discovered and revealed. The universe is the common "object", or point of reference, of all our experiences. It and its nature are revealed in all of them. But the *fullest* revelation of it, its *real* nature, its character as a *whole,* is displayed only in so far as its partial revelations are brought together so as to supplement, correct, interpret each other. The thinking and theorising which yields such a revelation, or insight, is neither a running away from reality, nor a "making of reality" in the image of human wishes. It is a seeking of reality by eliciting from experience as a whole its revelation of reality as a whole. It requires an openness of mind which, whilst rejecting no evidence, relies with due discrimination on the most significant and illuminating experiences, rarer though they may be than the surface moods and judgments of everyday life. Above all, it will eschew one-sidedness, and be on its guard against the danger of having its intellectual balance weighed down, contrary to the standards of proportionateness, by some fragmentary aspects of life, however intense and impressive. Philosophising is the pursuit of a will-o'-the-wisp, unless the philosopher can rely on the principle that there is nothing in the whole range of experience which does not, in its own degree and measure, help to reveal the nature of the universe.

The universe, to put it succinctly, is always with us, in us, around us. Every thrill of experience attests its presence; compels—in the language of highly reflective theory—acceptance of the judgment that something exists. What exists? What is this something? To these questions, experience in all its forms supplies the answer, or, at least, the materials for an answer. Philosophical thinking is the endeavour to elicit from these materials a revelation of the whole nature of the universe, which shall be as coherent and complete as we can obtain.

In the light of this analysis of what it is to philosophise, we can understand why now, as in the past, "philosophy" has been used in many different senses, and why, nonetheless, these different senses, as every student of the history of philosophy knows, are all connected, somewhat like variations on a single theme, or like different solutions of a single problem. If the tree of philosophy has many divergent branches, yet is there a single trunk from which they all spring. All sorts of men have set out to be "lovers of wisdom", and the manner of their loving has been no less varied than the things which they have loved as "wisdom." There is room in the enterprise of philosophising for all kinds of temperaments and all kinds of experiences, and each individual thinker draws upon the culture and science, the economic, political, religious substance of contemporary life. Proverbially it takes all sorts to make a world: certainly the world takes all sorts to make philosophers. Or to put the same thing in the mathematical language now fashionable: the function of philosophising is everywhere the same, but there are many values for its variables. Our " wisdom " may be social service, or it may be individual development. It may beckon to us as the refined pleasure of the Epicurean, or as the stern discipline of the Stoic. To some it lies in the faith, indistinguishable for them from knowledge, that the world is perfect. To others it lies in labouring hopefully for its perfecting. Yet others find their wisdom in facing unflinchingly the fact that it is neither perfect nor perfectible, but demands, even so, that men be loyal to ideals doomed never to be realised.

Thus not only does the emphasis fall differently among lovers of wisdom, but some exclude what others include. Some achieve unity, or wholeness, at a greater cost and sacrifice than others. Some are more balanced and well-rounded natures, others are more fragmentary and one-sided, perhaps even divided against themselves, torn by some inner conflict—of mysticism, it may be, and science; of intellect and emotion or desire. Yet all are fellow-travellers in the same spiritual pilgrimage, bent upon the same goal.

What is this goal?

Above we have already characterised it, in general terms, as the spirit of wholeness. Here we may express it, from a somewhat different angle, by saying that every philosopher, whatever his resources of insight and character, wants to discover, and to live, the life worth living. Every lover of wisdom wants to learn what wisdom is and to make it the actual quality of his living. His interest is both theoretical and practical. He is both spectator and agent. Indeed, it is only for exposition's sake that we can thus verbally contrast these two sides. In fact, knowing and doing are not thus separable in the pursuit of philosophy. For thinking, too, is a way of doing, of occupying oneself, of spending one's life, and the ways of doing which are not theoretical or contemplative, are the better for catching something of the spirit of selflessness which occupation with eternal truths brings into the fret and stress of practical life. *Vice versa,* only he who has lived deeply and broadly, has at his disposal rich and varied resources for meditation. There is indeed a theory according to which the end of all theory is action, and " propositions of practice " the truths most worth discovering. There is also an opposite theory according to which the thing most worth doing is to theorise. This is but another instance of those differences of emphasis in the pursuit of wisdom which are inevitable so long as men are not, in their spiritual make-up, mere repetitions of the same pattern, and so long as each age, each historical type of civilisation, has its own distinctive spiritual needs.

The identification of the problem of wisdom with the problem of the life worth living throws light on the connection between philosophy and value. A philosopher, it is agreed, is above all else a " thinker." Thinking is his business in life. What kind of thinking, then, is most worth while? What kind of employment of his intellect is most valuable? The answer can hardly be given except in terms of the objects, occupation with which is the best use a thinker can make of his capacity for thinking. Instead of " objects ", we might equally say " problems ", or even " truths." The important thing to recognise is that, if there is a capacity for thinking, there is also a specific need for it—a need not merely practical, but contemplative or creative. And if such thinking has value, it is because it is concerned, fundamentally, with value. To discern values and to realise them: to appreciate them where they do exist and to bring them into existence where they do not—this certainly is demanded of the lover of wisdom. To appreciate and recognise and forward what there is of value in the world; to see, perchance, in the end that nothing is wholly devoid of value—this is the employment of thought which is itself most valuable and which makes the thinker's life itself worth while. It is not difficult to see that in thus describing the philosopher's programme and quest, we are but carrying a step further what we said above about wholeness, order, organisation. For not only is order itself a type of value, but the reconciliation of " fact " and " value " is the gravest problem which confronts the seeker after wholeness. Here, again, we meet with differences of emphasis and inclusiveness. Are all things actual also invested with value? Does only desire confer value on things? Are values concretely embodied only in things made to satisfy desire? Questions such as these stand at the threshold of every inquiry into value, but once we step across the threshold, there is no stopping-place short of the problems of evil and of the relation of morality to religion. Thus here, once more, thinking is true to its character of seeking always the whole and being genuinely satisfied with nothing short of the whole. Indeed, ever since Plato set up the " Form of the Good " as the supreme principle of being and knowing, an unbroken line of philosophers has recorded this conviction, that the deepest need of our intellectual nature is for a reconciliation of fact and value, for a reasoned insight into their unity. And we may add that not to achieve such a unity, not at least to believe it possible, is to break with every great religion. But the roads to freedom by which, with Spinoza and the mystics, we mean here precisely this inward unity and reconciliation, are many, and we have as little right to lay down one rigid pattern of freedom as we have a right to lay down a pattern of wisdom. It is enough to acknowledge the spiritual kinship in diverse doctrines and lives.

Yet another way of expressing this love of wisdom which marks the philosopher is to say that he strives for stability in thought and feeling and action. On its emotional side, we all know what is meant by this " stability ":—the peace of mind which comes with understanding even if in the end it surpasses understanding; the harmony within oneself; the confidence, not so much in oneself, or in human power to master the world, or in the world as being, by happy chance, kind to men, but in the intrinsic value of the world and in one's own life as sharing in, and helping to sustain, that value. But this stability for a thinker must be intellectual as well—*scientia intuitiva* no less than *amor intellectualis*. Wonder, curiosity, perplexity, contradiction, conflict of theories, conflict of feelings and desires, lack of understanding, lack of self-knowledge and self-mastery—in all these ways come discord and instability. The goal of the philosopher is in its reflective form a theory, a *Weltanschauung;* in its practical form an habitual attitude or disposition of response; a power to meet and master whatever comes—elastic, adaptable, resourceful, yet steadfast, intrepid, unshaken; a self-adjusting equilibrium of insight into the true values of things, which in the greatest becomes the very spirit of their living.

Is the pursuit of philosophy in this sense worth while?

Those who have devoted themselves to it have found it so; and they alone are in a position to judge.

CHAPTER II

THE IDOL OF SCIENTIFIC METHOD IN PHILOSOPHY

A PHILOSOPHER, we said, is a thinker, but he is also, and for this very reason, a seer. He has his distinctive view or vision of the world, and it is only by hard thinking that he has gained and now possesses it. Insight and intuition on the one hand, thought and reason (which cover here everything from analysis and inference to argument and dialectics), on the other, are commonly regarded as the two poles of the philosophical attitude. Not infrequently they are opposed to each other even by philosophers. It is then said that there are two ways of knowing: intuition and intellect, or immediate experience and reflection, or knowledge by acquaintance and knowledge by description. Frequently one of these ways is deprecated for the glorification of the other. More particularly the nature, function, and value of thinking have become topics of burning discussion among present-day philosophers, and the debate has spread to such allied problems as whether, and how, philosophical theories can be proved or demonstrated; whether such theories are to be regarded as tentative guess-work or as deeper knowledge; and, in short, what is the proper method of philosophy.

Fundamentally, we shall surely agree, William James was right, when he spoke of philosophies as " just so many visions, modes of feeling the whole push, and seeing the whole drift of life "; [1] right, too, when he went on to say that these visions are " forced on one by one's total character and experience, and on the whole *preferred* . . . as

[1] *A Pluralistic Universe*, p. 20.

one's best working attitude ".[1]   Forced and preferred—it
seems a startling contradiction. It is as if one were compelled to choose in one way and in no other. Yet is not
this precisely the way in which philosophical convictions
come to be formed? The varied aspects of the universe
press upon the individual thinker. Alternative syntheses
suggest themselves to him, many of them backed by the
authority of a great name, but the one which, in the end,
he adopts is the one which he cannot help adopting. It is
the one which he is obliged to adopt if he is to be true to
himself, and this means true to the total revelation of the
universe to him through his experience. Thus he comes by
his vision, his world-view, his *Weltanschauung*. " A man's
vision is the great fact about him "[2]—yes, and the vision
includes the reasons which James says we do not care about.
We cannot share the vision, unless we share, or supply ourselves, the reasoning which yields the vision.

It is no mere accident that the language in which we
describe thinking is full of metaphors taken from sight, eye,
and light. A theory is a way of looking at things. Good
thinking must be clear and lucid. Truth must be perceived.
A conclusion must be seen to be implied in the premises.
Experiences illuminate each other. Insight, intuition, the
vivid appreciation or realisation of all that a given experience means and conveys—what would philosophising be
without these? They are its end, even more than its beginning. The most valuable insights, as a rule, are the result
of philosophising, rather than its starting-point, though
sometimes the insight into some central problem becomes
the nucleus around which a whole system crystallises.
Argument is but a method of getting fresh insights, a gathering of materials from which the vision must spring, and a
method of communicating and sharing one's vision, an at-

[1] *A Pluralistic Universe*, p. 21.
[2] *A Pluralistic Universe*, p. 20.

tempt to direct another mind to seeing the world in the same way. And, again, it is through argument, through reasoning with oneself or with others, that one's insights get tested, connected, stabilised. Thus the intuitional character is present everywhere, though it is in no way sacrosanct or removed beyond the reach of criticism. The eliciting of a fuller insight out of partial ones is precisely the chief business of systematic philosophising.

This is, of course, the point where individual differences come into play, where diversities in dominant mood, in temperament, in character, in the experiences which are the thinker's materials, lead to disagreement, to failure to see eye to eye. Yet failure to agree is not necessarily failure to understand. Most commonly when philosophers disagree, it is because each claims that what the other insists upon is included in his own view, but supplemented, corrected, presented in a truer form. In any case, the paradoxical fact remains that, in order to argue effectively against another, one must put oneself at his point of view. In this way the philosopher's intellectual world is enriched by the presence in it, and the pressure upon it, of the very visions which he may vigorously challenge and combat. And, apart from that, he would be a poor philosopher in whom the failure to share another's vision did not keep alive a humble conviction of the likelihood of defects in his own, of some poverty in it of range, some lack of penetration. Grant that philosophies are as full of an intensely personal atmosphere as poems, and that their sharp differences spring from this fact, still it would be a loss in the main to make philosophising impersonal, and to demand uniformity for the sake of agreement. It would seem rather that the universe has a use, so to speak, for these very differences, through which ever fresh nuances of experience are expressed and tried out. " Philosophies are intimate parts of the universe.

They express something of its own thought of itself. A philosophy may indeed be a most momentous reaction of the universe upon itself." [1] Press this, and the existence of differences acquires positive significance, is transformed from a defect into a merit. Moreover, with all their marked individuality, philosophies fall into " schools ", exhibit common tendencies, are affiliated by descent in the sense of influence of earlier on later thinkers. We tend to underestimate, in the midst of our polemics, the extent of our common ground. Indeed, without a common ground, how could we relevantly disagree? And if it is a pleasure to hit on a theory all one's own which no one else has ever thought of, it is also a pleasure, a very pure one, and not rare, to find one's independent thinking confirmed by the discovery that other thinkers, contemporaries or predecessors, had explored the same problem with the same result. Truth gains, though vanity may suffer.

And, lastly, the insistence on the quality of insight or vision in philosophising may serve to remind us that philosophical argument of the best sort is *material*, not formal. It seeks to use the very stuff and substance of actual experience as its datum. " The best of logic " and " the best of life " are its watchwords. [2] These two must go together in philosophising, for the quality of its logic is to be judged, not merely by the technical correctness of its inferences, but also and even more by the quality of its premises. There is an analogous situation in legal thinking which may illustrate the point. It is a familiar fact to lawyers that technical justice, in the sense of logically correct application of a law to a case, may be in effect actual injustice of a grievous kind. Hence the appearance of equity as a

---

[1] *A Pluralistic Universe*, p. 317. Thus wrote the same James who never tired of dwelling on the temperamental idiosyncrasies of philosophers and philosophies.
[2] B. Bosanquet, *The Principle of Individuality and Value, passim.*

higher, so to speak a juster, justice; hence the revolt among recent writers on the science of legal method against mere " logic "; hence the demand for a tempering of logic by considerations of social utility, humanity, tact.[1] So in philosophy: the use of experiences defective in range and quality, however formally correct that use may be, still means inferior philosophising in the end. On this point there is much which we can still with profit learn from the education and practical experience by which Plato proposed to train, and the moral and intellectual qualifications which he required in, the " lovers of wisdom " who were to be the guardians of his ideal commonwealth. Truth demands more than ingenuity or than formal consistency in reasoning. These, no doubt, belong to the technique of the philosopher's craft. But unless the material quality of the would-be philosopher's data be of the right sort, skill in dialectics will not give him the fundamental insights.

If this be true, it follows that improvements, or at least innovations, in philosophical technique alone, however valuable they may be in themselves, will not bring about the salvation of philosophy. None the less philosophers have again and again pinned their hopes to some reform in method. Ever since Bacon with his *Novum Organum*, and Descartes with his method of doubt, ushered in the period of " modern " philosophy, the problem of the right method or technique of conducting the enterprise of philosophy has been with us. Kant was not the first, as he certainly has not been the last, to raise the question, why hitherto philosophy had failed to enter, like physics or astronomy, on the sure and steady path of a science. At the present day, the spectacle of the progress of the natural sciences and of

---

[1] *Cf.* the author's review of *The Science of Legal Method* in the *Harvard Law Review,* vol. xxxi, no. 5 (March, 1918).

mathematics has once again brought the problem of method to the very forefront of discussion. Once more philosophers point to the sciences as models to be imitated. Their triumphs, their unbroken advance from success to success, must be due, it is held, to their method. How else account for the fact that the sciences obtain results which command the assent of all who are competent to form an opinion, whilst there is hardly an important philosophical theory, and certainly no philosophical system, which does not exhibit its author's temperament and idiosyncrasy, and from which other thinkers, no less competent, violently dissent? Must not the fault lie in the failure to employ the right method in philosophising? Does not the only hope for the future of philosophy lie in becoming " scientific "?

It is a tempting suggestion. We hardly know how to resist it, for the spell of science is upon us all. Science has as firmly put its stamp upon the intellectual culture and the practical organisation of our time, as ever had theology upon the civilisation of the Middle Ages. In peace and in war our lives rest upon the use of manifold appliances which science has put at our disposal. Bacon's *scientia est potentia* has become our watchword. To control the forces of nature by the study of nature's laws to the end of the " improvement of man's estate "—this is being acclaimed as the dominant temper of the " modern " age.[1] Our houses and our cities, our fields and our factories, our newspapers, our railroads, our steamships bear witness to the triumphs of science over nature. Compared with its predecessors, the XIXth century is pre-eminently a century of such triumphs of science, and its dominant temper has been well summed up in the description of it as the " century of hope ". Nor do the praises of science rest solely on its practical benefits, on the countless conveniences and inven-

[1] *Cf.* R. B. Perry, *Present Philosophical Tendencies,* ch. i; p. 5; also F. S. Marvin, *The Living Past* and *The Century of Hope.*

tions by which it has added to the comfort and ease of human existence. The buoyant optimism which comes with the power to do, is matched by the optimism which comes simply from the joy of intellectual conquests. There are many who rank the value of science as pure theory, as pursuit of knowledge for its own sake, far above its value in practical application.[1] On both grounds science is claiming, and obtaining, an ever larger place in modern education, at the expense of literary and historical subjects. Its advocates, not without reason, maintain that the scientific temper of mind and the scientific attitude towards the world have, not merely a utilitarian, but above all a profound spiritual value. Science, they remind us, demands severe submission to the objectivity of fact. It trains us in the virtues of being dispassionate and impartial. It bids us curb our desires before the stern face of truth. It discourages the facile human trick of letting the wish be father to the thought. Above all, it discourages us from judging facts as good or bad by reference to our wishes: it teaches us to be " ethically neutral ". As pure theory, too, it is indifferent to merely practical interests. In action we look to the future and turn our backs upon the unalterable past. But to the disinterested gaze of science the difference between past and future is irrelevant. Spinoza voiced the very spirit of science when he said, " In so far as the mind conceives a thing according to the dictates of reason, it will be equally affected whether the idea is that of a future, past, or present thing." [2]   Thus the intellectual discipline of science purges us from the fret of desire and the fear of an unknown future. Whatever there is *menschlich, allzu menschlich* about us drops away when we are brought face

---

[1] *Cf.* the well-known toast in honour of mathematics: " May it never be of any use to anybody."
[2] *Ethics*, Bk. iv, Prop. 62.

to face with the wonder and the necessity of things as they are. Only " the impersonal cosmic outlook " of science, with its " reverence towards fact ", can help us to " sweep away all other desires in the desire to know." "A life devoted to science ", concludes Bertrand Russell, " is a happy life, and its happiness is derived from the very best sources that are open to dwellers on this troubled and passionate planet." [1]

The attentive reader will have noticed that in this summary of the praises of science, the values claimed for it have undergone a subtle transformation. At first the practical and theoretical values of science were presented as complementary. It next appeared that the range of the desire to know is far wider than the range of things which our action can affect; still there was no incompatibility. But, in the end, science came to be praised for its aloofness from action and from the desires on which actions are based. Contemplation, or the cosmic outlook, we found to be valued as the solvent of desire, or at least as detaching us completely from practical, and incidentally from ethical, interests.

Now this is a situation to make a philosopher pause. Clearly, he cannot yield to the call to make his philosophy " scientific " without further investigation. Before he canforant that philosophy is a science, or at least ought to become one by adopting scientific methods, he wants to be very clear about the consequences of the step he is asked to make. In the first place, he notes that beneath the divergent valuations of science which have come to light, there are concealed incompatible concepts of what science and scientific method are. Is science homogeneous throughout? Is there but one scientific method? It would appear

[1] *Mysticism and Logic*, p. 45. The phrases in the preceding sentence are quoted from the same book.

that there is a profound ambiguity here; that the sciences differ widely in type and method, and that the advocates of scientific method have correspondingly different ideals in mind. For one group, the character of science is best embodied in mathematics, especially in so far as it can be reduced to pure logic, stripped of all empirical elements, made purely *a priori*. The other group is thinking of the laboratory sciences with their experimental methods, their manipulation of concrete objects, their hypotheses tested by action, their constant appeal to empirical observation. These two groups face in opposite directions. Though they use the common name of science, their differences are much more marked than their agreement. They are not only thinking of different sorts of facts and different methods of investigation, but the one group values science as an end in itself, for what is contemplative in it; whereas the other values science as a means only, for what is instrumental in it. Which of these two is the philosopher to follow when he is bidden to become scientific?

Again, it is easy to see that a difference in method here brings with it a difference in matter. What is at stake for the philosopher is not merely the manner of his philosophising, but the very problems with which he will be allowed to concern himself. And thus it becomes to undantly clear that the proposed reforms of philosophy are motived by fundamental choices or preferences, which must be examined in the light of day, if the value of the reforms themselves is to be fairly assessed. We are dealing, in the last analysis, with what are themselves philosothical attitudes, theories about the right employment of the intellect, spiritual valuations expressed in terms of the objects about which, and the conditions under which, it is most worth while for the thinker to think.

A brief examination of the sorts of philosophising to

which these two divergent ideals of scientific method respectively lead, will serve to verify this general account.

The one ideal of scientific method is best represented by Bertrand Russell, who means by it the " logico-analytic " method of modern mathematical logic. It draws its inspiration from the success of Frege and other mathematicians in showing that the concepts of space and of number, on which geometry and arithmetic appeared respectively to be built up, can be analysed into simpler logical notions; that, in fact, mathematics, thus pushed to its ultimate foundations, is indistinguishable from logic. This discovery re-enforced the traditional admiration for mathematics as the *beau idéal* of vigor, precision, clearness, consistency, conclusiveness—in short, as the embodiment of all the intellectual virtues. The ideal type of knowledge has once again been identified with a deductive system, derived according to logical rules of inference, from the smallest possible number of simple, indefinable notions and ultimate, mutually independent postulates or assumptions. Such an ideal suggests two tasks, *viz.*, (1) the study of the most general characteristics of deductive systems, such as the forms of propositions involved in them, the relations of implication by which one may be deduced from others, and (2) the analysis of particular complex systems into the simple notions and ultimate postulates, in which they can then be shown to be deductively implied. These two tasks would correspond, so to speak, to pure and applied philosophy respectively.

We ask, next, what the philosopher, armed with the logico-analytic method can do to make this actual world of ours, with all its pressing problems, intelligible.

In seeking an answer to this question we are at once confronted by a singular and perplexing oscillation in Russell's views. (a) At times he writes as if the philosopher had no concern with applications of his method to the actual world at all; as if he ought to restrict himself to pure philosophy, *i.e.*, to pure logic. (b) At other times, he makes himself most interesting experiments in application, rejoicing in " intellectual constructions " designed to illustrate the power of the new method and the " progress " which it promises to effect. (c) Yet, even then, Russell always emphatically insists that the range of fruitful application of the new method is strictly limited, and that many of the traditional problems of philosophy—and these precisely the humanly most interesting—are not soluble by his method at all and should, therefore, be severely left alone by the philosopher.

We proceed to illustrate these three strata, or aspects, in Russell's views, bringing to light, as we do so, minor oscillations which yet bear on the spiritual valuations underlying his whole theory.

(a) Philosophy, we note first of all, can deal by the logico-analytic method only with what is abstract and general, not with what is concrete and empirical. " *Philosophy is the science of the possible* ",[1] we are told in emphatic italics—not the practically possible, that is, but the theoretically possible, *i.e.*, that which is abstractly conceivable. " Philosophy deals only with the general properties in which all possible worlds agree." It follows, first, that " a philosophical proposition must be such as can neither be proved nor disproved by empirical evidence "; it must be " true of any possible world, independently of such facts as can only be discovered by our senses ". It follows, further, that " the difference between a good world and a bad world is

---

[1] The following quotations, except where otherwise stated, are from the Herbert Spencer Lecture on " Scientific Method in Philosophy ", reprinted in *Mysticism and Logic,* see esp. pp. 111, 112.

a difference in the particular characteristics of the particular things that exist in these worlds; it is not a sufficiently abstract difference to come within the province of philosophy ".[1] In thus providing " an inventory of possibilities, a repertory of abstractly tenable hypotheses ", philosophy emancipates us from pre-occupation with the actual world, alike in its appeal to our desires and its appeal to our senses. It gives wings to the imagination by carrying us into the realms of what *may* be, instead of focusing our vision narrowly on what *is*. It offers an escape from the intellectual bewilderment besetting those who allow themselves to be entangled, by their interest in the actual, in the insoluble problems of the destiny of the universe and of mankind. It introduces us, like mathematics, into a realm of eternal, unchangeable verities, the patient exploration of which is as satisfying to our feeling for beauty as to our desire for knowledge. In the solution, for example, of the contradictions which had been supposed to beset the concepts of continuity and infinity, the logico-analytic method has achieved its most characteristic triumphs.[2]

(b) Pure philosophy, then, which is pure logic, deals wholly with abstract, general *forms*. Out of itself, it is quite incapable of supplying concrete, particular *content*. Form and content, thus, are sharply sundered, and independent one of the other. " Pure logic and atomic facts (*e.g.*, facts of sense-perception) are the two poles, the wholly *a priori* and the wholly empirical ".[3] In the analysis of the actual world we are confronted with a complex product of these two factors, *i.e.*, with a body of beliefs of very varying degrees of trustworthiness. The first duty of the philosopher is to take up towards this common knowledge

[1] *Our Knowledge of the External World*, p. 26.
[2] *Cf. Our Knowledge of the External World*, chs. v-vii.
[3] *Loc. cit.*, p. 53.

which is his datum, an attitude of Cartesian doubt, so as to sort out the elements which resist criticism and may, therefore, be called "hard" data, from the "soft" elements which dissolve, or at least become doubtful, under examination. The common sense world having thus been reduced to its hard elements, the next task of the philosopher is to apply his method in the intellectual construction of complex entities which shall serve all the theoretical purposes of the "things" of common sense, or of the "points" and "instants" of physics, whilst yet being freed from all the "soft" elements contained in them as ordinarily conceived. With the details of Russell's catalogue of hard data we need not concern ourselves here, though it is only what we should expect that sense-data and the laws of logic figure among the hardest of the hard, whereas substances and other minds are "soft". So, again, it belongs to another context[1] to appreciate some of the features of Russell's intellectual construction of "things". It is enough for our present purpose to note that the application of logic to the actual world has these two stages: first, an analytic search, by methodical doubt, for all that is "logically primitive" or "hard"; secondly, a synthetic building up out of hard data, and by logically unexceptionable methods, of entities which fulfill all the theoretical functions of the objects of common sense and current physical science, without being infected by their logical softness. The fundamental question for Russell under this latter head is always: "Can we make any valid inferences from data to non-data in the empirical world"?[2] or, "Can the existence of anything other than our own hard data be inferred from the existence of those data?"[3] In the mathematical world of

---

[1] See below, ch. v.
[2] *Cf.* Russell's reply to John Dewey, in *Journal of Philosophy, Psychology and Scientific Methods*, vol. xvi, no. 1, p. 24.
[3] *Our Knowledge of the External World.* p. 73

abstract generalities we can and do make such inferences validly. In the concrete world of sense we make them too, but most of the time invalidly. Hence the problem is so to re-interpret the results of our inferences concerning the actual world that they are logically hard throughout.

(c) There are, however beliefs concerning the actual world which philosophy cannot, and must not, seek to reconstruct. They are not only open to grave doubt, but logic is powerless to save them. They are beliefs foreshadowing a destiny of the world which is satisfactory to our " mundane desires ". They are beliefs concerning the meaning, plan, purpose of the world; beliefs that it is good or at least working towards good; beliefs in its perfection or perfectibility; beliefs in God. With facts the logico-analytic method can deal: but in the realm of values it is powerless. Thus philosophy is bidden to eschew, not only all problems of practice and conduct, but above all the problems of the interpretation of the world in the light of moral and religious experience.   " It is my belief ", writes Russell, " that the ethical and religious motives, in spite of the splendidly imaginative systems to which they have given rise, have been on the whole a hindrance to the progress of philosophy, and ought now to be consciously thrust aside by those who wish to discover philosophical truth. . . . It is, I maintain, from science, rather than from ethics and religion, that philosophy should draw its inspiration." [1]   To let moral and religious experience enter into one's philosophising is to open the doors to temperamental differences, to let human hopes and fears dictate what the universe is to be. It is to surrender " that submission to fact which is the essence of the scientific temper." [2]   It is to prostitute the effort to

[1] *Mysticism and Logic*, p. 98.
[2] *Loc. cit.*, p. 109.

understand, in the interest of the desire to improve human existence or at least to inspire it with hope. With human weaknesses of this sort philosophy has no concern, and thus there are banished from it most of the problems upon which it has been traditionally engaged.

The second form of the demand for scientific method has for its watchword " experiment ", and finds its most plausible advocacy through the " instrumentalism " of Professor John Dewey. It differs from its rival in that it faces towards the actual world of our experience, not away from it, and in that it makes ethical categories fundamental in its philosophising, instead of eliminating them altogether. Inspired, at bottom, by the social reformer's zeal, instrumentalism seeks to supply reform with a technique modelled on the laboratory procedure of the experimental sciences. It does not, like its rival, shun the moral problems raised by the actual world as undeserving of the philosopher's study, but seeks to understand the world in order to better it. It does not want to banish desire as irrelevant, but to supply it with the knowledge which it needs for its realisation.

" Instrumentalism " is the name for the theory that thinking (or theorising) is an instrument; that its place and value is that of a means, a tool; that the insight or knowledge which thinking yields ought not to be treated as ends in themselves; and that their being so treated is a perverse development, full of undesirable moral and social consequences. Out of action knowledge springs and into action it must return. The special function of thinking is to make action intelligent by making it fore-seeing; to organise experience so as to provide a map, as it were, of possible actions and their consequences; to secure thus control, guidance, efficiency; adaptation of the environment to human needs and of human aims to what the environment permits.

Filling in this rough outline, we learn, further, that experience is practical, not cognitive. To experience is to experiment. Its physiological schema is that of stimulus and response. It is not a mere undergoing of a sequence of sensations with spectator-like passivity: it is a responding to a sensation with some sort of behaviour from which fresh sensations result. Thus a pattern of sensations linked by actions (or reactions) is formed, and each element in the pattern acquires meaning in this context, becomes a cue for possible actions, and a sign for, or evidence of, further experiences which may be had as consequences of these actions. On the basis of this pattern plans can be formed, and conduct be made purposeful and rational. To understand anything, to know what it is, means to be able to anticipate further experiences from it as the result of various actions upon or towards it. Knowing or thinking is thus continuous with, or incidental to, life conceived as commerce with an environment, as activity evoked by, and in its turn altering, that environment.

But, further, thinking occurs only on occasions of perplexity and doubt, when there is something going on of which the issue is uncertain, and when consequently right action is a problem. Hence it is a process of inquiry, search, discovery and its method is experimental. The situation is incomplete, its meaning in terms of future developments indeterminate. We proceed by analysis of what is given and by conjectural anticipation of what is to come. We form, in short, a working hypothesis and then work, *i.e.*, act, upon it. The result tests our thinking. This is the only way of " getting knowledge and making sure it *is* knowledge, and not mere opinion . . . we have no right to call anything knowledge except where our activity has actually produced certain physical changes in things, which agree with and confirm the conception entertained." [1]

Thus, in another way, thinking is intimately bound up with activity, and *bodily* activity at that. It is not something that goes on in detachment " in our heads "; it is not the exercise of a disembodied reasoning faculty, of a mind substantially distinct from a body. As experiment it involves doing, physical doing—looking, handling, dissecting, arranging, with or without special apparatus. Whether in the laboratory or in life, whether in the exploration of infant or scientist, there is no gaining of knowledge without bodily activity. And this means not merely using one's sense-organs on objects, but using the objects themselves, if only by playing with them, and thus gaining a fuller acquaintance with their nature.

Again, our world is in process of change and our activity is one of the channels through which this change is taking place—a channel important in proportion to the guidance of activity by knowledge. Knowledge thus looks always to the future. " All that the wisest man can do is to observe what is going on more widely and more minutely, and then select more carefully from what is noted just those factors which point to something to happen." [2] Knowledge, as involving activity and involved in activity, is a " mode of participation " in the cosmic process. It is not the mere onlooking of an unconcerned spectator.

And from this, lastly, flow ethical and social consequences of great importance. For, if we are helping to make the world what it is, we may as well help to make it better. Let our working hypotheses be ideals, let our experiments

---

[1] All quotatons in this account are from Dewey's *Democracy and Education*—a book in which there is much to admire and which sums up the quintessence of his philosophy. For the above passage, see p. 393.

[2] *Loc. cit.*, p. 171.

be reforms. Not understanding for its own sake, but improvement; not theory divorced from action, but action illumined by theory, is the end to which thinking is the instrument. In these respects, thus, the instrumentalist's theory of philosophical method is the polar opposite of the mathematician's. It is a synthesis of the method of experimental research on the one hand, and of aspirations towards social reform on the other. It has learnt from physiology the function of brain and nervous system as the mechanism for linking action with, and adjusting it to, stimulus; from psychology, the importance of movement and behaviour in the organisation of experience; from biology, the increasing rôle played by intelligence in making the organism master of the conditions of its life; from the natural sciences in general, the testing of hypotheses by experiment; from industrial organisation, the power of knowledge in transforming the environment of human life; from social reform, the duty and responsibility of using this power in the service of high ideals.

Summing up, one might not unfairly say that instrumentalism is an elaboration of the psychological theories of the function of thought to which William James gave currency. " Every idea is a half-way house to action ". " My thinking is first and last and always for the sake of my doing ". But whilst re-enforcing these positions by general biological considerations, instrumentalism adds a characteristic ethical application: the kind of doing which is at the present day most urgent is social, economic, political reform, and the kind of thinking of which the age stands most in need is " social research ", including social experiment. We need to know more and to think more to the end that we may make, if not a better heaven, at least a better earth. The same organised intelligence which we are applying to gaining the mastery over the forces of nature, we ought to apply to the better management of social institutions and to the cure of the many ills which spring from existing economic and political systems. It is this reformer's zeal, this meliorism, which is the instrumentalist's religion. His philosophy, put into practice, means intelligent philanthropy.

Our survey of these two main proposals for a reform of philosophical method has shown that they differ, not only in their concept of what makes a procedure scientific, but even more in their estimate of the place and function of thought and theory in human life, more particularly as these bear on moral values.

The enterprise of philosophy, as conceived in this book, has affinities with the positive points in both programmes, but does not share the extremes of their denials.

To begin with Russell's method, it is clear that, so far from being offered as a better instrument for achieving the traditional task of philosophy, it imposes on philosophy a complete re-orientation, a new task altogether. It is no longer a question of *how* to do a thing which is acknowledged to be worth doing, but of *what* is worth doing for a philosopher at all. The abstraction of facts from values which is characteristic of science is used to forbid the philosopher even the attempt at a synthesis. The inapplicability of the method to the problems of value is not confessed as a defect, nor even as a limitation, but recommended as a merit and a source of power. The implied claim is that these problems are not legitimate objects of theoretical interest. If it be replied that they are illegitimate only for a philosopher who seeks to be scientific—and nobody else, on this view, deserves the name of philosopher—we must counter by asking, What is gained by this transference of philosophy from its traditional problems to an altogether new and different set? Grant that progress will be made in these new problems, grant that competent enquirers will agree about them (for whoever does not agree will *ipso facto* be incompetent). That still leaves the old problems as urgent, as persistent, as ever. And men will continue to be troubled by them and to give their best thought to finding a solution for them. Traditionally, this has been the philosopher's province. Now the name of philosophy is to be attached to a different set of enquiries. If, then, a manipulation of names is the ultimate issue, what a pitiable storm in the academic teacup!

But, no—this new programme of scientific method is an important challenge, not because of the problems which it assigns or denies to philosophy, but because of the judgment of value which it expresses; because, in short, it embodies itself a philosophy, a world-view, precisely in the old-fashioned sense of these terms. On this point, no one can be in doubt who has followed how this present programme has developed out of the attitude so eloquently voiced in Russell's " The Free Man's Worship ". In that justly famous essay,[1] Russell affirms an irreconcilable antithesis between the ideals to which human beings acknowledge loyalty, and the physical universe which is the environing scene of their lives. The actual world is there apostrophised as " omnipotent matter, blind to good and evil, reckless of human life and human ideals." The only road to inward freedom is there represented as lying through the abandonment of hope, through stoic endurance, through heroic, though despairing, faithfulness to human values. Love there can flourish only between human beings, " fellow-sufferers in the same darkness, fellow-actors in the same tragedy ".[2] This same antithesis of scientific facts

[1] See *Philosophical Essays,* ch. ii; or *Mysticism and Logic,* ch. iii.
[2] *Loc. cit.,* pp. 69, 70; or p. 56.

and human values re-appears in Russell's latest writings. But it has there become a strict neutrality with respect to values, coupled with the withdrawal of theoretical interest into a realm of logical abstractions. It is now a passionate denial that reason can be at home, or help to make men feel at home, in this actual, concrete world of ours which, for better or for worse, grips and holds us by all sides of our natures. It declares the true home of reason to be another world, a world of abstract logical entities and relations, with a fascination and beauty of its own, a perfection which the intellect can enjoy, untroubled by passion and desire. " An impartial contemplation ", we are assured, " freed from all preoccupation with Self . . . is very easily combined with that feeling of universal love which leads the mystic to say that the whole world is good." [1] Still, all Russell's eloquence can but thinly veil the profound pessimism of this view, the confession that reason is impotent to find meaning or value even in the grim and terrible aspects of the actual world. *There* lies the real sting of Russell's plea for scientific method. *There* lies his real challenge to all philosophy which, in the hands of the great masters of speculation, has sought to elicit from all the resources of our experience a synthetic vision of the whole, which should justify that deep confidence in the world which is the fruit of religion at its best. It is because of this renunciation that no thorough-going philosophy can, in the end, find salvation by any method which is scientific in the spirit of Russell's utterances.

On the other hand, we can whole-heartedly accept all that Russell says in praise of philosophy as " contemplation ", as theory sought for its own sake. It does, indeed, in his own fine phrase, make us " citizens of the universe ",[2]

---

[1] *Mysticism and Logic*, p. 28.
[2] *The Problems of Philosophy*, p. 249.

a thing it could never do if it were merely subordinate to practical interests. It is just here, in denying to theory any but an instrumental value, that the weakness of instrumentalism lies. Thinking is often a means, but it may legitimately become an end in itself. It is often instrumental to the realisation or enjoyment of other values, but it may also be itself enjoyed and practised as an intrinsic value, as worth while for its own sake. We need knowledge in order to live. We need it even more in order to live well. But we need it most of all because the pursuit and the enjoyment of knowledge is itself one, though only one, of the values devotion to which makes life worth living. Again, it is a narrow conception of the range of the theoretical interest which identifies it exclusively with things about to happen and things to be done. Theory, as an end for its own sake, is not exclusively concerned with the future. Nor does it scorn to study things which have no essential connection with time at all. So, again, in proportion as the pressure of practical needs is released, we are free to turn our thoughts from the problem of what must be done, or of what it is best to do, to the contemplation of things that give no occasion for action at all except such as helps to a fuller knowledge of them. Nor does such thinking deserve to be depreciated as barren and otiose. It is well to have the experimental character of thinking insisted on, but not all theories can be tested by manipulation of the physical world, for they may not refer to that world at all. And even the reformer's attitude, however important, is not final, if only because it is not equivalent to, or exhaustive of, religion. A moral agent, without ceasing to be deeply concerned, can yet reflect on his moral activity and realise that it is not everything and affords no ultimate standing-ground. Grant that the world is in process of change, yet that does not preclude its bringing home to us in ever fresh ways the same fundamental lessons. It is insight into these lessons which philosophy seeks and, at its best, attains. And the supreme lesson, surely, is this that it does not lie within the power of man to make the world once and for all " safe " for his ideals. Such safe-making is for the moralist and reformer the end-all and be-all of human existence. Yet it may well be asked whether any world in which it is fundamentally worth while to live can be really conceived as " safe "—as a world in which man *no longer needs* to " save " himself by standing, with his life and with all that he has, for what he values most, because the forces which would endanger and overthrow these values are, once for all, destroyed? To believe such safe-making possible amounts to an idolatry of man and of men's self-sufficiency and prowess which is the mere moralist's peculiar fallacy, and from which religion with its " Not my will, but Thine, be done," offers the only escape. There can be no sound or complete philosophy, whatever its method, which ignores such lessons as these.

It must be very clear by now that the theories of method which we have been contrasting are, one and all, " visions " in the sense of James's saying quoted above.[1] They express spiritual attitudes—total reactions to each thinker's total experience; they are very literally ways in which each feels the " whole push of the universe." They are experiments in thinking, though not experiments in the laboratory sense of verifying by the actual event some prediction which is being put to the test. A philosophical theory is rarely such that it can be proved or disproved by some action devised *ad hoc*. It must indeed " work " and thus give evidence of its truth, but there is about the verification of it no watching for an anticipated consequence to come off,

[1] See p. 24.

nor does the criticism of it proceed, as a rule, by adducing "negative instances". Of experiment in the instrumentalist sense there is little in philosophy: of experiment in the adjusting of conflicting beliefs there is a great deal. There is a weighing of considerations, a trying out of alternatives, a mobilising of all the resources of one's experience and reflection, a feeling one's way from a distracted and unstable to a coherent and stable outlook. Experiment in this sense is one with "dialectic", with learning by experience, with the recasting and transforming of beliefs which mark the growing insight, as the thinker advances from haphazard and partial to orderly and inclusive reflection.

Does it follow from this experimental character of philosophical thinking that it can never get beyond tentative guesses? It is the fashion nowadays, even among certain philosophers, to evade the accusation of dogmatism by claiming for philosophical theory nothing more than the character of, at best, a probable hypothesis. Conviction, certainty—these are said to be unattainable. The facts of everyday life, the theories of science are allowed to be, by comparison, far superior in certainty. Proof, demonstration in philosophy are held to be impossible. The philosopher's path is not from doubt, or through doubt, to reasoned conviction, but from certainty to doubt. He leaves the firm land of common experience to navigate uncharted seas of speculation without assurance of reaching a harbour. Dogmatism, no doubt, is unjustifiable, but it does not follow that the philosopher may not reach convictions which are stable enough at least for him. To demonstrate them to others, to compel their assent, may be beyond his powers, for demonstration requires, not merely technical correctness of the argument, but acceptance by the other of its premises. But the difficulties of securing this, where the premises depend on the range and quality of each thinker's concrete experience, are obvious. Yet a reasoned and reasonable theory (or, if the word be preferred, " faith ") is not unattainable and has rewarded the venture of philosophising again and again. Are there not, after all, certainties in life, not ordinarily reflected on, which in philosophising are raised to the level of explicit insight? " The things which are most important in man's experience are also the things which are most certain to his thought ".[1]

Does it follow, lastly, that there is no progress in philosophising? And if there is none, is the fact a fatal condemnation? The denial of progress can hardly apply to the individual thinker. He does progress in developing his world-view. Again, it cannot mean that no new theories are formulated, no original discoveries made, no old theories re-examined, improved, supported by fresh argument. For all these things are happening in philosophy. It must, then, mean that all new theories do but add to the babel and confusion, that there is no cumulative coöperative advance from generation to generation, no funded stock of philosophical truths which can be taught as its established rudiments to beginners, and which are taken for granted by all experts as the basis of further enquiry. The same problems are ever examined afresh. No doubt, typical solutions are supported again and again by fresh adherents, yet for philosophers as a body the old problems remain persistently open.

" Persistent problems "—why do they persist? If philosophy does not get on, why not apply to it the wholesome rule: get on or get out?

The answer to this challenge is to be found in our whole interpretation of philosophy. In whatever respects we may claim to have progressed since the days of Parmenides and

---

[1] B. Bosanquet, *The Principle of Individuality and Value*, Preface, p. v.

Plato, yet the need for discerning the permanent lineaments of the universe in the ever-changing tissue of social and scientific, moral and religious experience remains with us, and is ever renewed by the very changes which we acclaim as progress.   Problems persist because, being universal, they recur from age to age in human experience, however its details may be modified.   And as often as they recur, the individual thinker has to master them once more himself, for the solutions of his predecessors are but lifeless formulae, unless he can re-think them on the basis of his own experience.   Without such re-thinking, there is no " living past ".   Only through it does the thought of the great philosophers become dateless and deathless, living across the ages and helping the thinker of the present day as the record of a pilgrimage may help later travellers passing the same way.   But only he who undertakes the journey himself learns to perceive that every philosopher is engaged in the same pilgrim's progress, whether or no he call his goal the city of God.

CHAPTER III

PHILOSOPHY of Nature grows, like all philosophy, out of the effort to make explicit, in coherent theory, just *what* is the character of that world which reveals itself in human experience.

"Nature", "the physical world", "the world of sense", is to us both the environment—the scene, or stage, upon which we act out our lives—and the greater whole, or system, of which we recognise ourselves as parts. If in the former aspect we think of it chiefly as something to be mastered and used for our ends, in the latter aspect it is brought home to us that, after all, it depends on the constitution of Nature what is the ultimate fate of all our efforts, what is the destiny of all those values the realisation of which alone makes life worth living. Bacon's wisdom still holds: *naturae non imperatur nisi parendo.*

However, lording it over Nature at the price of submission to her laws has never been man's only, even though it has often been his most urgent, concern. Not on any pattern so simple are the relations of man to the world around him constructed. From control to worship, from intellectual curiosity to aesthetic enjoyment and religious awe, his ways of being interested in Nature are many and various. His attitudes towards Nature run through the whole gamut of emotions, and his theories reflect the oscillations of his moods. It is precisely out of these complex and often contradictory data that philosophy must seek to elicit an interpretation of Nature which shall be true as theory and also offer a firm foundation for conduct.

But in attempting this task, philosophy finds itself at a parting of the ways. One of these ways—a way advocated by a growing and influential school of thinkers—is the way of distinguishing sharply between " fact " and " truth ", on the one side, and, on the other, all human wishes, preferences, emotions. " Ascertain first the constitution of the universe and then adjust your feelings to your facts ", say these counsellors. They bid us bear in mind how subtle, because generally unconscious, is the influence of our wishes upon our theories, how ready we are to believe what is pleasing and to disbelieve what is displeasing, how apt our reasonings are to favour rather than thwart our desires. Who has not, on occasion, been tempted to argue that, unless certain beliefs be true, the world would be utterly bad and life in it not worth living? Who has not cried out that certain beliefs cannot be true, because it would be intolerable if they were? Who has not, in effect, tried to infer the falsity of a theory from the undesirability of its consequences? Put in this way, intellectual integrity and moral courage alike seem to demand, that he who would enter the temple of truth must first lay aside all demands and desires, and be ready, in utter humility and submission, to face and accept facts as they are, whatever be the hurt to his feelings.

Hope, comfort, security, trust—these are the things for which men most long in their dealings with Nature. A world in which they can hope, a world which comforts rather than bruises, a world in which they can feel at home—that is the kind of world which men want above all to believe in, which at all costs they try to believe in, inventing philosophies and religions which hold out this promise, which bring this assurance.

But this, so say the advocates of the one way, is to be the victim of illusion. Beliefs which are untrue are bound,

sooner or later, to play the believer false. His comfort, his
security, his happiness are built on unstable foundations,
and at the remorseless touch of fact will crumble into dust.
The only way to salvation lies through the wholly disinterested search for truth. Let us ask first what we have a
right reasonably to believe, and then let us adjust our
feelings and wishes, for better or for worse, to the inexorable facts. This is the one way of escape from illusion and
fear, not perhaps to happiness and hope, but at least to
dignity and nobility of living.

There is something in this appeal which must evoke a
thrill of response from everyone who cares at all for
truth and who knows, as Spinoza knew, that the service
of truth demands a severe discipline and education of the
emotions. But is the situation quite so simple as it is
here pictured? However much we may all need the warn-
ing against the cheery, but cheap, optimism which exclaims
" God is in his heaven, all's right with the world ", is there
not also the opposite and more subtle danger that we shall
distrust, and reject as false, beliefs on no other ground
that they are pleasant and comforting? There is a tendency
abroad among some present-day thinkers to set down all
theories which do not paint the world as an ugly, dark, evil
thing, as " compensations " for, or " escapes " from, an
intolerable actuality. Shrinking from the cruelty and
horror of the world as it is, we build, according to this
view, palaces of illusion where we can be at peace. We
remould the world nearer to the heart's desire—in imagination, deliberately turning our backs upon the actual which
we cannot bear. We seek and find in make-believe theory
a vicarious satisfaction for the wishes which life, as it
really is, brutally thwarts and represses. Philosophies
which find value in the world are likened to art, as ways
of escape into the realm of the ideal from the imperfections

of the actual. Religions which give comfort are likened to the dreams of Freudian psychology, as make-believe fulfilments of baulked desires. But if we are thus to "psychologise", or "psycho-analyse", those whose beliefs are comforting, why not peer similarly into the hidden springs of the thought of those who, in the words of Russell's ingenuous confession, "like some of their beliefs to have the quality of a hair-shirt?"[1] If philosophy has, as Russell in the same passage suggests, its ascetics as well as its voluptuaries, is it *a priori* certain that the truth is always and wholly on the side of the ascetic? If there is a bias for what is comforting and pleasant, is there not in some minds also a bias for what is arduous and painful? It is possible, as every psychologist knows, to enjoy the infliction of pain, not only on others, but even on oneself. It is possible to enjoy a theory which tortures by demanding renunciations, and even, unconsciously, to let the fact that it tortures weigh among the reasons for accepting it as true. There never yet was a pessimist who did not enjoy at least the conviction of the truth of his pessimism, not unmixed, occasionally, with the pleasure of contemplating the pitiful illusions of his opponents. Bradley was not far wrong when he summed up the pessimist's attitude in the aphorism: "Where all is bad, it must be good to know the worst"—a remark unintentionally verified by Russell's: "There is a stark joy in the unflinching perception of our true place in the world." It is, of course, only a bad world which requires unflinching perception.

If this were merely a dispute about tastes or temperaments, there would be little point in paying so much atten-

[1] "Some ascetic instinct makes me desire that a portion, at least, of my beliefs should be of the nature of a hair-shirt; and, as is natural to an ascetic, I incline to condemn the will-to-believers as voluptuaries". *Journal of Philosophy, Psychology and Scientific Methods,* vol. xvi, no. 1, Jan. 1919.

tion to it. What is important is to challenge, here and now, the suggestion that philosophies, or religions, which meet spiritual needs, are, *for this reason,* false, or, at least, likely to be false. Granted that a wish is often the father of a thought, does it follow either that a given thought which is such that we should prefer it to be true, has therefore a wish for its parent, or is therefore untrue? The situation reminds one of the relation of duty to the inclinations in Kant's moral theory. When duty and inclination coincide, we are but too likely to deceive ourselves concerning the moral quality of our conduct. Hence it is only when we do a thing we utterly dislike from a stern sense of duty alone, that we can be sure our action is moral. So here; it is only when we believe the world to be as we would much rather not have it, that we can be sure of the truth of the belief—or at least sure that no wishes have imposed illusions upon us. The only wish against the influence of which, even then, we shall have no guarantee is the wish to believe what runs counter to other wishes, of one's own or of other people.

The only aim of our argument, so far, has been to keep open the door for an alternative to this much-advertised way of contrasting facts and wishes. Behind that contrast, there lies the deeper contrast of *fact* and *value,* and the problem of their relation, indeed of their identity. It is from this side that we can best approach the second way which lies before philosophy.

In the first essay, we had laid it down that the spirit of philosophising is the spirit of wholeness, and that wholeness implies a unity of outlook upon the universe and a stability of attitude, such as are unattainable if no synthesis is possible of the realm of fact and the realm of value.

The category of value is as old as morality and religion themselves, and in this sense has been a topic of philosophical speculation as long as these modes of experience have attracted the philosopher's interest. But, in another sense, the realm of values is new to exploration, and it is only in our own day that this exploration has been undertaken with all the resources of modern psychological and logical analysis. The "Theory of Value", *eo nomine*, is the latest addition to philosophical disciplines, and its development has barely begun to emerge from the experimental stage. Value-judgments, value-feelings, acts of valuation, still stand as so many diverse points of departure for analysis, nor can any single theory claim to have gained undisputed acceptance. All the conflicting tendencies which characterise modern philosophy at large, re-appear in the special field of the theory of value. Here, as elsewhere, realism and idealism, naturalism and mysticism, pragmatism and intuitionism confront one another, though sometimes in strangely assorted alliances.

Still, through the dust it is possible to discern that the conflict is raging, as it was bound to rage, about a fundamental point, the recognition of which is as old as the Platonic-Aristotelian theory of pleasure. Is value relative to desire and want, and thus "subjective"? Or is it "objective"—a quality of perfection in the universe to be appreciated, though this appreciation may need to be learned, and though this learning may need an arduous effort?

If value is relative to desire, then nothing has value (or is a value) except what is desired, and so far, and for so long, as it remains an object of desire to somebody. Desire will confer the quality of value on its objects. The existence of a desire will be the condition precedent to anything having value. To have value will mean to be valued, and this will mean to be desired.

No doubt, this position may be superficially approximated to its rival, by saying that every desire implies an appreciation and thus a judgment of approval. Whatever you desire, so the plea may run, you approve; to desire is to think (judge) that what you desire is good. Thus all desire is *sub ratione boni*.

But this is an evasion, as may be seen by putting the test-question: on the theory of the subjectivity of value, is a thing desired because it is judged to be good, or is the judgment of value a mere consequence, and expression of, the fact that it is desired? The latter position alone would appear to be consonant with the subjectivity-theory. But lest we lose ourselves here in idle hair-splitting, let us rather put the point thus: Are there not approvals, *Bejahungen*, which are not preceded, or conditioned by, desire? Are there not acceptances, appreciations, satisfactions, findings good of which desire, at best, is only an index under the special condition when the object is absent, lacking, unrealised? Does value cease with fulfilment and thereby cessation of desire? Is there no enjoyment or recognition of value in things, when reflected upon and contemplated? Is there no value discernible in things which, from the nature of the case, cannot be effectively or reasonably desired, as not being within our power? Do not the resources of experience and reflection enable us, on occasion, to perceive a value in things which, in their immediately given character, provoke aversion and condemnation? A theory which has not explored these clues and possibilities, or which refuses to do so, can hardly set up an unchallenged claim to acceptance.

Another way of pressing the same point is to enquire whether, except on a theory of objective value, there can be any standard for the criticism, and thereby for the correction and education, of desires. In the field of desires the process of learning by experience is, perhaps, even more obvious than in the field of our theoretical beliefs. Mistakes here are peculiarly glaring and painful. Desired objects so frequently play us false. Attained, they still leave us dissatisfied. Disappointment proves them "false"; shows that they were not what we "really", *i.e.*, truly, wanted. Not that the theory of the subjectivity of value is wholly at a loss in the face of this situation. It may set up the ideal of a harmony of desires, an organisation of them without friction or mutual interference, a goal of maximum satisfaction through desires regulated and adjusted each to the others in due proportion. In that it thus offers a standard of apparent "wholeness", the theory is tempting and plausible. And indeed it is right so far as it goes. But it does not go all the way. It leaves out too much to measure up, even in mere theory, to what wholeness implies and demands. It leaves out the enjoyments and appreciations which come unsought and undesired. It leaves out the problem of the appreciation of, or satisfaction with, the world in all those aspects of it for which, because they are not modifiable by human action, desire cannot furnish the criterion or measure of value. Those who hold that "good" is indefinable, or, in general, that value is a quality in things the presence of which can only be perceived or intuited, like the presence of a sense-quality, such as "yellow",[1] might support our view here against the theory which makes value dependent on desire. But in so far as they declare such intuition to be infallible (for who can perceive what is not there?), and therefore beyond the reach of, or need for, correction and education; in so far as they deny, by implication at least, that the appreciation and

[1] G. E. Moore, *Principia Ethica*, ch. i, §7, p. 7.

recognition of objective value can be deepened by the lessons of experience, or that there is a " dialectic " through which we come to apprehend more clearly not only what we ought to desire, but the actual value of actual fact, their theory still differs from the one here suggested.

This is not the place to argue the difficult question of the comparative merits of these rival theories of value. It is enough to have shown what alternatives are open to choice. Which of them a given thinker will prefer is sure to depend on his total philosophical attitude, such as it springs by reflection from the synthesis of all his experience. In choices of this sort it is never possible to demonstrate that one alternative is unquestionably right and the other wrong. If that were possible with any ease, there would not be the prevailing divergence of view. But this is not to deny the reasonableness of such choices. For what is a thinker to reason with except the experiences through which the world reveals itself to him? All he can do is to weigh how far any given view sums up, and is consistent with, any experience by which he can test it. On such weighings of total impressions the fundamental differences in philosophy commonly turn. When the question is whether value exists, or comes into being, only in dependence on desire, or whether it may be discerned throughout the world in proportion as the effort to view the world as a whole succeeds, the decision will always depend on what types of experiences furnish the dominant clues, what point of view each thinker is accustomed to treat as decisive. On the one theory, value is essentially a man-dependent phenomenon. On the other, it is a cosmic, or, if we prefer to say so, a metaphysical character. On the one view, certain kinds of things in the universe have value, as being objects of desire. On the other, it is the universe itself, and as a whole, which to the best insight has value. The " best insight " of the latter theory will seem romantic fiction, or even mere foolish or mischievous make-believe, to the adherents of the former. By contrast, the theory of the former will seem abstract and ill-balanced to the adherents of the latter, as ignoring or depreciating through the device of opposing feeling to fact, or desire to truth, the metaphysical import of moral and religious experience.

Here, after all, we have the kernel of the issue. Philosophical choices turn, we said just now, on total impressions, on the point of view which, in estimating the dominant character of the universe, we treat as decisive. There are for modern men two such points of view, determined for us by the whole historical development of our civilisation, alike on its side of social organisation and activity, and, even more, on its side of speculative theory. Throughout the history of modern philosophy, no less than in the wider movements of educated thought which philosophical theories both focus and stimulate, we can trace the varying relations of these two points of view, now in sharp opposition, now in ingenious compromise, now joined in close synthesis. Knowing them already as interest in fact and interest in value, we may now, summarily if crudely, contrast them as *science* and *religion*.

Philosophy of Nature, thus, as it pushes on to fundamental problems, will always become philosophy of Religion, even when, as " Naturalism " or " Materialism ", it condemns all religion as savage animism or effete superstition; even when, as " Positivism ", it elevates philanthropy to the dignity of a " religion of humanity ". From this angle the ultimate question is: what religion, if any, is possible for reasonable men when their choice is in favour of accepting as dominant and decisive the methods and results of Natural Science?

The hold of Science on the minds of educated men, and its influence on their philosophical attitude, is, not without justice, immense. It is amazing to reflect with how small a stock of scientific knowledge, yet with what confidence in the effectiveness of their endeavours, men have in past ages carried on the business of living and built up the complex structure of their civilisations. That knowledge which, as Bacon said, is power and from the acquisition of which he hoped so much for " the relief of man's estate " —how recent are its inception and its triumphs! Most of our sciences hardly date more than a century back, and even those which are older have only within this period made rapid and unbroken progress. The control of natural forces for human ends was hardly more advanced in the London or Paris of 1750 than it was in the Rome of Augustus or the Athens of Pericles. Most of the inventions and discoveries on which modern industry and commerce are built up, are the achievements of the last century.

Let us stop for a moment to recall what this means. Here is the picture as a distinguished scientist draws it for us. " At that date [1754] the steam-engine had not yet assumed a practical form, and apart from some small use of water and wind power, when mechanical work had to be done this was accomplished by the aid of the muscular effort of men and animals. The question of power supply was, in fact, in the same condition that had existed for thousands of years, and, in consequence, the employment of machinery of all descriptions that required power to drive it was extremely limited. Nor as regards travel for persons, or transit for goods, were things very different. The steamship was unthought of, and ocean journeying was no faster, and but little more certain, than in the days of Columbus. Railways in the modern sense were non-existent, and even the coaching era had scarcely begun. Travelling of all sorts was no more rapid or more convenient than in the days of the Romans. Indeed, emperors such as Hadrian and Severus, who visited this Country [England] in late classical times, probably made the journey to and from Rome quite as expeditiously, and very likely even much more comfortably, than did any traveller of the eighteenth century. Furthermore, at the time of which I speak, the communication of intelligence was limited to the speed at which postmen could travel, for, of course, there were no electric telegraphs, such as have shortened the time of communication with the ends of the earth to a few seconds, and have reduced even ambassadors to the status of clerks at the hourly beck and call of the Home Government. In the eighteenth century, moreover, illuminating gas and electric light had still to be invented, public lighting was practically non-existent, and even in London and other large cities linkmen with torches were required to light the passenger to his home after dark. If printing was in use it was slow and expensive, without any of the modern mechanical, photographic, and other adjuncts that have rendered possible our numerous newspapers and the other derivatives of the press. Nor were there any proper systems either for water supply or for the disposal of sewage. Disease, born of filth and neglect, stalked through the land practically unchecked. Medicine was still almost entirely empiric. Little or nothing was known of the causes and nature of illness, of infection by bacilli, or of treatment by inoculation. Anaesthetics had not yet been applied, and the marvels of modern surgery were undreamt of. It would be easy to multiply instances, but in the aggregate it is not inaccurate to state that at that time the general mode of life had not much improved on what obtained in civilised Europe in the days of the

Antonines, while, in some respects, it fell much short of this." [1]

It is easy to paint for oneself the contrasting picture of how much science, since then, has achieved for the relief of man's estate, in medicine, in chemistry, in metallurgy, in engineering, in fact in all the old, and many new, lines of investigation. Yet its triumphs, alike in theory and in the application of theory to life, with all they have done for the enlargement of human power and the multiplication of human comforts, have not brought any obvious increase in happiness, or made the living of a good life appreciably easier. The mastery over natural forces with which science has endowed us is, like all power, morally neutral. It may be abused as well as used. Social justice and the welfare of manual workers have not kept step with the development of machinery and of tools. Science has armed the will to destruction with weapons of an efficacy undreamt of by previous generations, but it has not made international relations more stable or less dangerous. It has repeatedly revolutionised the art of war, but it has not taught men to control their own war-like tendencies. It has brought increased power for good or evil. It has not strengthened the will for good against evil. Hence in the midst of the keen zest of research and the confident hope of a better future to be gained by intelligent efforts, the mood of men has again and again turned into discouragement and despair. For all our pomp of power and pride of knowledge, the applications of science seem but to make life more complex and difficult, and to leave the moral and religious aspirations of men as unfulfilled and unsatisfied as ever. Moreover, the scientific theory of Nature, and of man's place and prospects within it, so far from dispelling, rather deepens this pessimism. What is its promise to the human

[1] *Science and Its Functions*, by A. A. Campbell Swinton, F.R.S., *Nature*, vol. 100, no. 2511, Dec. 1917.

race but ultimate extinction?   It paints human life as a brief episode in a cosmic drama which is as vast as it is meaningless.   It condemns human achievements to destruction, human efforts to vanity.   Loyalty to ideals becomes a futile rebelliousness against an inexorable fate.   The very ideals may be ranked as no better than pathetic dreams.

Typical utterances, illustrative of this view, are not hard to find in our literature.   For it is a view which stirs the feeling of self-pity, and lends itself to tragic eloquence. Bertrand Russell's " The Free Man's Worship " is no mere voice of one crying in the wilderness of a thoughtless optimism.   In allowing his imagination to fill in the colours where science has drawn the outlines, he does but put into words a widespread estimate of human destiny.   Here is another, less well-known, but no less characteristic statement from his pen.   " The universe as astronomy reveals it is very vast.   How much there may be beyond what our telescopes show, we cannot tell; but what we can know is of unimaginable immensity.   In the visible world the Milky Way is a tiny fragment; within this fragment, the solar system is an infinitesimal speck, and of this speck our planet is a microscopic dot.   On this dot, tiny lumps of impure carbon and water, of complicated structure, with somewhat unusual physical and chemical properties, crawl about for a few years, until they are compounded.   They divide their time between labour designed to postpone the moment of dissolution for themselves and frantic struggles to hasten it for others of their kind.   Natural convulsions periodically destroy some thousands or millions of them, and disease prematurely sweeps away many more.   These events are considered to be misfortunes; but when men succeed in inflicting similar destruction by their own efforts, they rejoice, and give thanks to God.   In the life of the solar system, the period during which the existence of man will have been physically possible is a minute portion of the whole; but there is some reason to hope that even before this period is ended men will have set a term to his own existence by his efforts at mutual annihilation. Such is man's life viewed from the outside." [1]

A similar utterance in the pages of Mr. A. J. Balfour's " Foundations of Belief " used to thrill our fathers in their youth. " Man—past, present and future—lays claim to our devotion. What, then, can we say of him? Man, so far as natural science by itself is able to teach us, is no longer the final cause of the universe, the Heaven-descended heir of all the ages. His very existence is an accident, his story a brief and transitory episode in the life of one of the meanest of the planets. Of the combination of causes which first converted a dead organic compound into the living progenitors of humanity, science, indeed, as yet knows nothing. It is enough that from such beginnings famine, disease, and mutual slaughter, fit nurses of the future lords of creation, have gradually evolved, after infinite travail, a race with conscience enough to feel that it is vile, and intelligence enough to know that it is insignificant. We survey the past, and see that its history is of blood and tears, of helpless blundering, of wild revolt, of stupid acquiescence, of empty aspirations. We sound the future, and learn that after a period, long compared with the individual life, but short indeed compared with the divisions of time open to our investigation, the energies of our system will decay, the glory of the sun will be dimmed, and the earth, tideless and inert, will no longer tolerate the race which has for a moment disturbed its solitude. Man will go down into the pit, and all his thoughts will perish. The uneasy consciousness, which in this obscure corner has for a brief space broken the contented silence of the universe, will be

[1] *Athenæum*, No. 4643 (April 1919), p. 232.

at rest. Matter will know itself no longer. "Imperishable monuments" and "immortal deeds", death itself, and love stronger than death, will be as though they had never been. Nor will anything that *is* be better or be worse for all that the labour, genius, devotion, and suffering of man have striven through countless generations to effect." [1]

Few, in this chorus of agreement, are the dissentient voices. Here is one of the most recent. Challenging Russell, Professor R. B. Perry writes: " To pretend to speak for the universe in terms of the narrow and abstract predictions of astronomy, is to betray a bias of mind that is little less provincial and unimaginative than the most naive anthropomorphism. What that residual cosmos which looms beyond the border of knowledge shall in time bring forth, no man that has yet been born can say. That it may overbalance and remake the little world of things known, and falsify every present prophecy, no man can doubt. It is as consistent with rigorous thought to greet it as a promise of salvation, as to dread it as a portent of doom. And if it be granted that in either case it is a question of over-belief, of the hazard of faith, no devoted soul can hesitate." [2]

Perry thus denies the alleged " fact ". He challenges the pretended " truth " of the scientific prediction on the general ground of the limitation of human knowledge. From ignorance he draws hope. He argues, in effect, that because the worst is not certain there is an even chance of the best, and that we have a moral right, not to say a moral duty, to stake our all on this possibility. But suppose we do not embark upon this venture of the will to believe. Suppose we accept the " fact " and the " truth ", on the ground that we must be guided by the knowledge which we

[1] *The Foundations of Belief*, pp. 33, 4.
[2] *Present Philosophical Tendencies*, p. 347.

have. Even then our course is not clear. For on the all-important issue our advisers speak with a divided voice. And the all-important issue is to determine what our practical attitude, our conduct, ought to be on the basis of these scientific truths, and how we ought to remodel the beliefs on which our conduct is normally built. It is here that our authorities differ and leave us perplexed. Balfour, finding it impossible to give, within the frame-work of this scientific world-view, an adequate explanation either of the existence of values, aesthetic, moral, even cognitive, or of our devotion to them, draws from this failure an argument in favour of Theism.[1] He puts us out of humour with Naturalism in order to make us turn back more kindly to the verities of traditional piety. Russell, on the other hand, bids us accept the facts and defy them to break our spirit. To admit unwelcome truths, is to purge ourselves from fear, hope, and desire. In breaking loose from bondage to these tyrants of the human spirit, we escape from the littleness of self, and the need for consoling illusions. We become free to contemplate, without plaint or regret, a world of facts which promises nothing but extinction to ourselves and all we care for. Yet it is only when we have ceased to expect or ask anything on behalf of our ideals, that we are free to be loyal to them, with a stoic austerity and ardour into which enters no base alloy of compromise or delusion of success.[2]

The moral of all these speculations is plain. The problem of fact and value is inescapable, at least for him who would be a philosopher. Is not this, indeed, the fundamental difference in modern life between science and phil-

[1] See for the most recent statement of his view his Gifford Lectures on *Humanism and Theism.*

[2] For an examination of this position, see the author's *The Religious Aspect of Bertrand Russell's Philosophy,* in *The Harvard Theological Review,* vol. ix.

osophy—both taken in their aspect of pure theory? The sciences, each taking some special territory for exploration, are content to accumulate facts and give, as far as may be, a systematic account of them. Balfour's dialectics on behalf of dogma, Russell's despairs and heroics, Perry's hazards of faith and over-beliefs—all alike the scientist can, if he pleases, ignore as irrelevant sentimentalities. His enterprise, within its own limited sphere, carries for him its own justification. "Within its limited sphere"—for it is only by narrowing his horizon that he purchases his security. When science becomes philosophy, or when the problems of philosophy come to be attempted on the basis of scientific theories, the horizon at once widens to the whole range of human experience, and troublesome questionings and misgivings come crowding in. The need of a synthesis of fact and value comes into view, and cannot be ignored by the philosopher. For he is the guardian of the whole of experience, and his task is to elicit from each of its forms the contribution which it has to make to a comprehensive theory of the universe. Values and valuations he cannot ignore. Nor can he *a priori* subordinate them to facts, for such subordination itself expresses an estimate of value. "Ethical neutrality" is not for him. True it is that of the danger of believing what one wants to believe, he needs ever to remind himself. But he cannot seek safety by settling facts first and then letting values, under the title of desires, adjust themselves as best they may. For there are experiences in which he seems to himself to perceive that the facts themselves, fully understood or, to put it technically, viewed from the point of view of the whole, are embodiments of value. And, at any rate, to the philosopher the moral spirit is itself a fact, a force, or quality of life, become operative in human beings and through them in the world. He cannot refuse to enquire what light such a fact, or rather such a value present as an effective force, throws on the nature of human beings and of the universe of which they are parts.

"We are not here concerned", says Darwin at the end of his *Descent of Man*, "with hopes and fears, but only with truth as reason enables us to ascertain it." The antithesis had its value so long as prejudice disguised as dogma stood in the way of unbiased research. But, if there is anything in the argument of this essay, then to talk of hopes and fears as the enemies of truth is itself misleading, For it diverts attention from the problem of objective value, or of "reality" as being both fact and, to the deepest insight, embodiment of value. Hope, fear, desire, are truly secondary, and need to be disciplined if they are not to distort our vision. But it would be false to deny that they serve to direct attention to the value-aspect of the universe, They are an intimation and a reminder that there is more to "fact" and "truth" than scientific theory is able to reveal; and this not so much because, as Perry has it, our science is small and our ignorance large, but because science builds its edifice of theory on a relatively narrow selection of data from among human experiences. It is not true to our experience as a whole. It is "abstract".

Nor is the result substantially different when we appeal, like Darwin, to "reason". For, as we said a short while ago, what is the reasoner to reason with except the materials which human experience, in the widest sense of that word, puts at his disposal? What he is to think on any given problem, and ultimately on the universe as a whole, is bound to depend on what he has to think with. There is nothing else on which it can depend. Reasonings differ partly, no doubt, because some minds are more "logical" than others, but partly, and on philosophical issues fundamentally, because as between one mind and another there are differences in the range, kind, and quality of the experiences which are their material for reasoning, and even more because out of the same sort of experience one mind can elicit more of insight than another. In any case, it is well to recognise clearly, that reason and logic are not restricted to the " facts " for which we have the warrant of sense-perception and experiment. It would be a fatal mistake of method, as well as contrary to the practice of all the great philosophers, to exclude the things which are of profoundest human concern from the competence of " reason " and from the field of philosophy, by setting them down as matters of mere feeling, unreasoning itself and incapable of furnishing insights which reason can, and indeed must, use in its endeavour to frame a world-view which shall be true to the whole of our experience.

CHAPTER IV

IT is not hard to understand why the world which we call external, physical, material, is, to ordinary thought, *par excellence* the " real " world, and why the problem of vindicating its " reality " against attacks such as those which " idealists " are supposed to make upon it, is one of the persistent problems at any rate of modern philosophy.

No doubt, it is well to remind ourselves how narrow, after all, this concept of the " real " world is—how much that is undeniably real it fails, on any plausible interpretation of the terms " external ", *etc.*, to include. Still, in a very genuine sense the case of the external world is a crucial one. At all times men have been found to believe in the existence of things which do not in fact exist. The very sense-data which we treat as evidences of the reality of physical things are deceptively aped by dreams and hallucinations. The difficulty of distinguishing with certainty what is real and what is unreal, when in either case the experiences, be they sense-data or images, are equally vivid, lends colour to the theory that nothing exists except what is perceived by some mind, for so long as it is perceived; and that the existence of " matter ", if not to be denied outright, must be interpreted in keeping with this *esse-est-percipi* principle. At the same time, whilst this " subjective idealism " throws doubt on the existence of anything other than, or beyond, the percipient's actual sense-data here and now, from quite a different angle scientific theory threatens to discredit these sense-data as mere " mental impressions ", effects produced in a perceiver's mind by the action, on his sense-organs and nervous system, of material objects conceived in terms of imperceptible, and hence hypothetical, particles and forces. Every student of modern philosophy is familiar with the maze of polemical discussion which has enveloped the issues thus summarily indicated. Taking the conflicting theories as they find them, philosophers may well wonder what exactly it is in which the " reality " of the external world consists. Extreme views on this problem confront one another. For the orthodox physicist, reality, as it has been picturesquely put, is a " mad dance of electrons ", and sense-data, for all that they are the physicist's only direct evidence of the existence of any external world whatever, are counted as " merely mental " and " subjective ". On the other side, the physicist who has turned " phenomenalist ", joins positivists, empiricists, and subjective idealists among philosophers in declaring for the indubitable reality of sense-data, and rejecting, as hypothetical fictions, all imperceptible forces or entities—in short, the orthodox physicist's whole theoretical apparatus of " matter " and " energy ".

Moreover, our difficulties do not begin and end with the relation of the facts of sense to the concepts of physics. Behind the problem of sense-data and matter there looms up the problem of the relation of matter to life and to mind or consciousness. Mechanism and vitalism compete directly as rival interpretations of the facts of biology.[1] Just as the mechanical theory of nature, from its home in the physico-chemical sciences, is ever tending to overflow the whole field of Nature and engulf biology and psychology, so, in return, there are not lacking attempts to borrow from biology the concept of life or vital impulse, or from psychology the concept of mind or consciousness, as a directive factor, and apply them to all natural phenomena.

[1] See chs. vi and vii.

Physics, biology, and psychology have in turn supplied the fundamental concepts for metaphysical theories. We are here in a region of metaphysical experiments where the alternatives range from the materialism of, say, Haeckel, to the vitalism of Bergson and the panpsychism of C. A. Strong. Confronting all these alike are philosophies seeking to maintain and defend the orders and distinctions which in common thought we acknowledge and live by, and which are reflected accurately enough in the system of natural sciences. There Nature is taken as a hierarchy of inorganic or non-living, and organic or living. The latter in·turn is divided into the living but not conscious, and the living which is also " besouled ".[1] Moreover, this hierarchy presents not merely a classificatory scheme, but also an evolutionary series, in which the lower and earlier stages endure and persist, as basis and environment for the higher and later. We may even, within the realm of living bodies which are besouled, distinguish degrees or levels of soul— beings which can sense and feel but not think from beings which can also think and reason, or beings who are merely conscious from beings who are also self-conscious. At this last point, however, we shall probably be held definitely to pass beyond the legitimate limits of a philosophy of Nature. For self-consciousness is a " reflexive " phenomenon in which the spectator-standpoint, with its self-forgetfulness, its interest in the object for its own sake, be it an interest of knowledge or of aesthetic enjoyment, is transcended. This is not to deny that the attitude of objectivity can be restored, or regained, at a higher level after the inclusion of self-consciousness. Indeed, we may hold this to be essential, and the supreme task of philosophy. Meanwhile, philosophy of Nature moves at the level of thought for which the spectator-attitude is characteristic. The

---

[1] ἔμψυχος, beseelt.

spectator here does not take into account that, after all, he is not merely taking stock of a spectacle, but is, in the very act of doing so, himself a part of the spectacle, an agent in the play. When he does take account of this, he passes from interest in the object to interest in the study and theory of the object, from philosophy of Nature to philosophy of Science; in short, to theory of knowledge. But this is not the only, nor the most important, effect of the turn to self-consciousness. More important is the reminder how completely the meaning of " Nature ", even in the utmost extension which current usage permits us to give to the term, fails to include all those achievements and activities which we may conveniently sum up in the term " Civilisation ". The biological concepts which suffice for dealing with human beings as an animal species fail to serve for the analysis of morality or religion, art or science; and equally patent is the failure of any psychology the orientation of which is towards " naturalism " rather than towards what Hegel called a " phenomenology of spirit ". At some point or other the difference between *Naturwissenschaft* and *Geisteswissenschaft* demands recognition; and there is no way of avoiding this recognition and still doing justice to the facts. The turn to self-consciousness, as we called it above, means, in fact, not this or that individual's attention to his private self, but the philosopher's awakening to the ideal values which the lives and institutions of human beings very literally embody—which through men and women of flesh and blood (" physico-chemical machines ", if we like) are being realised in, and by use of, that " Nature " of which they are parts. It is, we suggest, precisely in the participation in the service of these ideal values, that the true function of " soul ", " mind ", or " consciousness " in individual human beings is to be found." [1]

[1] See ch. viii *ad fin.*

To mention " ideal values " is, of course, to open up the whole problem of *teleology* which forms, as it were, the upper limit of the philosophy of Nature, the bridge from Nature to Spirit. So far as the mechanical theory of Nature prevails, there is no room for the category of purpose. On the other hand, it is only by doing violence to the facts that biologists can avoid expressing themselves in language of teleological import. At the same time, biologists are rightly reluctant to use the term " purpose " in any sense which might suggest the presence of conscious desire, plan, or design where no evidence for such consciousness is to be found. This raises the very difficult question whether the psychological sense of purpose, as aim or object of desire, can be extended by analogy, as the panpsychists propose to do, through the organic even to the inorganic, or whether conscious purpose in human beings is not a special form of a deeper-lying unconscious purposiveness in the total structure of the world. The suggestion may be ventured that a teleology in terms, not so much of conscious purpose, as of *objective value* may meet the situation.[1]

But we do not need to pursue these ramifications of the philosophy of Nature in order to see that the special problems of the relation of matter, life, mind, which the spectacle of Nature raises, are forms of the general problem, how to order and how to interpret the sense-data which are what we immediately experience of Nature. To doubt the " reality " of the world of sense is to doubt a theory or interpretation of the sense-data. The very distinction among objects of experience between those which are real and those which are unreal is a matter of theory. Hence, before entering in later essays on the special problems of physical objects, living beings, and minds, we cannot do better than explore, in

[1] See ch. vi.

this essay, in what ways it is possible to doubt the reality of the world of sense.

There is an old tradition in philosophy which holds such doubt to be the gate to wisdom. But many of the grounds which have, in the history of philosophy, been assigned in support of it, have lost their appeal for our scientifically-minded age, or at least do not weigh with us as heavily as once they did. The Eastern doctrines of the senses as spreading a veil of illusion over reality, and of the elaborate ascetic regimen for mind and body by which the student must discipline himself for penetrating to the reality behind the veil, have never profoundly affected the main current of Western thought. Most of the great philosophers of the West, certainly since the time of the Renaissance, have been men of the world as well as students and thinkers. They have not tried to be " holy " men, set apart from their fellows and the problems of contemporary life. They have not, even when they were professors, spent their days in meditation and mortification of the flesh in order to achieve, individually, the blessedness of union with the One behind the veil. Again the dualism, commonly, though perhaps erroneously, ascribed to Plato, between the flux of sensations and the immutable, imperishable Forms, is not characteristic of the best Western philosophy, though its influences have been, and will continue to be, felt again and again. It is not on such grounds as these that, in recent discussions, the reality of the world of sense has been doubted. Present-day doubts fasten, in part, upon the distinction between what is real and what is unreal in experience, and in part upon what the " real " nature of the real is. In either case the issue turns on the truth of a theory, an interpretation; be it the truth of the classification which excludes from the " real " world the objects of

dreams, hallucinations, and other abnormal experiences as
" unreal "; or be it the truth of one of the many theories
concerning the nature of some, or all, of the objects which
are real.

That the problem of the " reality " of anything can
always be turned into a problem of the truth of a theory
concerning that something, is easily illustrated by reflecting
what is meant by speaking of a " *world* of sense ". Particular sense-data here and now cannot be doubted. Taken
thus abstractly, they assert nothing, they mean nothing.
They simply *are*. It has unfortunately become the fashion
to speak of them as being " real ", when what is meant is
merely that they are, occur, are " had " (as Driesch puts
it) or experienced. In this sense, of course, their " reality "
is not in debate. But as soon as they are taken to
mean something, are classified in some way, are regarded
as being related, as having implications and consequences,
they are caught up in a network of theory, and their reality
in *this* sense is, at once, open to doubt, but open also to
confirmation. Suppose, *e.g.*, that you hear a faint sound,
and then begin to wonder whether it is a real sound or an
imaginary one. (The point remains the same if you wonder
whether you really heard a sound or only imagined that
you did). Here, at once, a theory is at stake. If the sound
you heard was real, it will be connected with other things
in the universe in a way very different from that in which
the imaginary sound is connected. Or take a somewhat
more complicated case. Were the voices heard by Joan of
Arc real or were they auditory hallucinations? In either
case there is no doubt that Joan really experienced something. But what that something was or meant, a divine
presence calling her to save France, or a symptom of
religious hysteria—this is the issue of reality in the

pregnant sense of the true nature of that which she experienced.

The occurrence, then, of sense-data at the moment when they are being had, is indubitable. But to talk of a " world " of sense-data is at once a theory. It signalises the step from data to interpretation. Do we sense a world? The present moment's tissue of colours, sounds, smells, touches—is this a world? No and Yes. No, if we think of their disorder, as given, of their mutual irrelevancies, of their fragmentariness. Yes, if we think of the order and meaning which we have learnt to discover in them and which we now habitually find there. But, certainly, in discovering order and meaning, we have had to go beyond the present moment's data. We have had to call in memories of previous experiences, correlating, synthesising, identifying their data with those of present experience. We have learnt to regard the latter as a fragment of something *more*—of things sensed in the past or to be sensed in the future, or, more generally still, capable of being sensed (" sensibilia "). Thus in all directions the force of " world " carries us beyond the here-and-now of sense-data. The moment's actual data are but the spear-point of the world of " possible experience ". Again, " world " connotes system, an ordered whole. But what is there of order in our actual sense-data here and now? We might mention co-existence in space, and succession in time, but so far as sense-data exhibit such order, they constitute little more than a " Together " —a continuum, or changing manifold, which is barely distinguishable from a chaos. More pregnantly, order means relevance, or logical connection—more particularly connection according to some " law " or " universal principle ". It means, too, the grouping of sense-data into complexes such that we are able to recognise and identify a complex when only one, or a few, of its constituent members are given. Perceiving some, we "know" what others belong to the group, and may, or will, be perceived by us. Such complexes of sense-data, actual and possible, are, according to phenomenalist thinkers, all that we mean by individual "things", either in science or in practical life. But of course, such synthesis of sense-data into things is once more "interpretation", *i.e.*, expansion of what is given here and now, with the help of previous experience and subject to verification by future experience. There is nothing that brings home to us so clearly the theoretical character of this whole process of the discovery of an orderly world in the chaos of sense-data, than to reflect on the fact that the synthesis of which we have been speaking, involves the identification of a datum here and now with other data experienced on other occasions and in other contexts, nay even its identification with data of different kinds, as all aspects, or qualities, of the "same" individual thing. But this identification of differences is no arbitrary and subjective device of human thinking. On the contrary, in it we follow and obey the objective principle of identity in difference without which there are neither "things", nor a "world" of things; without which, in short, any interpretation of sense-data is impossible.

The view here maintained, that a question of "reality" always discloses, on analysis, a question of the truth of a theory, may also be illustrated by considering the terms "physical", "material", "external world", which are commonly treated as synonyms of "world of sense". Every one of these adjectives has a theoretical import. It expresses the interpretation of sense-data in terms of some set of concepts, involving, as a rule, a classification of things, *e.g.*, material and mental, spatial and non-spatial, *etc.* At the same time, a moment's consideration suffices to

show that none of the alleged synonyms is co-extensive with
the " world of sense ". The physical world, for example,
is no doubt a world of sense in that the physicist, in his
observing, experimenting, verifying, is guided by sense-data
throughout. But there are many familiar sense-experiences
of which he takes no account, and which he methodically
excludes from the evidence on which he builds his theories.
No element can be known in chemistry, no force or energy
in physics, unless its presence becomes sensibly apparent,
however indirectly, through some difference in what we
observe. The most advanced theories of the constitution
of " matter ", whether they be framed in terms of atoms,
or ions, or electro-magnetic discharges, or whatnot, rest in
the last resort on specific differences in sense-data. But
the sense-data which are thus relevant for physical theory
are not co-extensive with the world of sense-data. The
latter is much wider, and more miscellaneous than the
world of physics. The physicist practises a vigorous selection among the actual data which he shares with non-
scientific mortals. He ignores the beauty or ugliness of
physical things. Abnormal and supernormal experiences
do not count as evidences to him. He does not admit the
objects and events witnessed in dreams as facts to which
his theories have to be adjusted. Yet, as Russell has well
reminded us, " dreams and waking life, in our first efforts
at construction, must be treated with equal respect; it is
only by some reality not *merely* sensible that dreams can
be condemned." [1] In fact, physical theory both rests on,
and results in, a classification of objects of experience, such
that those which satisfy the laws of physics are admitted,
whilst the rest is left to be dealt with in the context of some
other theory.

Again, the term " material world ", if not used as a

[1] *Our Knowledge of the External World*, p. 86. Russell's italics.

mere equivalent of "physical world", imports into the
problem of the reality of the world of sense a burden of
theory of its own.   For by long-standing association it suggests its opposite, the immaterial, commonly identified with
the mental or spiritual.   Between them these terms in-
vite to a sorting out of all things in the universe into two
kinds, material things or bodies, immaterial things or souls.
When this familiar dualism of popular metaphysics, canon-
ised in philosophy by Descartes, is applied to sense-data,
we find ourselves asking such questions as, In what sense,
if any, can bodies or souls be perceived by the senses? and,
Should sense-data be pigeon-holed under " body " or under
" mind "?   We shall, clearly, come to very different conclusions about the reality of the world of sense, according
as we set down colours, sounds, *etc.*, as " sensations ", and,
therefore, as psychical states, modes of consciousness, contents of minds, or, else, as the very stuff that bodies are
made of, or as qualities of physical things.   If we follow
the psychologists of the analytic and introspective school
in enumerating colour, sound, smell, *etc.*, as so many differences in the " quality " of " sensations ",[1] we ought,
strictly, to speak not of a sensation of blue, but of a blue
sensation; not of seeing a blue thing, but of having a blue
state of consciousness.   Similar language would seem to
be demanded by the view that all sense-data are " subjective ", *i.e.*, mental or intra-mental, on the ground that the
" real ", *i.e.*, material, objects must be conceived in terms
exclusively of " primary qualities ", and hence as colourless, soundless, tasteless.   This is the view which a dis-
gusted critic, quoted by Bosanquet,[2] sums up in the im-

[1] Some writers of this school, *e.g.*, Professor G. F. Stout, combine
with this the view that the qualities of sensations mediate our knowledge of " sensible qualities " inhering in physical objects. *Cf.* his
Manual of Psychology, 3rd edition.
[2] Adamson Lecture, *The Distinction Between Mind and Its Objects*,
p. 7.

patient exclamation: " What a world is that which science pronounces real; dark, cold, and shaking like a jelly." Against either view common sense rebels, and so does all philosophy which cares about vindicating for the familiar things of our " material " environment their panoply of sense-qualities. Those neo-realists who declare sense-data to be " non-mental ", in order, by the magic virtue of this term, to plant them safely " out there " in the " real " world, are, at least, guided by a sound instinct, whatever one may think of their language. As a matter of fact, the dualism of body and mind, or matter and spirit, considered as the two substances of which the universe is made up, has been the greatest trouble-maker in philosophy since Descartes' time. Indeed, the history of modern philosophy might be described as the history of the efforts to cast off the meshes of this metaphysical net and return to an unprejudiced " phenomenology ", *i.e.*, a study of appearances, in their diversity, their order, their mutual interdependence, their total meaning.

When, lastly, we try to take " external world " as a synonym of " world of sense ", once more we find ourselves caught in a net of theories. External, strictly, means spatial. The external world is the world of things in space, of *res extensae*. But do all sense-data belong to the same spatial system? Are the spaces of dream-worlds, or of the many worlds of imagination, identical with the space of the waking world which we call " real "? Those who, with Bertrand Russell believe in the privacy of sense-data, have as many private spaces to deal with as there are sets of private sense-data. Moreover, there is the problem for them of explaining the relations of these private spaces to the " public " space of the physical world. The situation is hardly more comfortable for those who endow " sensa-tions ", taken as mental states, with the quality of " extensity ", and then labour to show how our " idea " of the real space of the non-mental, physical world is developed from this basis. In all these ways the " reality " of the world of sense, taken as " external ", shows itself to be a matter of theory, and, as such, open to argument. And in all this we have not even touched on that other sense of " external ", in which the reality of the external world means its independence, in existence and character, of being perceived or known by any mind whatsoever.

If in our discussion of the reality of the world of sense up to this point we have roamed far and wide, our excuse must be that a philosopher's argument, like the wind, bloweth him whithersoever it listeth, but that, at least, it is his duty to expose himself to all the winds of heaven and catch them, if he can, in his sail. And our result, so far, may be summed up as follows. The " world of sense ", we find, covers all sense-data, but it covers also their interpretation as a world. If we ask concerning the " reality " of this world, and do not by this term mean simply the givenness (so to speak) of the sense-data, we can get no answer except in terms of some theory as to what sort of a world it is—what are its constituents, what its structure and order, what its meaning. These theories, we find, fall, broadly, into two groups. One set is concerned with the distinction between what is real and what is unreal. The other is concerned with the real nature of the real world. The difficulty of drawing a clear line of demarcation between these two groups results chiefly from the tendency to restrict the " real " world to that selection from the whole world of sense which is dealt with by the physical sciences, thus excluding as unreal dreams and suchlike sense-experiences, but threatening with unreality also all those characters and relations of real things which are not dealt with by the physical sciences.

The conclusion which appears to emerge is that the " reality " of anything may be doubted in one of two senses. We may doubt either its being real, or its being really so-and-so. In the former sense, " to be real " is a synonym for " to exist ", and what is real is then opposed to the unreal, the non-existent, the imaginary. In the latter sense, " really " is synonymous with " truly ", and emphasises adverbially the truth of the judgment that something is so-and-so. Both senses appear to be combined intentionally when the universe, as a whole, is spoken of as " Reality " or " The Reality ", the meaning being " all that exists in its true, or real, character."

Another way of putting the difference is to say that the real, in the existential sense, is opposed by the unreal, but the real, in the sense of the true, by the apparent or the false. The distinction between " reality " and " appearance " will then belong to this latter problem of the true nature of the actual or existent.

Or, again, we may say that the former distinction leads to a classification of objects as real or unreal, existent or non-existent. The latter distinction leads to an ordering of judgments concerning any object of experience according to the " degree " of their truth.

It is in the former sense that we ask whether such-and-such things exist; it is in the latter sense that, assured of existence, we ask whether a thing is really so-and-so. The one sense concerns the " that ", the other the " what ". In the one sense we may decide, after enquiring, that " there exists no such thing "; ˉin the other sense we may be sure that there is something there without knowing what it is, or whether our judgments of its nature are true.

Can we throw any further light on this distinction? Can we, perhaps, get behind it? Let us consider some examples of it. Let us experiment with it.

As synonym of " true ", " real " often has the force of " genuine ", and asserts the fulfilment, as it were, of a claim. Thus when we say, that somebody is " a real man " the meaning is that he embodies all a man ought to be, realises our ideal of manhood. The same thought might be expressed by saying, that he is a man in the true sense of the word, *i.e.*, in the full or maximum sense. The judgment would reflect the fact that an object may realise the character by which we classify it, more or less perfectly. Being of the kind it is, a thing is always more or less good of its kind. For every character by which we can classify may also supply a standard for estimating perfection in that respect. Thus, if our example were to be challenged by saying " the person you refer to is not a real man ", or, " not really a man ", the normal meaning would be that he falls short, certainly of the ideal, perhaps of the average, of manhood by being, say, cowardly or effeminate. Only secondarily, or in unusual contexts, would the meaning be that the object referred to is not a man at all, but, say, a wax-figure made to look like a " real " man, or a stump of a tree mistaken on a foggy day for a human figure. Here the very classification would be challenged, but the challenge would only bring to light the fact that the mistaken classification was suggested—one might almost say, demanded—by the cunning fake, or by the shape and height of the stump. In either case, the judgment rests on evidence which further evidence belies. There is a claim not sustained, a character suggested, but not proved genuine. So, again, a sleeper who awakes with the vivid recollection upon him of a scene just witnessed, may be at a loss to decide between dream and real fact. The point to notice here is that the data in dreams are interpreted as spontaneously as data in waking perception.[1] The whole complex of data and interpretation is taken by the dreamer not only as really so, but as real, until conflict with the experiences of waking life suggests doubts. *Vice versa*, the events of waking experience are occasionally so startling or incredible as to suggest doubts whether one be not dreaming.[2] In all cases what is doubted is the genuineness of the claim of something to be real or to have really the character which it appears to have.

In considering examples such as these, and especially examples drawn from the comparison of dream and waking experience, it is impossible not to feel a certain pull towards an assimilation to each other of the problems whether something is real and whether it is really so-and-so. In both cases we deal with matters of theory, of judgment, but our suggestion now is that the judgment that something is real or unreal, depends on the thing's character, and hence cannot be discussed in abstraction from the judgment that the thing is really so-and-so. The two senses of " reality ", in short, though they may be distinguished, are too closely connected to be profitably separated.

But before we can follow up this suggestion and present a more detailed defence of it, it will repay us to learn what we can from a consideration of two recent discussions of the nature and status of " unreal " objects—discussions which deserve the attention of students of philosophy no less because of the eminence of the debaters than because of their striking divergence from each other in spite of a general affinity in their philosophical positions. We refer to the

---

[1] This is the reason why dreams can be reported in the language of the " real " world.
[2] *Cf.* the proverbial pinching oneself to make sure one is awake.

Gegenstandstheorie of Meinong and his school, on the one side, and to Bertrand Russell's criticism of it, on the other.[1]

It is characteristic of the method of *Gegenstandstheorie* to insist with equal emphasis both on the difference between " mental " acts of apprehension and " non-mental " objects, and also on their invariable correlation, in that every act of apprehension has an object and thus affords a glimpse into the realm where *Gegenstände* of all sorts have " being ". In fact, we are invited to think of the universe as a realm of " being " in the widest, and therefore also emptiest, sense of the word. Within it, we are to distinguish kinds or modes of being, such as " existence " and " subsistence ". Or, using " subsistence " as a synonym for " being " in general, we shall distinguish existent from non-existent, real from unreal, being, as in the following sketch of the universe by a neo-realist writer who declares it to be composed of " all things physical, mental, logical, propositions and terms, ex-istent and non-existent, false and true, good and evil, real and unreal." [2] The unicorns, the mermaids, the golden mountains of fairy-tale, the spirits and forces and magical influences of things on one another of primitive supersti-tion, the objects and events of nightmares, will " have being " or " subsist " in such a universe as truly as the things of the " real " world of common-sense and natural science. There simply will *be* things which are " real " and other things which are " unreal ", and if we are realists we shall add that neither sort owes its being in any way to being perceived, conceived, or in some other manner ap-prehended by a mind. The result may strike those who

---

[1] See especially A. Meinong's *Untersuchungen zur Gegenstandstheorie und Phychologie,* and for the most recent statement of Russell's position, his *Introduction to Mathematical Philosophy,* esp. chs. xv, xvi.
[2] E. B. Holt, *The Place of Illusory Experience in a Realistic World,* in *The New Realism,* p. 372.

have not familiarised themselves with such a view as de-
cidedly queer, but it is, at any rate, the outcome of a
straightforward application of the principle that whatever
any mind is in any way conscious of, or whatever it can
think of, or talk about, must at any rate *be*.

But, perhaps, as Russell suggests, the grammatical structure of language here induces metaphysical illusions, which
it is the business of logical analysis to dispel. Language
consists of symbols, and it is the function of symbols to
have meanings. The danger is that we may attribute meaning to groups of symbols which, by themselves, have no
meaning, though when joined with other words in propositions they help to express the total meaning of the proposition as a whole. The propositions of a fairy-tale about
fairies and golden mountains, and so forth, are capable of
being understood, and thus have an intelligible meaning.
The illusion is that this meaning depends on there *being*,
in a " world of imagination ", fairies and golden mountains,
just as in the " real world " there *are* men and women and
mountains of chalk or granite. The problem is to find an
interpretation of propositions apparently mentioning, and
referring to, unreal objects, which shall save for them, as
wholes, the intelligible meaning they clearly have, without
saddling us with the task of finding a place in the world
for things which have no place there. For to the question,
Do fairies exist? we shall reply, There are no such things,
only to be met by the retort, How then can you talk or
think of them? The familiar device of distinguishing " uni-
verses of discourse "—a real world, a world of fairy-tale,
a world of literary fiction, *etc.*—does not solve the problem,
but only evades it. No doubt, such sorting out into worlds
prevents direct contradiction. It permits us playfully to
fancy that there are hobgoblins round the corner of the
door without being unduly disappointed if, on looking, we

find nothing there. But, after all, we cannot forget that these make-believe objects and worlds depend on the way in which real minds, real human beings, use the symbols, linguistic and otherwise, which they have fashioned. By this link, as meanings conditioned by symbols employed by men of flesh and blood, unreal objects are tied to the real world. To ignore this is to be lacking in that " sense of reality " which, as Russell insists, " is vital in Logic." " Logic, I should maintain, must no more admit a unicorn than zoölogy can; for logic is concerned with the real world just as truly as zoölogy, though with its more abstract and general features. To say that unicorns have an existence in heraldry, or in literature, or in imagination, is a most pitiful and paltry evasion. What exists in heraldry is not an animal, made of flesh and blood, moving and breathing of its own initiative. What exists is a picture, or a description in words. Similarly, to maintain that Hamlet, for example, exists in his own world, namely, in the world of Shakespeare's imagination, just as truly as (say) Napoleon existed in the ordinary world, is to say something deliberately confusing, or else confused to a degree which is scarcely credible. There is only one world, the " real " world: Shakespeare's imagination is part of it, and the thoughts that he had in writing Hamlet are real. So are the thoughts that we have in reading the play. But it is of the very essence of fiction that only the thoughts, feelings, *etc.*, in Shakespeare and his readers are real, and that there is not, in addition to them, an objective Hamlet. When you have taken account of all the feelings roused by Napoleon in writers and readers of history, you have not touched the actual man; but in the case of Hamlet you have come to the end of him. If no one thought about Hamlet, there would be nothing left of him; if no one had thought about Napoleon, he would have soon seen to it that some

one did." [1]   This, we shall agree, is common sense, and
when common sense can quote the high authority of mathematical logic, it is time for philosophers to sit up and take
notice.

What, then, is Russell's solution of the problem?
Stripped of his technical language about " propositional
functions ", " descriptions ", and so forth, it comes to this,
that the meaning of propositions about fairies depends on
the *concept* fairy, but not on the existence of " a fairy "
or " fairies " somewhere in the real world which is the only
world.   In other words, though we can talk of fairies and
make significant assertions about them, we never meet in
experience with a situation in which we can say, " *This*
is a fairy ", or " *there* are fairies ", where " this " and
" there " are the linguistic equivalents of pointing at actual
sense-data or particulars.   If we ever perceived something
of which we could truly say, " This is a fairy ", then at
least one fairy would exist.   But, for lack of such cases,
we must say of fairies, " There are no such creatures ", or
" Fairies are unreal ", the meaning being that the concept
" fairy " is inapplicable in the real world, which, at the very
least, is the world of actual sense-data.   In Russell's language, " fairies are unreal " means that the " description ",
fairy, describes nothing, that the function x is a fairy, is
always false.

There is a great deal of technical refinement in Russell's
statement of his view into which it is not necessary for our
purposes to follow him.   But if the above correctly represents the substance of his theory, we may heartily agree
to it, so far as it goes.   It is, however, easy to see that there
are a great many questions suggested by such a theory,
to which Russell neither refers nor replies.   There is, *e.g.*,
the question, how we get these concepts, or descriptions, of

[1] *Introduction to Mathematical Philosophy*, p. 169.

unreal things—how we know what it would be to be a fairy —seeing that there are no fairies to give us a clue. The interest of such a question lies in its suggestion of the parallel question, how we get the concepts, or descriptions, which do apply in the real world, and how we determine when we have got a concept in its "true" or "real" form. To the technicalities of formal analysis in which Russell is interested throughout his argument, these "epistemological" questions are perhaps irrelevant. But when we are interested in the concrete problem of the reality of the world of sense, these questions inevitably come to the front.

At any rate, there is one thing which we may well learn from Russell, and hold fast against Meinong. Apparent classifications of objects into "real" and "unreal", "existent" and "non-existent", are not really classifications of particular objects at all, but of concepts, or descriptions, according as experience presents, or does not present, cases for their application. And, further, "being real" and "being unreal" are themselves concepts, or descriptions, predicable of other concepts according as these are, or are not, to be found realised in sensible particulars. The same remark applies to "existent" and "non-existent". It is only concerning concepts that we can ask, "Does *such* a thing exist?" meaning whether in the world of sense some datum, or group of data, can be found of which we can say, "This is *it*", or "This is one of that sort". It will be noted that this is but a more elaborate statement of the position from which we started out above, *viz.*, that a question of reality, once we pass beyond bare, uninterpreted data, is always a question of the truth of a theory, *i.e.*, in the language of the present argument, of the applicability of a concept, or description.

But are we not, it may be asked, making a predicate, or attribute, of "existence"? Are we not forgetting, or running counter to, the well-known argument by which Hume and Kant upset the ontological proof? By no means—on the contrary, we may claim that ours is but a modern version of their position. For what they challenged when they argued that " existence " is not an attribute analytically contained in the definition of a concept, was the view that an *a priori* concept can guarantee its own applicability, *i.e.*, that it can guarantee the occurrence in experience of a " this ", of which it shall be true to say, " This is it " (" it " in the ontological argument being God).[1] When Kant declares that there is no difference in attributes, *i.e.*, in description, between " real " and " imaginary " dollars, and that the difference lies in that the former are empirically given, the latter not, he is clearly affirming, in effect, the position here laid down.

What we have said may suffice for the abstractly formal side of the problem of reality. But the situation, as we have already indicated above in anticipation, is a great deal more complicated when we are dealing with concrete problems of reality in respect of the actual world of sense. It will help to clear up these complications to some extent, if we distinguish at least three typically different ways in which problems of " reality ", *i.e.*, of the truth of judgments affirming a concept (or " universal ") of the this-here-now, may arise.

(1) The first of these three situations arises from the fact that what is given always has a definite character of its own—is a " this-such "[2]—but that the extent and de-

---

[1] Of course, it is quite another matter to begin at the empirical end by asking whether the world as a whole, or anything in the world, possesses the special character which, once recognised, we call " divine ". Here we begin with what is given, and work, through deepening and enlarging experience and interpretation to its true character. We do not begin with a definition and seek to apply it. See ch. x.

[2] We shall have occasion to return to this point in the following essay (ch. v).

gree to which this character is revealed or known, depends both on the range of experiences which furnish materials for synthesis, and on the type of unity thus discerned. In all argument, whether in ordinary intercourse, in science, or in philosophy, if the disputants are not simply " at cross-purposes ", the " this ", or, more generally, the point of reference, is agreed on and recognised to be the same, but the rival theories, or descriptions, of its character conflict. The familiar story of the theological disputant exclaiming to his opponent: " Your God is my Devil ", is an extreme instance of such conflict. Everyday instances may be found in any argument between men disputing the accuracy of one another's memory of the same event, or whether an object seen at a distance is a human being or a tree-trunk. Other examples may be found whenever we distinguish between denying a " fact " and denying a " theory about the fact ", as when a behaviourist, like E. B. Holt, warns his fellow-behaviourists against repeating the " materialist's error, of denying the *facts*, as well as the *theory*, of consciousness." [1] That there are things in the world, things met with in experience, to which the term " consciousness " applies, is here conceded as fact. But *what* is the nature of these consciousnesses, that is in dispute, the extremes of theory ranging from immaterial, immortal soul-substance to stream of ideas and integration of reflex-responses to the environment. All these are questions of something being really so or really thus, with two, or more, positive alternatives of theory opposing each other. And most commonly these questions arise at a level where, not only the bare data, but up to a point the interpretation is agreed upon. For, clearly, there are levels, or strata, of interpretation. At the level of description of the given which suffices for the correct identifica-

---

[1] *The Freudian Wish,* Supplementary Essay on *Response and Cognition,* p. 207.

tion of the familiar objects and happenings of daily life, savage and civilised man commonly agree. When interpretation is pushed further, *e.g.*, into causes, they begin to disagree, the savage taking the turn into magic and animism, the civilised man into science. Potatoes, water, and cooking they recognise alike, but when, at a high altitude, boiling water fails to cook potatoes, the unscientific mind blames the devil in the cursed pot, the scientific mind traces the correlation of boiling point and atmospheric pressure.[1] Mr. T. P. Nunn proposes [2] to distinguish " primary syntheses " (or interpretations) of sensational data on which all men agree, from " secondary syntheses " which may be either " animistic " beliefs or " scientific " hypotheses. But it would be better to distinguish not merely two, but many, levels, or strata, of interpretation, some mutually incompatible, others rather complementary or built up on one another in some such hierarchical order as we have in the order of the sciences, from physics and chemistry through biology to psychology. Here, as before, the aim is to get the best total interpretation, where " best " means both the most comprehensive or inclusive, and the most systematic and organising. And if we are to be honestly systematic, there must be no slurring over of empirically recognisable differences, in order to be able to say that " nothing but " some abstract generality is involved. Thus, *e.g.*, the distinction between the living and the non-living is one of the corner-stones of the order we recognise in the world and on which we found our conduct, yet the theory of mechanism confronts that of vitalism, and panpsychism claims to be able to replace both. Indeed, all interpretations in terms of " life " and " mind " raise, for the philosopher, the

[1] The instance comes from Darwin's *The Voyage of the Beagle.* I owe it to Mr. T. P. Nunn's *The Aims of Scientific Method*, ch. ii, p. 46.
[2] *Loc. cit.*, p. 47.

choice between being "positivistic" (or "phenomenalistic"), *i.e.*, construing every fact as a complex of sense-data, and being "metaphysical". And there are, again, two ways of being metaphysical—one, which consists in positing non-perceptible entities and forces, from "atoms" to "entelechies" and "souls"; the other, which claims that characters such as life and mind are empirically recognisable where they occur, though not perceptible in the sense of consisting merely of patterns of sense-data with their, relations of co-existence and succession.

(ii) The examples on which we found Russell chiefly relying—creatures of fairy-tale, characters in literature, and all figments of the imagination generally—raise the "reality" problem in a very different form. Much depends here on how explicit the distinction between fact and fiction is in a person's thought. To a child, believing in the existence of the grotesque creatures of nursery-tales, afraid of the dark because of unseen presences in it, these creatures are real as objects of possible perception.[1] But when a novelist assures us that the characters of his tale "have no existence outside the pages of his book", *i.e.*, that he has not described the doings of actual persons of his acquaintance, we understand clearly that we must not expect to meet his characters in the street, or have any of the relations to them, of buying or selling, marrying or giving in marriage, which we have to "real" people. We can see, on reflection, that we are dealing with a phenomenon of language,

---

[1] I may, perhaps, illustrate this by an experience of my boyhood. I believed so firmly in the reality of the Christ-child as the giver of good things at Christmas that one of my first uses of the laboriously acquired art of writing was to indite a letter to the Christ-child, setting forth my wishes. The letter was duly placed outside the window for the convenience of the angelic mail, and, of course, removed by a grown-up relative. But I, presently finding it gone, was firmly convinced that I had just caught the flash of the departing angel's wings in the sky. I had there my data on which the reality of the whole belief hung.

or, generally, of symbolism. For, though the meanings of our symbols are, in the first instance, found realised, or, at least, considered as realisable, in the " real " world, they can, by supposition or make-believe, be detached, and as a result, through the whole range from idle fancy to highest literary art, we can indulge in a real occupation with meanings unrealised and unrealisable—with the " unreal things " of common parlance.

(iii) But a third group of reality-problems is not so simply disposed of. The problems of this group have this in common, as distinct from those of the preceding group, that they spring from *actual* data, the interpretation of which is wellnigh impossible within the framework of theory which we call the " real " world of practice and science, and which suggest interpretations of their own, more or less flagrantly in conflict with that framework. In two directions we find especially striking instances of such vagabond phenomena, roaming on the fringes of our orderly universe, and not admitted into it, like the arts, as licensed jesters or tragedians. One of these groups of instances is to be found in all the phenomena under investigation by Societies of Psychical Research. Any one who knows these phenomena only by description, may well feel, when perusing reports of apparitions of ghosts, materialisations, levitations, communications from departed spirits through the trance-utterances of mediums, that he might be more convinced if he, personally, were to have such experiences—to see what he could not but explain as a ghost, to witness heavy objects moving through the air without discoverable physical cause, to receive communications of unmistakable authenticity from departed friends. But this is the smaller difficulty. Having the experiences, he would, indeed, have the data, the " facts ", and so far he would be in a better position to judge. But the mere seeing and hearing would not, even

then, settle for him the question of the truth of rival interpretations, from telepathy and telaesthesia to supernormal
action of " spirits ", which are so utterly without analogue
among the interpretations to which especially the natural
sciences have accustomed him. And when he finds reputable witnesses recording themselves as convinced, from their
personal observations, of the truth of such tales as that men
can take on at will the shape of wild beasts [1]—tales which
he had been wont to class among the most grotesque super-
stitions of savages—Hamlet's reminder that " there are more
things in heaven and earth, Horatio, than are dreamt of in
your philosophy," may seem the only possible comment.
To set these phenomena aside as abnormal does not help.
The field of psychical research is full of data, as multitudinous as they are varied, which the best will to disbelieve cannot either fit into the pattern of orthodox physical
or psychological science, or dispose of by wholesale label-
lings as fraud, coincidence, credulity. What is real here,
what unreal, *i.e.*, what theory will turn out to be true, what
others false, who will confidently presume to tell? Of one
thing only can we be reasonably sure: reality here, as elsewhere, will in the end prove to be that theory which supplies the most comprehensive, as well as systematic, interpretation of all the relevant data.

And the other group of difficult instances is formed by
dreams, which are difficult even when we wholly omit from
consideration prophetic and veridical dreams as being, once
more, abnormal and rare. In spite of all the illuminating
study of dreams which in recent years we have had from
psychologists, like Freud, or from philosophers, like Berg-

[1] See Richard Bagot's article on *The Hyenas of Pirra* in the *Corn-
hill Magazine*, Oct. 1918. The article is based on the independent
testimony of two British officers in Nigeria. See also the *Journal*
of the Society for Psychical Research (London), vol. xix, no. 157
(July 1919).

son, the problems which dreams present for a theory of
reality can hardly be said to have been exhausted. Dreams
are composed of sense-data,[1] which are all through the dream
interpreted and identified, be it as objects we are familiar
with in waking experience (*e.g.*, in dreaming of a friend), be
it as objects like those we are familiar with (houses, trees,
etc.). The verisimilitude of dreams is sometimes so complete that there is nothing to exclude the experience from
the real world except the fact that we awake from it in bed.
Still, this is enough of discontinuity, at any rate for practical
purposes, to justify our setting dream-objects and events
down as " unreal ", a conclusion reinforced by the many
dreams in which the sequence of events and the behaviour
of objects are chaotic as measured by the order of the daylight world. " Unreal " here means that the theory—for
we know, by now, that the order of the daylight world
is a theory—the application of which to the sense-data to
which it does apply, yields the " real world ", does not apply
to the data within the dream. But with dreams we are
fortunate enough to be able to take a further step. Granted
that what we dream is unreal, *i.e.*, that taken *bona fide* for
what it ostensibly is, it does not fit into the pattern of the
real world, and has none of the consequences and implications there which as a genuine member of the pattern it
should have, yet at the same time the dreamings, as events
in a real dreamer's life, have a place and date in the temporal order. And if, in addition, we can interpret the subject-matter of dreams, as Freud has taught us to do, as the
symbolic disguise of the satisfaction of wishes repressed in

---

[1] It would take too long to defend this statement, which might easily
be supported from the literature, against objections. Suffice to say
that a vivid dream is indistinguishable for the dreamer from waking-
experience along the lines of images versus sense-data; that the inference to dreams being composed of images, in spite of their vivid-
ness, is open to criticism; and that images, in any case are revivals
of sense-data.

real life, we have taken yet a further step towards integrating these excursions into the unreal with the tissue of the real world.

At any rate, throughout this discussion, we have found no reason to abandon the general, if so far purely formal, principle that " reality ", or " the real world ", is the most comprehensive and coherent system of interpretations which alike is based upon, and also continually confirmed by, the manifold sense-data which come and go from moment to moment. At any point the true interpretation of these data is that which (a) either implies, or is at least compatible with, the largest number of other interpretations accepted as true; and (b) which is open in principle, if not always in practice, to verification by fresh evidence in the form of further sense-data (including the testimony of others).

CHAPTER V

"SAVING THE APPEARANCES" IN THE PHYSICAL WORLD

THROUGHOUT the argument of this essay we are to keep steadily within the context of perceptions, the objects of which are regarded, *bona fide*, as physical or material things. Hallucinations, dreams, imaginations are to be excluded. We are to deal with such familiar experiences as looking around a room and touching this thing or that; looking out of the window, too, at things which, like clouds, we cannot touch; listening to the multifarious noises of traffic in the street; recognising, throughout, each thing for what it is, and taking it for granted that each is real, and is really, *i.e.*, truly, what we perceive it to be. Memories, too, we shall admit into our argument, provided again they are memories of perceptions of physical things, not of dreams or other experiences of what is not physically real. For memories help to generalise the situations which we are to examine. But it is best to steady our argument by conducting it in a context of actual perception of physical things. To give himself actual examples of the kind of experience he is about to analyse, is the philosopher's only equivalent to the scientist's experiment.

The setting for our argument is provided by the common-sense belief that what, at any given moment, we perceive is a bit of a world of individual " things ", of which the colours we see, the sounds we hear, the solidity we feel by touch, *etc.*, are " qualities ". Throughout the first stage of the argument we shall take it for granted that " seeing is believing ", or, in other words, that every act of perception is also an act of judgment. We shall assume that to perceive a thing—to identify, recognise, know it for what it is —no less than to perceive its qualities, or its relations, is to judge that what we perceive is really such-and-such a thing, with such-and-such qualities and relations. The commonest class of such judgments of perception consists of those in which some sense-datum is affirmed, or interpreted, to be the quality of a thing. We are first, then, to examine the various problems which centre around the status of *sense-data* [1] in the perception of physical things. An amazing amount of philosophical ingenuity has been expended upon efforts to show that the things which we perceive are not really what we perceive them to be. The point of these arguments is not merely that perception does not give us the whole truth about things, but that things must be judged to be definitely *other* than, or *different* from, what to our senses they " appear " to be. We must face, at least in its main forms, this challenge to our naive confidence that through sense-data we become acquainted with the nature of physical things. If sense-data are not what we take them to be, *viz.,* qualities of physical things, then this confidence is unjustified, and all our ordinary judgments of perception are, in fact, false.

This first group of problems will lead us on to a second group, concerned, in part, with the distinction—insisted upon as fundamental by eminent present-day thinkers—between perception and judgment; and, in part, with a deeper analysis of what is involved in the perception of a " thing ".

---

[1] The term " sense-data " is used throughout as being theoretically the most neutral and non-committal. The term " sensations ", by current usage, commits us at once to the theory that colours, sounds, etc., are " mental " states, and therefore cannot be qualities of physical things or belong in any way to the texture of the external world. Its meaning, in short, belongs traditionally to the context of the theory which sorts out the contents of the universe into " physical " and " psychical " as mutually exclusive classes. The present discussion neither takes this theory for granted, nor supports it. To introduce it here would be indefensible irrelevance.

In this context, we shall have occasion to carry a step further the discussion of data and interpretation upon which
we had entered in the preceding essay. And we shall also
be compelled to define our attitude towards two tendencies
in the contemporary treatment of the thing-problem which
we may call, respectively, the phenomenalistic and the metaphysical. The former begins, historically, with Berkeley's
analysis of a thing as a complex of " ideas of sense "; is
continued by Hume and by Comte; elaborated in J. S.
Mill's theory of a thing as a " permanent possibility of sensations "; and it counts among its present-day representatives a physicist like Ernst Mach, a mathematician and
biologist like Karl Pearson, a logician and philosopher like
Bertrand Russell.[1] Indeed it may be said to have attained
its highest refinement in Russell's account of a thing as a
" logical construct ", a class of sense-data and sensibilia.
The metaphysical tendency, by contrast, is the philosophical
defender of that scheme of common thought which has
shaped our language into substantives, adjectives, and verbs,
expressive of the theory that ours is a world of things,
possessed of qualities, and active in their relations to each
other. Formerly this type of philosophical theory used the
concepts of " substance " and " attribute ", but so far as
substance was conceived as distinct from its attributes, and
as somehow the bearer of them, it has long given way before
the assaults of phenomenalistic critics who, first pressing the
distinction, pushed the substance into the position of an unknown and unknowable x, and then denied its very existence
as an otiose fiction. Berkeley's denial of " matter " is
typical of the logic of this situation. But substance always
meant more than merely something which has qualities. It
meant above all something which exists in its own right, is

[1] See Mack's *Analysis of Sensations*, Pearson's *Grammar of Science*,
Russell's *Our Knowledge of the External World*.

therefore independent of other things, self-contained and self-existent—*individual*, in short, in the most pregnant sense of this word. Spinoza's *Per substantiam intelligo id quod in se est et per se concipitur* is perhaps the most famous historical link between a tradition almost as old as philosophy itself, and its vigorous modern representatives. It is the mark of the modern metaphysician, as distinct from the phenomenalist, to use as fundamental the categories of individuality and self-existence. But there are two ways of doing even ˌthis. One way, by bold speculative guesses, takes us away from experience, and seeks to construe individuality everywhere on the analogy of psychical activity, attributing some degree of consciousness, will, or soul, to every physical thing.[1] The other way, which will be our way, is to save things as individuals, of at least relative self-existence, equally from being dissolved into classes of sensibilia, and from having their unity referred to the possession of a soul of which we have no empirical evidence. We shall try to show that there are perceptible clues to individuality which the current analyses of the perception of things overlook.

Throughout both groups of problems, we shall try to " save the appearances ", *i.e.*, to construct a theory of the physical world as we perceive it to be, which shall not discard, or reject, sense-data, and still less set up an " unknowable somewhat " behind appearances, but which shall include all data offered by experience in such a way that

---

[1] There is no need to review in detail the various hypotheses, from Leibniz to Lotze and modern panpsychists and voluntarists of all sorts, not to forget Schopenhauer's Will, von Hartmann's Unconscious, Bergson's *élan vital*, Clifford's Mind-stuff, recently resuscitated by Strong. Perhaps the most attractive and plausible statement of this type of theory in recent literature is to be found in Professor Mary Whitton Calkins's Presidential Address to the American Philosophical Association, published under the title, *The Personalistic Conception of Nature*, in the *Philosophical Review* for March, 1919 (vol. xxviii, no. 2).

each, in its place and character, may be retained, and that the contradictions and incoherencies which, *prima facie*, beset our data may yield to the discovery of order. This is in keeping with our ideal of philosophical theory as striving to find a place and use for all that is given in experience, by incorporation in a self-consistent system.

I

"When we see a tree we think that it is really green and really waving about in precisely the same way as it appears to be ".[1] In short, when we perceive we judge that what we perceive is really so. Clearly the truth of a class of judgments is here at issue, *viz.*, the judgments which affirm that colours, sounds, tastes, smells, touches are qualities of physical things. We can distinguish four main problems which have been raised about judgments of this sort, four lines of argument along which their truth has been either doubted or denied. We may formulate them in the following four questions:

(1) Are sense-data really qualities of physical things,

[1] C. D. Broad, *Perception, Physics and Reality,* p. 1. "As it appears to be" is, of course, only a synonym for "as it is seen to be", though "appears", with its reminder of a possible difference between "appearance" and "reality", hints also, by anticipation, at the problem of the truth of what we think, or judge, when we see a tree. It is worth noting that, whilst our linguistic resources for expressing what we perceive are very varied and flexible, they gravitate towards the judgment-form, "I see a tree", "I see this (object) to be a tree", "I see that this is a tree". Here the initial substantive is drawn out into what is unmistakeably a judgment. If we express what we perceive without the prefix "I see", "I hear", the remainder, "this is a tree", even if shrunk into the exclamation, "a tree", is obviously a judgment. Moreover, phrases like "I see" are frequently mere synonyms for "there is . . ." They rarely, in current speech at any rate, demand an interpretation placing the emphasis on the ostensible grammatical subject "I". They are not, in this first intention, statements of fact about me, but about what it is that is perceived by me. When challenged in this, their first, intention, the emphasis may, of course, shift to the seeing:—"but I *see* it is a tree "—as the evidence on which I rely in my belief. Certainly, intelligent perception, "knowing what one sees", is indistinguishable from judgment.

i.e., are physical things really coloured, tasting, smelling, *etc.*, things, or are their so-called qualities merely impressions produced in the minds of observers of appropriate psycho-physical constitution?

(2) Granted that physical things really have these sensible qualities, what is the "real" quality of a thing, as distinct from the varying appearances of that quality?

(3) Do things possess their sensible qualities only when, and so long as, they are being perceived? Or are their qualities "real" in the special sense of existing when not perceived by anybody?

(4) Are sense-data "private" to each observer, and hence unshareable, incommunicable? If so, can two persons be said to perceive the same thing, or even merely to see the same colour or hear the same sound?

To simplify the discussion, let us restate these four questions quite briefly in terms of a single quality, *viz.*, colour:

(1) Is a physical thing which we see really coloured?

(2) If so, what is its real colour?

(3) Is it coloured at times when no one perceives it?

(4) Has it all the colours which different percipients see in it from different points of view and at the same time?

(1) The grounds on which it is denied that the colours we perceive are really qualities of physical objects fall, broadly, into two groups. One group consists of arguments drawn from the difficulty of determining the "real" colour, or, else, from the alleged "privacy" of colours. They thus fall to be considered under (2) and (4). The other group consists of the familiar distinction between primary and secondary qualities, together with the causal theory of perception by which that distinction is commonly supported. The psycho-physiology of perception, which is but the

causal theory drawn out into a detailed account of the sense-organs and the nervous system as a mechanism of response to stimuli, lends additional weight; and so apparently does the fact that the fundamental concepts of physics define " matter " in terms which make no mention of secondary qualities.[1] If the advocates of these theories always remembered them in making their judgments, they would say, not " This tree is green ", but " This tree produces a sensation of greenness in us." Among recent writers, Mr. H. A. Prichard, with his usual intellectual honesty, draws precisely this conclusion, and, denying colour to be a quality of bodies, sets it down that, " with respect to colour, things look what they never are, or, in other words, are wholly different from what they look ".[2]

There is no need to review the prolonged debate on this issue in all its twistings and turnings. But we may usefully dwell on certain points which do not appear to have met with the recognition they deserve.

(a) First, it is worth noticing that the arguments do not attack the concept of quality as such, for physical objects (" bodies ") continue to be thought of as characterised by primary qualities. All they deny is that colours and other secondaries can be qualities, whatever " being a quality " may mean. So when Locke denies the " reality " of secondaries, he merely means that they are not qualities of bodies, but ideas in our minds. In short, all that the arguments 'do is, first, to substitute, in the interpretation of sense-data, the relation of cause and effect for the relation of thing and

---

[1] Locke's defence of the distinction between primary and secondary qualities (*Essay on the Human Understanding,* Book II, ch. viii), which, though not the earliest in modern philosophy, exercised the most influence on subsequent thought, relies on a most heterogeneous assemblage of arguments. See *Note* at the end of this chapter.

[2] *Kant's Theory of Knowledge,* p. 87. For other secondaries, see pp. 85, 6. Mr. Prichard's premises, however, are drawn mainly from arguments which, for us, belong to questions (2) and (3) in our list.

quality; and, secondly, to class sense-data as intra-mental impressions in contrast to extra-mental bodies.

(b) Now when we consider the bearing of these theses on the practice and theory of the physical sciences, we find that they amount to a subtle distortion of the intellectual perspective. In the first place, every scientist, as observer and experimenter, identifies and discriminates the objects he uses and investigates, by their look and feel and other sensible properties. But more important than this is the fact that secondaries, so far from being excluded as " mental ", and therefore non-physical, actually belong to the physicist's field of investigation. This is true, at any rate, for colours and sounds. In optics and acoustics, colours and sounds become objects of investigation, not as " sensations " or " ideas ", but as *phenomena*. The physicist's actual procedure cuts right across, and ignores, all classificatory boundary-lines dividing the supposedly physical from the supposedly mental. He does not permit himself to be hampered by such barriers as these in following up the connections of phenomena with one another or with their hypothetical conditions. When light is, by a prism, broken up into a spectral band of colours, or when, in spectroscopy, faint lines in such spectral bands are taken as evidence of the presence of certain chemical elements in distant stars, there is no suggestion that, at some point in this argument, the astronomer steps across the line which divides " mind " from " matter " or " ideas from " things ". He deals in good faith throughout with phenomena to which all these divisions are utterly irrelevant. No doubt, in dealing with colours as phenomena, he is thinking of them as *effects* rather than as qualities. But in what sense are they " effects "? Not in the sense that they are produced by bodies in a non-physical medium called " mind ", but in the sense that they occur under conditions which can be precisely stated and with which they are correlated according to precise laws. It is true that in this sense the physicist " explains " sense-data by their " causes ", *i.e.*, he correlates colours with ether-waves of which, as they are invisible, he does not need to think as coloured. He correlates sounds with air-vibrations which; as such, are conceived as soundless. He correlates temperatures with molecular motions which, as such unfelt, do not need to be thought of as either hot or cold.

When physiology shows that among the conditions of which account must be taken in studying the occurrence of colours and sounds, are the ways in which eyes and ears and nervous systems are constructed and function, the situation becomes more complex, but is not altered in principle. And for physiologist, as for physicist, the study of the conditions is possible only so far as eye and ear are themselves visible and, therefore, coloured, tangible, hard, soft, and so forth.

To sum up: colours, and other secondaries (so far as they are considered at all) are, for physical science, phenomena, and, as such, effects rather than qualities. But they are effects only as correlated according to law with other phenomena, actually observed or hypothetically assumed, not as removed from the physical context into a world of ideas. And their being treated as effects is not incompatible with their being also treated as qualities. By an obvious abstraction, we can define, as the object of our investigation, colours rather than coloured things, just as we can define psychology as concerned with mental processes rather than with minds or selves. And if we will agree to say that things possess, or exhibit, varying qualities in varying conditions, and that, as thus correlated with conditions, qualities may be considered " effects ", no difficulty of principle stands in the way of accepting the conclusions of physical theory for the familiar characters in which things present themselves to our senses. So far from saying, " This tree produces a green sensation in our minds ", we shall still be able to say, with common sense, " This tree is green "; only we shall now understand that this judgment is elliptical in that it omits to specify the conditions under which the tree possesses, or exhibits, the quality of being green.

(c) Why, thirdly, do we apply the causal point of view to sense-data at all? The question arises most pointedly in the context of psychology, in connection with theories of the "stimulus" of sensation. The reason most commonly given is that sense-data are largely independent of our will: they are given, they come unsought, they force themselves upon us, they interrupt trains of thought, they may have to be, like disturbing noises, shut out by concentrating attention on the matter in hand. But fully as important, and far less frequently noticed, is the fact that often by one sense we can observe the sequence of events leading up to experiences of another sense, e.g., when feeling for a match-box and striking a match in the dark gives us the setting in which seeing light occurs as an effect; or when we watch a body approaching to the moment of contact, and then feel its tactual quality or its temperature. In such situations we may recognise the empirical basis from which start all attempts scientifically to correlate phenomena. The mere fact that colours, sounds, etc., are given, does not, by itself, lead to the discovery of causal connections between phenomena, in the sense of correlations according to law.

(2) Having tried to defend the truth of the judgments in which, perceiving colours, we affirm them to be qualities of things, we turn now to the second question, What is the real colour of a thing?

The main reason for discussing this question at all is

that the difficulty of determining the " real " colour has been used—most recently by Bertrand Russell [1]—as a premise for the conclusion that objects cannot really have any colour at all. The argument is that, *e.g.*, a so-called " brown " table exhibits actually a large variety of colours, according to the incidence of light, the spectator's point of view, the condition of his eyes, and so forth. Whence it is held to follow that " colour is not something which is inherent in the table, but something depending upon the table and the spectator and the way the light falls on the table." [2] All colours actually seen have an equally good right to be considered real, and, therefore, " to avoid favouritism, we are compelled to deny that, in itself, the table has any one particular colour." [3]   From the point of view which we are advocating, the difficulty is wholly due to the identification of " the real " colour with a colour supposedly " inherent " in the table " by itself." Russell himself shows that, at any moment, the colour of the table is relative to varying conditions, and that these varying colours have an equal right to be considered real. Now these are the only colours with which, empirically, we ever can, or do, deal. [4] With a table " by itself ", *i.e.*, a table abstracted from these conditions, and with its colour, when so abstracted, we have no concern. We might as well speculate what colour things have in the dark, and argue, with Locke, that because they have no colour then, they never have any colour at all. The thing " by itself " is a self-contradictory fiction. A thing's qualities vary with different conditions. The demand for qualities which shall be unchangeably the

[1] *The Problems of Philosophy*, pp. 11 ff. *Cf.* also H. A. Prichard, *loc. cit.*, p. 86.
[2] B. Russell, *loc. cit.*, p. 13.
[3] *Ibid.*, p. 14.
[4] When, remembering, or reflecting, we "think of" an object as blue, we are attributing to it the colour we saw in it and expect to see again in the same conditions. See below (3).

same, however the conditions may vary, is one for which experience gives no warrant or excuse. Identity, of course, we want, but not the static, abstract, identity of a supposed thing "by itself", but a mobile identity in difference—the identity of a thing which, in a concrete network of relationships, shows different sides of itself in different settings, and yet is, in all this display of differences, always "itself."

Any colour, then, actually perceived is "real", in the sense that the judgment attributing this colour, seen here and now, to the object is, *so far and in these conditions,* true. If further observations demand further judgments, to the effect that, in other parts, at other times, from other points of view, in other illuminations, the same object has other colours, then these judgments, too, are true within the limits of the evidence. What is necessary for a synthesis of them is the discovery and recognition of the system in which each colour-difference is correlated with differences in the conditions under which it occurs.

It is by a similar, but more selective, synthesis that we can speak of *the* "real" colour of a thing, so far as that phrase implies "a normal spectator from an ordinary point of view under usual conditions of light."[1] There is no reference here to the object "by itself", but either to the average, or the most frequent, or, else, to the best and most favourable, conditions of perception. There is, in other words, an attempt at *standardisation.* Now it must be conceded that, with colours, such attempts have not succeeded far, though sufficiently for the rough-and-ready uses of practical life. The main obstacle lies in the difficulty of measuring, and the consequent lack of precision. This appears clearly enough when we turn to the corresponding problems of the "real" size, or "real" shape, or "real" temperature of an object. All these are standardisations amidst a vari-

[1] *Loc. cit.,* p. 14.

ety of perceptual " appearances ". The same thing, seen at different distances, has different sizes. A circular coin looks elliptical from most points of view; the warmth of a fire increases as we approach. In fact, we can here, as above, agree on what shall be normal conditions of perception, but the decisive solution is through measurement. The " real " distance is the measured distance, and so for figure, or temperature. It is to be remembered, however, that measuring comes down, in the last resort, to the accuracy with which an observer can perceive the coincidence of two lines, e.g., of the top of a mercury column with the notches on the scale alongside it.[1] But, whether or no we can measure, the way to " save the appearances " is not to deny them wholesale of the object " by itself ", and consign them to some metaphysical limbo of illusions, but to correlate them with their varying conditions. Thus, for example, we learn to understand why " the " sound which a bicycle-bell makes is heard as a different sound by hearers at different distances or of different auditory acuity. The miracle would be if there were no such differences—if what each hearer hears and calls " the " sound of the bell were actually identical in quality for all. Except as identity in difference, there is no way of getting an intelligible synthesis of the data.

(3) We turn to our third problem, which was whether an object, perceived to be coloured, is " really " coloured in the sense that it is, or remains, coloured at times when it is not perceived by any one. In short, does the *esse-est-percipi* principle apply to colours and other secondary qualities? If it does, then the further question arises, how are we to think of the object, *i.e.*, what character we are to attribute to it, in the intervals of its being perceived.

[1] Mr. T. P. Nunn has some excellent observations on this whole subject in his book, *The Aim and Achievement of Scientific Method*, pp. 5-7.

To judge from the present state of the discussion of this problem, the question is an entirely open one. Even a professed realist, like Russell, is found scandalising his fellow-realists by admitting it " as probable that the immediate objects of sense [= sense-data, or secondary qualities] depend for their existence upon physiological conditions in ourselves, and that, for example, the coloured surfaces which we see cease to exist when we shut our eyes." [1] Nor does he shrink from the consequences of his view: " The starry heaven, for instance, becomes actual whenever we choose to look at it," [2] where, of course, the phrase " the starry heaven " means strictly nothing but the yellowish spots of light in a dark expanse which are " the immediate objects of sense " in this case.

The first point to note, in approaching this problem, is that, quite apart from the presence of a spectator, or from dependence on his physiological condition, we do not, on reflection, believe that objects are coloured (or that colours exist) always and under any conditions. Both common sense and physical science recognise that colours vary with variations in the illumination, and that in the absence of light they disappear, *i.e., cease to exist*. No doubt, it is barely possible to argue that the colours are there all the time, and that the presence of light is necessary only to their being seen. But such a view could certainly not be established by an appeal to experience, and would have to be based, in the last resort, on the principle of identity abstractly interpreted. The principle of identity lays it down that " every thing is what it is." The issue—one of those fundamental issues which run through the whole history of philosophy and seem destined to be re-tried by each new generation—is whether this principle demands that

[1] *Our Knowledge of the External World*, p. 64.
[2] *Loc. cit.*, p. 112.

we should attribute to each thing an absolute character, *i.e.,* a character not variable with varying conditions, but unchanged and fixed in whatever setting or relationships the thing may exist, or that we should acknowledge its character to be relative to conditions, and its identity, or self-maintenance, to consist just in the resourcefulness (so to speak) with which it responds differently to different settings. On the latter interpretation, a synthesis of the manifold data of experience becomes possible; on the former, the changeless identity of each thing must either be sought in some hypothetical character which does not appear in the flux of empirical data at all, or else we must elevate each separate datum here and now to the rank of a tiny absolute. The philosophers who have explored this path, have had little success, and meanwhile the weight of common sense and of science is against them, and in favour of the philosophers who have interpreted the principle of identity concretely, *i.e.,* as identity in difference.

But to return from this debate on principles to the empirical situation. We are from experience familiar with perceptions of the " same " object [1] in different conditions of light. We perceive it coloured in bright daylight, and colourless in the dark, identifying it then either by touch, or, in very dim light, by seeing outline and shape. And there are all intermediate stages. The problem is so to interpret our judgments of perception concerning the colour of objects as to save all these empirical data. The way to do this is neither to affirm that the object has " really " no colour at all, nor to attribute to it, as " real ", an absolute, unchangeable colour which is different from all, or most, of the colours perceived in it, but to correlate the observed

---

[1] The right to say the "same" rests, of course, precisely on such a synthesis of different perceptual data as we are trying to defend throughout.

differences with differences in the conditions under which, in each case, the object is what it is. The result of the application of this point of view to the interpretation of judgments of perception is that, *e.g.*, the judgment, " This is blue ", made in the moment of perception, will not now be taken to mean, " This is blue always, however light and other conditions may vary ", but " This is blue here and now." And the " here and now " will, with increasing knowledge and completer analysis of the whole context, give way to " under conditions such as these ", where the conditions are as exhaustively and precisely specified as our evidence permits. Thus qualified by the inclusion of explicit conditions, the judgment not only permits of other colours being predicated of the same thing under other conditions, but also is true both at the moment of perception and " always ". For the statement of conditions, " such as these ", generalises the particular datum and invests it with the truth belonging to an instance of a universal.[1]

The principle, then, here advocated for the saving of appearances demands that the possession of qualities by an object be taken, not as absolute, but as relative. It is dependent on conditions, some of which are comparatively uniform and stable, others of which are variable and transitory. What the conditions in any given case are is as much a question for empirical analysis and synthesis, as is the corresponding question how to recognise and identify certain data in the flux of experience as appearances of the " same " thing.

If, then, there are, as there would seem to be, good reasons for saying that colours, and other secondary qualities, are found to occur only under conditions which include the presence of a properly functioning physiological organism,

---

[1] A fuller discussion of this view of truth will be offered in a sequel to the present volume of *Studies*.

no *a priori* prejudices ought to stand in the way. If colours vary with physical conditions, why not with physiological conditions, which, after all, are physical, too?

At this point, however, an objection will be raised, not so much on the score of the general principle, as on the ground of its consequences when applied, as here, to making human beings, or, in general, living beings with sense-organs, one of the conditions of the occurrence of secondary qualities. The objector will urge that, according to the theory of evolution, the physical world existed before there were living beings in it:—what, at that time, were its qualities? And, in any case, there are even now many physical things which are never perceived by any living being, so far as we know, and there is no physical thing which is perceived all the time. If unperceived objects have no secondary qualities, what qualities have they?

Two replies may be made to this objection. In the first place, judgments of perception, whether primitive, or amplified by conditions, are retained by memory. In other words, we " think of " objects as possessing the qualities which we perceived in them. Does this mean that we think of them as possessing these qualities even when no one perceives them? No—as little as the perception of an object as hot compels us to think of it as always hot. We cannot, in memory, endow the object with any qualities except those which we found it to have at the times, and under the conditions, under which it was perceived. And if we have perceived it frequently, and for continuous stretches of time, we may ultimately be able to piece together these data and think of all the details of the object's existence and behaviour, *as if* we were continuously observing it. In this manner we fill out the gaps by analogy, imagining the qualities we should see, if perception were possible. We can anticipate what, under statable conditions, we shall see, and verify our anticipations by realising the conditions and perceiving what we had expected to perceive.   In this context, "thinking of" an object as blue means remembering that one has seen it to be blue, and expecting to see it as blue again.   Certainly, in ordinary intercourse, we talk and think of objects as blue, *i.e.*, judge them to have that colour, at times when we do not perceive them.   But a judgment expressed thus roughly, and without nice qualification, cannot fairly be taken to mean that the objects are blue now, or apart from any conditions. If this were its meaning, it would simply be false.   But these judgments can be saved, too, by interpreting their meaning to be that the objects are blue, *if perceived under proper conditions*—which is, in fact, all that the evidence of past experience justifies, and the evidence of future experience can verify.   We have a right, then, to think of objects in the intervals of perception, as we should find them to be if we were perceiving them.   And, on the same principle, basing ourselves on present perceptual evidence, we reconstruct in imagination what we should have seen, heard, felt, had we lived in ages of the world when, in fact, no living things yet existed.   Again, having never seen atoms, we think of them as colourless, but if some new discovery in microscopical instruments were ever to make an atom visible, can we doubt that we should see it coloured?

But this is not quite the end of the problem.   For the objection we are discussing rests, at bottom, on the principle that everything which exists has a nature or character; that all existence is *qualified* existence.   Hence, if an object has certain qualities only at certain times, and under certain conditions, and yet is to be thought of as existing at other times, and under other conditions, then it does not seem a meaningless question to ask: What is the nature, what are the qualities, of objects unperceived?   The temptation is great to try and get behind the tantalising "if" and "should" in our sentence, above, about " thinking of objects in the intervals of perception as we should find them to be if we were perceiving them." If we yield to the temptation, we shall be drawn into speculative guesses beyond the reach of perceptual evidence. We shall, with Berkeley, say that objects are at all times perceived by God, or with panpsychists of all shades, that each object is inwardly a will, or soul, and exists in its own right as such. But a more cautious temper in philosophising, guided by the empirical distinctions between things in the context of Nature, will content itself with a solution which keeps closer to the evidence. It will either extend to objects unperceived the deliberate abstraction from secondary qualities and the conditions of perception, which characterises the point of view of " mechanical theory ". It will then think of unperceived objects in terms only of primary qualities, *i.e.*, of those qualities which are involved in the purely " mechanical " relations of things to each other. Or, else, it will recognise that the knowledge of things which we have through the senses is subject to conditions, and that the path of wisdom is to accept these conditions and make the most of the resources which perception puts at our disposal, rather than indulge in speculations, however fascinating, for which the evidence furnishes neither basis nor verification. Perception furnishes genuine knowledge of the nature of physical things, and we know more, not less, about them when we discover that the qualities which we perceive them to have are subject to, and variable with, conditions of which we can formulate the laws. This is all which the argument, so far, fairly entitles us to say, though something more remains to be added below.[1]

---

[1] See p. 135. The view in the text tries to do justice to what is sound in the phenomenalistic position. Mill's formula for that position,

(4) In the light of the preceding discussions, our fourth problem can be briefly disposed of. It concerns the question whether different percipients, since for each the object, according to the different conditions under which he perceives it, has different qualities, can be said to be perceiving the same object, or even merely to be seeing the same colour or hearing the same sound. In Russell's picturesque terminology, if the sense-data are " private ", is there a " public " object at all, and if there is, can the private sense-data possibly be qualities of the public object? In *The Problems of Philosophy*, Russell argues that our " instinctive belief "—for it is no more than that to him—that we perceive the same objects, can be reconciled with the differences in our sense-data only by assuming that the object is something " over and above " the sense-data, distinct from them in existence and qualities.[1] In *Our Knowledge of the External World*, on the other hand, Russell wings over to the view that the physical thing is not something other than the sense-data which we call its qualities, but *is* the system, or set, of these, though each be perceptible only to one spectator at one time and place. In short, Russell is here no longer divorcing the thing from its " appearances ": he now sets himself the explicit task of " finding

defining a physical thing as a " permanent possibility of sensations ", is awkward, and lays itself open to the retort, that what is " possible " (*i.e.*, may occur) is sensations, and that what is " permanent" and makes sensations possible, must itself be actual, with a nature of its own (*Cf*. G. F. Stout, *Proceedings of the Aristotelian Society*, vol. iv, article on *Primary and Secondary Qualities*). Russell's account of a thing as a logical construct of actual and ideal sense-data is a vast improvement on Mill's. Russell's suggestion that, if we know under what conditions an " ideal" sense-datum (*i.e.*, a sense-datum thought of) becomes an " actual" sense-datum (*i.e.*, one actually sensed by a mind), it is unnecessary even for physical science to assign existence to the ideal elements, is closely similar to the view in the text. (*Cf. Our Knowledge of the External World*, p. 112).

[1] " One great reason why it is felt that we must secure a physical object in addition to the sense-data, is that we want the *same* object for different people."—*The Problems of Philosophy*, pp. 31, 2.

a place "² for all data; in fact, saving the appearances by
correlation in a system on what we have called (though
Russell would not) the principle of identity in difference.
The point is exactly the same, at bottom, as that which has
occupied us in the preceding problems.   Are we to seek
the identity of the object—its character as existing, its what-
it-is—apart from its various appearances in the world of
sense, or are we to identify these, construe them in spite of
their difference from one another as none the less *its* appearances—*different* appearances of the *same* thing?   If
the latter is possible at all, there need be, in principle, no
limit to the number of different appearances, provided only
and always that the judgments affirming this interpretation
do not contradict each other.   And such contradiction is
avoided by resting them on the system in which each appearance is correlated with its exclusive conditions.

From the first group of problems, in which we have
argued on the basis that we know physical things by perception, because every perception is a judgment interpreting
sense-data as qualities of things, we must now turn to our
second group.   The problems of this second group may
conveniently be formulated as follows:
(1) Is the view that every perception is a judgment correct?   If not, what is the difference between them, and what
the motive, or ground, for passing from a perception to a
judgment "about" what we perceive?   Is there such a
thing as "pure" perception, into which judgment does
not enter, and if so, what is its cognitive function and
value?
(2) What is the relation in a judgment of perception between datum and interpretation?   For it appears to be

¹ *Loc. cit.*, p. 97.

agreed on all sides that, whatever our answer to (1) may be, a judgment, at any rate, transcends a bare datum, and the analysis of it, therefore, demands that we distinguish between the given and what, by interpretation or construction, the given is identified as meaning. We affirm, or believe in, the existence of more than is simply found within the four corners of the given here and now. What makes this transcendence, this expansion of the given, possible? What, above all, justifies it? We shall have, at least, to touch on the whole problem of meaning which, despite many nibblings at it in recent psychology and philosophy, has hardly yet begun to yield up the solution of its riddle.[1]

(3) Has our analysis of what is given in perception, up to this point, exhausted all the clues for the discrimination and recognition of things as " individual " objects, self-identical despite change?

These problems, again, we shall survey in order, seeking, as before, to " save the appearances."

(1) The question, " What do we perceive? ", if understood in the sense of, " What do we know by pure perception, without judgment? ", is not nearly as easy to answer as is sometimes assumed. It throws us back inevitably on some theory about perception, into which much more enters than can be got from a naive inspection of examples of perception. The obvious advice, " Take a perception and analyse it ", is deceptive in its simplicity. For there is no infallible way of analysing correctly or getting a true theory by simply looking and recording what is there. Too many philosophers (and psychologists, too) indulge the pleasant habit of assuming that " introspection " can do no wrong, and that all that is needed is to put the findings of

[1] *Cf.* my article, *Image, Idea, and Meaning,* in Mills, N. S., vol. xvi, no. 41.

introspection into words. To dispel this illusion it is enough that we remind ourselves of the utterly disparate and mutually contradictory analyses of perception which are being offered, if not always in the name of introspection, at least in the name of what is euphemistically called an "unprejudiced inspection of the facts". Introspection has been much criticised, chiefly on the grounds that it is difficult to introspect experiences whilst one has them, and impossible to introspect the experiences of others. But the biggest difficulty of all—a difficulty attaching to every theory claiming to be based on a plain inspection of facts—is hardly mentioned in the literature. It arises from the fact that the findings, in order to yield usable theory, must be put into words. But what dictates the words to be employed? What makes the difference between a true and a false report? One theorist " finds " that what we perceive is " things ", qualified things. Another " finds " that we perceive neither things nor qualities, but just sense-data. What a third " finds " are " sensations ", and he will talk of colours, sounds, *etc.*, as qualities of sensations and there is, so far, for him no evidence of objects *extra mentem*. What a fourth " finds " are " acts " of sensing and either " contents " or " objects ", where it remains a moot question whether these are sense-data or physical things. The " raw, unverbalised " facts, as James happily calls them, appear to suffer any one of these analyses as patiently as any other. Is it not clear that the question, Which is the true report? can be settled only in a general context of theory in which such rival descriptions are supported as much as supporting?

Here, for example, is a typical account of "pure perception ": " The stage of pure perception of a coloured surface corresponds, it would seem, to the state of a man who just reads the enumeration or sees the figure of the 47th proposition (of the first book of Euclid), but to whom the words and figure convey no meaning ".[1] This amounts to saying that the object of pure perception consists of bare sense-data, as they come and go, stripped of every vestige of interpretation. Moreover, to judge that the object of perception is just what we perceive it to be, could at best only amount to taking each sense-datum for just what it is. We should have no right to say that things and qualities are perceived. Judgments like " this is a tree ", or " this tree is green and is waving about in the wind " (to take Broad's own examples), could not be offered as judgments of perception, the truth of which was infallibly derived from, and guaranteed by, the accompanying perception. For in all such judgments there is interpretation. A meaning is affirmed of which pure perception, *ex hypothesi*, contains no trace. Even the mere " this is green " bursts across the boundaries of the object of pure perception when they are thus narrowly drawn. For green is a universal, and no universal can be tied down to any momentary particular in which it is realised. To see and recognise " this " as " green " is to think of " this " as a case or instance of being green, as a member of the class of green particulars. But what hint does the pure datum here and now contain of other data of the same sort, or of membership in a class of similars? Thus, the more we push back to the pure datum, the harder does it become to identify any cognition which could fairly be said to arise just from it, by itself, and to be assured by it of infallible truth. Facing in this direction, we move further and further away from getting out of perception anything remotely like the world of common experience with its relatively permanent things, exhibiting in different settings a wide range of different qualities. The world of immediate data is a chaos in which nothing

[1] C. D. Broad, *Perception, Physics, and Reality,* pp. 24, 5.

is permanent, nothing so connected that we can identify any two data as appearances or qualities of the same thing. The question—to quote Russell's wording of it—becomes urgent: " By what principles shall we select certain data from the chaos, and call them appearances of the same thing? "[1] The appeal to pure perception, thus, throws into more vivid relief the fact that, in intelligent perception, we always mean very much more than we perceive, at least if we whittle down what we perceive to bare sense-data. This becomes unmistakable when we put into language what we perceive, or think we perceive. For language is not only, for beings given to philosophising, the most convenient vehicle of judgment, but the meanings of words, being universal, transcend the data even when particularised by application to them. This is true even of " this " as the instrument *par excellence* of emphatic particularisation. For, taken abstractly, there is hardly another word in the language which has so wide a range of potential application, being used to designate anything and everything which can appear in the focus of attention. Thus a datum of perception is never more than a cue for a meaning, and the meaning, though identified with *this* datum here and now, as a whole transcends it. Yet the whole meaning is judged to be real on the strength of the real datum, taken as a fragment of the whole, and as a sign of its presence. The given carries a meaning, from which it derives its full character and to which it guarantees existence by its own existence, by being itself emphatically there.

It is easy to understand that this curiously double-edged character of transcendence should attract philosophical interest now rather by one of its sides, now rather by the

---

[1] *Our Knowledge of the External World*, p. 108. It might have been even better to ask, " By what principles *do* we select? " for there can be no doubt that we do select and identify, and, in the main, do so rightly.

other. To some, like Russell, the problem, above all others, is how, and by what right, we pass from data to non-data. And, since the data seem to guarantee so very little, these thinkers gravitate towards a profound doubt concerning the validity of the elaborate superstructures which common sense and science so readily erect. Yet what choice is there? We neither do, nor can, stop at the point of pure perception, even supposing that unordered, uninterpreted sense-data do form the actual first stage in the process of our learning to know the physical world. Transcend, synthesise, order, invest with meaning we do, and must, even at the least speculative level of perception. Does it help to suspect, or depreciate, root and branch this transcending of data, on the ground that it is everywhere shaped by hope and fear, whim and convenience, that it rests on nothing better than " instinctive belief "? To say this is to say that transcending is, at bottom, irrational, and that, at best, reason has no other function than that of organising into the most harmonious possible system the instinctive beliefs in virtue of which we *do* transcend the data and cannot help transcending them.[1] Is it not preferable to explore the obvious alternative? According to this, the data themselves demand to be transcended, furnishing clues for doing so precisely through their universal character, which it is the function

---

[1] This is, clearly, the general position set forth in the remarkable passage at the end of ch. ii (pp. 39-41) of Russell's *The Problems of Philosophy*. Note especially: " All knowledge, we find, must be built up upon our instinctive beliefs, and if these are rejected, nothing is left"; and " There can never be any reason for rejecting one instinctive belief except that it clashes with others; thus, if they are found to harmonise, the whole system becomes worthy of acceptance." Yet Russell's actual practice is to cut down the number of admissible instinctive beliefs to the point where they almost vanish. Thus, he would dearly like to be able to dispense with the instinctive belief in the existence of other minds, and build his world on a solipsistic basis of his own sense-data plus the principles of pure logic. That, however, only raises the further awkward question, What justifies the application of logic to sense-data, the treatment of sense-data as " values " for the " variables " of logic?

of reason to seize upon and follow up into that system of meanings which, as most comprehensive and internally coherent, constitutes " truth " and " reality ", and hence is affirmed as the true nature of that real world to which each moment's data bear witness.[1]

So far, then, we can conclude only that neither can transcendence be avoided by falling back on pure perception, nor ought it to be condemned as merely instinctive. It is the very life of reason, the very process of discovering truth under the pressure of the " logic of the facts "

But mention of truth may remind us that there is another angle from which it has been asserted that perception, as " knowledge of things ", is completely different from judgment, as " knowledge of truths " (*i.e.*, propositions), and that a special function and value belong to it as a mode of knowledge which cannot possibly ever be mistaken. Perception, it is said, is a two-term relation of mind to object, and since there must be an object for a mind to have this relation to it, perception cannot be deceptive. There can be no misperceiving, we are told, for that would be perceiving the non-existent, or, rather, perceiving what is not there, or, else, what is not so. " I may ", says G. E. Moore, in advocating this view, " judge with regard to an animal

---

[1] It is not a mere paradox to suggest that Russell's "instinctive beliefs" (*Cf.* preceding footnote) are identical in function with what "idealists" have called "categories of thought" or "principles of reason". Kant's "synthetic activity of the understanding", applying the categories to the manifold of sense and thus constructing objects judged to be empirically real, has undeniable affinities with the ordering and interpreting of sense-data along the lines of instinctive beliefs. The categories of thing and quality correspond, for example, to the instinctive belief that diverse sense-data are appearance of the same thing. And in both cases the question is how to select the sense-data which are to be identified as qualities, or appearances, of this thing rather than of that. The differences in detail between Kant and Russell are, no doubt, profound. But are not both, at bottom, trying to solve the same problem with assumptions the similarity of which is disguised by differences of terminology?

which I see at a distance, that it is a sheep, when in fact it is a pig. And here my judgment is certainly not due to the fact that I see it to be a sheep; since I cannot possibly see a thing to be a sheep unless it is one ".[1] In more technical language Russell analyses perception as involving only the object $a R b$ and the perceiving mind, whereas judgment involves the mind which judges that a stands in the relation R to b. The objection that there are errors of perception, Russell tries to meet by saying that, whilst no perception can be mistaken, we may wrongly think we are perceiving when, in fact, we are not.[2] Unfortunately, he does not tell us how to recognise a genuine perception when we have one. And, thus, after all, the infallibility of perception turns out to be, not so much an empirical fact, as an *a priori* definition, framed—as if in confirmation of our observation above concerning the influences of theory on the analysis of perception—to provide the setting for a new version of the correspondence theory of truth. For Russell's analysis does not appeal to introspection, nor is it even based on current psychological theory. Its motive appears to have been to provide, first, a fact-complex aRb by the correspondence to which the proposition " that a is in relation R to b " may be true, and, next, an infallible way of knowing the fact in

[1] *Some Judgments of Perception,* in *Proceedings of the Aristotelian Society* for 1918-19, p. 6. From the point of view of these essays the correct analysis of the situation posited by Moore would be this: I see something which from its look I identify as a sheep but which, on closer inspection, I identify as a pig. Of course, I may be cautious and say, " That looks like a sheep but may be something else "; but no one will deny that there are cases where, without any misgivings, but with the utmost confidence, we judge things from what we see of them, to be what we find afterwards they are not. If it be said that seeing a pig as sheep is wrong inference, the obvious reply is that seeing a pig as a pig is right inference. If it be said that we can speak of seeing a pig as a pig only when it actually is one, and no mistake is possible, the reply is that there is always interpretation and with it a chance of error, however remote—unless we whittle down what is perceived to mere sense-data, in which case we neither see nor know any " thing "—be it pig or sheep—at all.

[2] *Cf. Principia Mathematica,* p. 45.

order that we may know when the proposition is true. But, in fact, the symbols aRb oversimplify the situation and the problem.   In giving concrete values to these symbols in any particular case, we shall unawares assume the real problem to have been solved already, *i.e.*, the object to be correctly perceived for what it is.   Whereas the real problem is when a perception, involving always, as it does, data transcended by interpretation, can be trusted as correct.   And this can be only in a system of interpretations, mutually supporting each other.[1]   It is precisely because this attempt to distinguish perception and judgment traverses the distinction between datum and interpretation that it finds, we may bluntly say, no support in the actual facts.

(2) Having tried to show that pure perception is a will-o'-the-wisp which it is unsafe to follow, we are in a position to appreciate critically the way in which the problem of datum and interpretation is raised in the very subtle and acute analysis of some judgments of perception, given by G. E. Moore in the article from which we have just quoted. At the risk of slurring over some of Moore's cautious qualifications of statement, we may summarise the substance of his theory as follows:

(a) Let us assume that we are perceiving an inkstand and judging, " This is an inkstand."   What factors are involved? Clearly, we are not perceiving the *whole* of the inkstand. Very rarely, if ever, do we perceive the whole of the object which we judge ourselves to be perceiving.   Our judgment, in such cases, is on the one hand about " this "—the datum, *the* item in the total field of presentation at the moment, about which, as distinct from every other simultaneous datum, the judgment is being made.   On the other hand,

---

[1] A fuller treatment of this point, with special reference to perception, is planned for the second volume of *Studies.*

the judgment is also about the "inkstand" which we certainly believe ourselves to be perceiving. Now, whilst the datum is thus "the real or ultimate subject" of every judgment of perception, yet, clearly, *it* is not, in general, the kind of thing for which the predicate term (here "inkstand") is a name. The "this" may be a colour, or a sound, or any other sort of sense-datum; it will not be what we mean by a physical or material thing. If "this" is all we perceive, then we are not perceiving an inkstand, and the judgment "this is an inkstand" will be false. Is there any line of analysis open by which we can avoid this conclusion?

(b) If "this" is all that is strictly perceived, then the *whole* object is only "known by description" as "*the* object which stands to *this* in a certain relation." What 'is that relation? It seems plausible, especially in examples drawn from sight, to say that "this" is a *part* of the object, *e.g.*, a part of its surface. In that case, "This is an inkstand" would be only a loose way of saying, "This is part of the surface of an inkstand."[1] This analysis would provide plausibly for the difference between the datum and the object with which in the judgment of perception it is identified. A part might be a datum, and might be seen, in a sense in which the whole was neither a datum, nor seen. But there is a formidable difficulty: many things are true of sense-data which are not true of genuine parts of physical objects. There are many occasions when we judge that we are perceiving the same thing, or the same part of the same thing. We do so, frequently, even when the "same" part has perceptibly changed. But whether it

[1] With temperature-, sound-, smell-, taste-data, such language would be very much less plausible, though Moore does not touch on this. At any rate, we could speak of a "part" here only in a metaphorical sense. "Aspect", "quality", "appearance" would be less awkward, but it is to be admitted that there is no device of language by which it is possible to dodge the problem which Moore raises about "part".

has perceptibly changed or not, the data involved on these different occasions always are perceptibly different. When we look, *e.g.*, at the " same " inkstand from different distances, or from different angles of perspective, or when we perceive it by touch rather than by sight, the sense-data differ perceptibly throughout, yet we do not judge the inkstand to have perceptibly changed.[1] Hence the sense-datum cannot be, or truly be judged to be, " part " of the object perceived. In fact, in so far as it is true that we perceive a part, not the whole, of the inkstand, that part, once more, will be known only by description as *the* part which stands in the sought-for relation to " this ".

(c) The situation at this point drives Moore to the desperate expedient of suggesting that sense-data, after all, may not really differ perceptibly but only *seem* to differ. " What now seems to me to be possible is that the sense-datum which corresponds to a tree, which I am seeing, when I am a mile off, may not really be perceived to be smaller than the one, which corresponds to the same tree, when I see it from a distance of only a hundred yards, but that it is only perceived to seem smaller; that the sense-datum which corresponds to a penny, which I am seeing obliquely, is not really perceived to be different in shape from that which corresponded to the penny, when I was straight in front of it, but is only perceived to seem different—that all that is perceived is that the one seems elliptical and the other circular; that the sense-datum presented to me when I have the blue spectacles on is not perceived to be different in colour from the one presented to me when I have not, but only to seem so; and finally that the sense-datum presented when I touch this finger is not

[1] A reference to a similar argument in Professor G. F. Stout's British Academy paper on *Things and Sensations* may here be in place. See *Proceedings,* 1905-06.

perceived to be different in any way from that presented
when I see it, but only to seem so—that I do not perceive
the one to be coloured and the other not to be so, but
only that the one seems coloured and the other not." [1]
If this suggestion held good, it would be possible to
interpret a datum (a "this") as a part of the physical
thing.

(d) But if we hold to the usual view that sense-data
really differ, their relation to physical things is still to be
discovered. Moore considers two possible theories, only to
discard them both. One is the causal theory, that the sense-
datum has one, and only one cause, *viz.*, the physical thing.
The other is the theory that the sought-for relation might
be an ultimate and indefinable one, "being a manifestation of". The causal theory Moore rejects as, on the
whole, improbable; the other, on the ground that no such
relation is actually experienced. Perhaps, then, the analysis
into sense-datum, object, and a relation between them
is at fault? If so, the Mill-Russell theory of a physical
thing as a complex of actual or possible sense-data,
none of which is itself a physical thing, seems the only
well-accredited alternative, unless we are to fall back,
after all, on the desperate expedient discussed under (c)
above. Not being convinced of the truth of the Mill-Russell
theory, and confessing himself otherwise completely puzzled,
Moore finally inclines to favour this desperate view, because
at least it allows the sense-datum to be regarded as really
identical with part of the object.

The essential problem could hardly have been put with
more startling clearness. Judgments like "this is an inkstand" or "I see (this to be) an inkstand", express

---

[1] *Loc. cit.*, p. 23. I can, frankly, make nothing of this suggestion.
In offering it Moore himself admits it to be possible that he is "talking
sheer nonsense".

straightforwardly and, normally, with undeniable truth—
what?   What we perceive, or—does it not amount to the
same thing?—what we judge that to be which we perceive.
Yet the audacity of this judgment is brought to light by the
analysis which whittles down what we strictly perceive to
the mere " this " here and now, so that we are judging
more to be real than, in fact, we do perceive.   Yet the
paradox is that we do not stop at mere data, and that it
would not help us if we did.   For the road to knowledge
lies precisely in expanding this " more "—in making a
whole universe, in the last resort, hang upon each moment's
data.   Certainly we perceive " things " only by interpreting
data to mean wholes which, as wholes, are not data.   Is
there any way of throwing further light on this mystery
of *transcendence?*

The first step on such a way is to recognise that every
datum is a this-such—an Aristotelian τόδε τοιόνδε—hence
a realised, or embodied, universal.   It is emphatically this,
and no other, and so far a " particular ".   But it has also
a nature, quality, character—a " what "—which is not con-
fined to " this " but appears in other particulars; not only in
particulars similar to this one, or of the same sort, but also
in particulars different from this one, yet recognisable as
aspects of the same higher unity as this one.   Transcendence, in short, is the function of universals.   We may mar-
vel at it and find it unintelligible—but it can be so only
in the sense in which it may be said to be unintelligible that
there is anything at all.   We must not only accept universals as embodied in particulars and yet transcending each,
but recognise that they are the condition of the intelligibil-
ity of anything whatsoever.   Knowledge consists in the
progressive and constructive discovery of the universals—
of all sorts and degrees—which are embodied in the data
of our experience.   Thought, intelligence—call it what we

will—are the response to, or acknowledgment of, universals, or, as we may also put it, of the same in the different—a response made possible, indeed exacted, by the fact that the flux of experience brings an ever fresh multiplicity of data from moment to moment. The discovery of universals here takes place through the ordering, organising, synthesising—again call it what we will—of data. And these terms describe an activity which is, so far as it is " logical " or " rational ", under the control, the " objective " control, of the universals embodied in the data. We are obliged to think as we do think, when we think truly. There is nothing capricious or arbitrary about this logical activity. Still less is it an imposition, upon a neutral mass of data, of principles of order invented or imagined by human minds, or given with them as their habitual ways of working. We are not dealing with the tricks of an animal species, but with the nature of the world revealing itself to us. In thinking, it is not we who operate on the world, but the world (*i.e.*, the system of universals concretely presented in data) which operates in us—subject, of course, to the limitation which Spinoza expresses in the words *natura quatenus humanam mentem constituit*. Though it strains language, it would be truer to say, that the world thinks in us than that " we " think it, or about it. Least objectionable, perhaps, is the formula: reality reveals itself in what, on the basis of perception and feeling, we are obliged to think it to be.

The problem, thus, of " transcendence " is solved (so far as we can speak of " solving " it at all) by recognising that data are particularised universals, that it is of the nature of universals to transcend any one particular, and that this power of universals is exhibited in what we call " our activity " of thinking, when, with the help of memory and " association of ideas ", we identify different data as individual [1] things, or as higher types of concrete unities. The reminder will hardly be required that language, so far as it does not consist of symbols for mere denoting or pointing,[2] consists of symbols for universals of various sorts. Being, by common consent, the instrument for the expression and fixation, even more than for the communication, of thought, language surely bears witness to the universals which judgment predicates of the given as its true nature.

In keeping with this general view, we may now reaffirm the position adopted above that " seeing is believing ", or, in other words, that the perceptions which guide us in action and enter as " observations " into scientific research are judgments. It is certainly only on this view that we can plausibly be said to perceive physical " things " or a physical " world ".

In truth, the so-called " facts " of perception are " theories ". This follows at once from the admission that intelligent perception is a species of judgment, and involves interpretation of data by identification with a universal,

---

[1] It should be noted carefully that the term "particular" in the above account refers only to what may also be called a datum, or a "this". It does not refer to "things" or to anything which can be called an identity in differences. On the other hand, an "individual", being an identity in differences, is a kind of universal—a "concrete" universal, though it must be remembered that there are degrees of individuality. It would assist present-day philosophical discussion if it were to be authoritatively settled what is the position of the "simple" and unanalysable "terms", which a modern fashion in logical theory hails as the ultimate constituents of the world, in respect of the distinction of particular and universal.

[2] Whether a symbol merely denotes, and what it denotes, can be determined only by its use, *i.e.,* in the context of an actual application. The "values" for the "variables" of Russell's logic are, I understand, to consist in the last resort of entities merely denotable each by its "proper name" (*Cf., e.g., Introduction to Mathematical Philosophy,* p. 182). These entities, it may be observed, will not be physical things, or persons, or other complex objects, such as in our unphilosophical language may have proper names, but will probably, when Russell comes to exhibiting them, be found to be "particulars" such as sense-data: this, and this, and this. And then it will be time to repeat the question raised at the end of the preceding note.

with which we have become acquainted also in other data on other occasions.   Incidentally, it follows that sense-data, though facts in the sense that here and now they occur, are not *the* fact which is known or affirmed.   They are evidence, and circumstantial evidence at that, for the fact. Experience of illusion soon brings home to us the inferential character of perception, just as do the not infrequent occasions when we have to support our judgments of perception, like our judgments of memory, by argument, as well as by more attentive observation, or additional sense-data which furnish corroborative circumstantial evidence.[1]

The current distinction between " fact " and " theory " arises from this, that there are obvious stages, or degrees, of interpretation within what would commonly still be called a judgment of perception, the subject being denoted by " this ".   Keeping to judgments expressed in language, there is clearly an advance from " this is brown " to " this is a table ", and to " this table is brown ".   Though we should still be said to *perceive* what is asserted in the last judgment, we certainly *know* much more in the last judgment than we do in the first.   For, if the first is taken to express, *bona fide,* the degree of knowledge supplied by merely seeing a brown (something), without any recognition of the kind of *thing* it is, the progress to " this is a (brown) table " is undeniable.   The difference is, perhaps, most frequently experienced with unfamiliar noises.   To hear a novel noise and to appreciate its peculiar sound-quality is rather sharply marked off from learning of what thing it is the noise.[2]   The inferential transition or synthesis is here most marked.

---

[1] See B. Bosanquet, *Logic* (2nd edit.), vol. ii, pp. 16, 7.
[2] Incidentally, it may be observed that, even in current speech, the sound-qualities of things are nearest to being treated as effects.   We pass from a noise, not so much to a noisy thing, as to the thing which " makes " the noise, though we still speak of " hearing a lark ", etc.

Whatever may be the details of such expansion of knowledge within what is still "perception", according to the current meaning of the term, and whatever account we may give of it in terms of "acquisition of meaning", "association of ideas", "learning by experience", *etc.*, the fundamental point remains unaffected that all these processes are possible only because of the universals which, in supplying logical, or objective, control, at the same time become themselves explicit and articulate.   What is called the "logic of the facts" is the logic of the universals which we learn to recognise as the true nature of the data in which they are realised.

It is worth adding, that the recognition of degrees of knowledge within perception supplies an additional argument against the infallibility of perception.   The more there is of meaning in a perception, the more its truth will depend on matters falling outside the moment's "this".   And on the attempts to save the theory by eliminating meaning we have definitely turned our backs.   To eliminate meaning is to refuse to follow the lead of the principle of identity in difference.   Is it from a fear that this intellectual adventure may end in the absolute?

(3) We must turn to our last problem, whether we have exhausted all the clues which perception furnishes for recognising and discriminating "individual" things.

The view that a thing is a class of actual and possible sense-data reminds us, correctly enough, that we know any "thing" by a synthesis of actual and remembered sense-data, in which the gaps are filled out on principles of continuity and correlation.   But, quite apart from the awkward

---

The reason is obviously that the occurrence of noises is conditioned, as a rule, by visible movements or activities of the thing which makes the noise. *Cf.* the dependence of speech-sounds on movements of the speech-organs.

fact that the author of this view now regards a " class " as a " logical fiction ",[1] this view fails to do justice to the character of individuality which things possess and which we—why shrink from saying it?—perceive in them. At least, there is the striking fact that the objects which we most commonly and readily recognise as " things " belong to three main classes, *viz.*, (1) organisms of all kinds; (2) artefacts of all kinds; (3) objects which are neither organisms nor artefacts but, like mountains, or rivers, possess an aesthetic unity and individuality.[2] Now, in part, this individuality is perceived, especially by the eye, in a certain characteristic *form* or *structure*, which the analysis of things into assemblages of actual and possible sense-data has, so far, completely ignored. It would not be a relevant reply to say that every sense-datum, *e.g.*, a colour-patch, has its " form ", *i.e.*, definite boundary lines. The important point is that in and through the colour-patches which we perceive as a thing, and which may change in outline with the movements of the thing, we recognise a characteristic shape and structure, which we learn to analyse into a distinctive proportion and balance of parts within a whole. And, thence, further analysis will take us, on the one hand, by way of measurement, into the quantitative formulae for the proportions, *e.g.*, of size and weight, and, on the other, into the function or purpose which these parts in just these proportions fulfil, either relatively to each other (*e.g.*, internal proportions within a tool or organism), or relatively to other things (*e.g.*, adaptation of organism to environment, of tool to human need). Dr. Bosanquet may exaggerate

[1] Bertrand Russell, *Introduction to Mathematical Philosophy*, chs. xiii and xvii.
[2] Our habit of giving proper names to such natural objects is surely significant here. On the whole subject of the individuality of things there are some incidental remarks in Dr. Bosanquet's *Logic* (2nd ed.), vol. i, pp. 129, 218, which are, unless I am greatly mistaken, too commonly overlooked by students of philosophy.

in suggesting that, but for our familiarity with the embodiment of our purposes in tools made by ourselves, we should
not find it so easy as we do to recognise " things ".[1] The
individuality, at any rate, of living things is likely to have
struck men long before they had made much advance in
the making of tools.   But the main point is, surely, sound:
" It is by acquaintance with the perceptible character impressed by . . . proportions . . . that we readily pro-
nounce on the use of objects made by the hand of man,
and that we detect, somewhat less readily, the actual purpose served by adaptations in the organic world.   Such attributes as are expressed in these proportions form, for
perception, the content of individualities ".[2]

The character of individuality, then, is conveyed at the
very least in the perceptible proportions and arrangements
of the parts of a thing—or, in other words, in its structure,
form, organisation.   This, clearly, is something more than
is fairly conveyed by terms like assemblage or conjunction
of sense-data, even when these terms are applied to a complex of sense-data presented together.   It is something
more than, and by attentive analysis distinguishable from,
the sense-data, yet it is given in them as *their* arrangement,
and is perceived just as they are.   But the most interesting
point of the whole theory is that, whilst the arrangement, in
detail and as a whole, is, and must always be, capable of
a causal explanation, by laws formulating its correlation
with its conditions, yet it challenges also an interpretation
of that other sort for which " purpose " or " purposiveness " are the only convenient terms.   The proportions of
the parts and their qualities—and in the economy of nature
this is true equally of primary qualities such as size, weight,
resistance, and of secondary qualities, such as the coloura-
tion of animals and flowers, their smell, their sound—

[1] *Loc. cit.,* p. 218.   [2] *Loc. cit.,* p. 129.

demand explanation in terms of "function" and "use". Yet this teleological character of things, in structure and behaviour, raises tantalising problems.

With tools of our own making, we know what purpose they are intended to serve, and can explain why, in order to serve that purpose, they had to be endowed with the structure and qualities they possess, though it ought not to be ignored that natural materials, by their "given" qualities, partly lend themselves to our purposes, partly handicap us, or at least impose severe conditions on the way in which, and the extent to which, they are usable. But when we pass to organisms, the application of the concept of purpose becomes difficult and precarious. The functions of an organ are generally easily enough traced, though even here we may run up against riddles, which may extend through the whole economy of an organism's existence, especially when research brings to light, e.g., microscopic structures or chemical processes unknown to ordinary perception. But the chief difficulty is that organisms as wholes seem to have no obvious or necessary function except that of being just themselves and fulfilling the routine cycle of their existence. And even then, though conscious intention or purpose may sometimes, as in men, play a part, we cannot, in general, say, on obvious evidence, that every natural organism is what it is, grows as it grows, behaves as it behaves, because of its own conscious purpose to be, grow, behave just so. No human being is the designer of his own body: a fortiori, no animals or plants are. And there is still less empirical warrant for saying that Nature, as master-artist, designed the tout ensemble, and fitted each thing into its place in the general plan. Yet teleological categories will not let themselves be ousted. Structure and function, being frequently still perceptible in whatever sense "things" are perceptible, connect teleological categories directly with sense-data and give them a place in the interpretation of sense-data. At the same time, through their suggestion of purpose they are also connected both with "consciousness" and with "value", and thus introduce us to an order of appearances requiring to be saved even more urgently for not being any longer so directly sustained by sense-data.

Note on John Locke's Distinction of Primary and Secondary Qualities

It is of interest in connection with the first half of the preceding essay, to analyse in detail Locke's argument for the distinction of primary and secondary qualities, because there is hardly a point in the prolonged subsequent discussion of the problem, which Locke has not anticipated, however briefly. From the very start of his argument Locke takes for granted the psycho-physiological causation of "ideas" in our minds, by the "impulse", or "motion" which bodies impart to our sense-organs, and which "our nerves or animal spirits" carry to the brain or "seat of sensation", there to produce the ideas we have. He takes for granted, also, the physical theory that bodies consist of "insensible particles" of matter, each having its figure, bulk, solidity, motion. These are "primary" qualities because (a) they are constantly found "in every particle of matter which has bulk enough to be perceived"; (b) even if we imagine particles so small as to be utterly imperceptible, we must still endow them with all these qualities, for matter is inconceivable without them; (c) they are necessary to the action of one body on another, and, therefore, to the production of ideas in our minds; (d) they are real qualities in that they are really in bodies, "whether any one's senses perceive them or no"; (e) primaries are free from contradiction: a figure is never perceived as other than it is. The ideas of themselves which primary qualities produce in us are "resemblances" of the "patterns" which "do really exist in the bodies themselves". On the other hand, the secondary qualities "in truth are nothing in the objects themselves, but powers to produce various sensations in us by their primary qualities." The colour and scent of a violet are but the effects in us of the bulk, figure, texture, and motion of the insensible parts of which the violet, as a material thing, is composed. Why is it a "mistake" to attribute "reality" to secondaries, as we commonly do? (a)

Because bodies produce in us sensations of whiteness or sweetness just as they produce the sensations of pain or of sickness. Why attribute warmth to the fire, but not pain? Why sweetness to manna, but not the sickness of which it is in the same way the cause? (b) Because, " Take away the sensations of them; let not the eyes see light or colours, nor the ears hear sounds; let the palate not taste, nor the nose smell; and all colours, tastes, odours, and sounds, as they are such particular ideas, vanish and cease, and are reduced to their causes, *i.e.*, bulk, figure, and motion of parts ". (c) Because, if pain does not exist when it is not felt, there is no reason to think that sweetness exists when it is not tasted, or colour when it is not seen. (d) Because secondary qualities are variable with physical conditions: " Can any one think any real alterations are made in the porphyry by the presence or absence of light, and that those ideas of whiteness and redness are really in porphyry in the light, when it is plain that it has no colour in the dark? " (e) Because secondary qualities are often mutually contradictory: " The same water, at the same time, may produce the idea of cold by one hand, and of heat by the other; whereas it is impossible that the same water, if those ideas were really in it, should at the same time be both hot and cold." Locke fairly boxes the compass collecting premises for the conclusion he is bent on reaching. Yet most of his arguments, taken singly, each on its merits, are open to criticism, and, taken together, they are irrelevant to one another. For example, the arguments against the reality of secondaries, drawn from their relativity and mutual incompatibility, not only lend no support to his account of the causation of perceptions, but since, on Locke's own showing, all our knowledge of things is derived from sensations, make the very possibility of formulating such a causal theory unintelligible. The most curious point is, I think, the assimilation of colour and taste to sickness and pain as effects in us, not real qualities in things. The corresponding assimilation of " the stomach and guts " to the " eyes and palate " teaches one to appreciate the greater subtlety and psychological accuracy with which Berkeley has restated the pain-argument in his *Dialogues*. Modern writers, like Broad, Russell, and others, have done well to separate the relativity arguments from the causal theory in its psychophysiological form.

CHAPTER VI

THE problem of mechanism and vitalism may be regarded
as single, but it is certainly far from simple. Recent discussion [1] has shown it to be the meeting-point of a veritable
maze of questions, touching experimental facts on one side
and logical principles on the other. What is meant by
" mechanism "?   What are the limits, if any, of a mechanistic explanation of natural phenomena?   How many
different types of theory sail under the common name of
" vitalism "?   Do living beings in their structure, growth,
behaviour, exhibit features incapable of being explained in
physico-chemical terms?   If so, must we refer them to a

---

[1] It is, surely, no mere coincidence, but a symptom of the trend of
contemporary thought, and especially of the way in which science and
philosophy react upon each other, that during 1918 the Aristotelian
Society of London and the American Philosophical Association
arranged, independently of each other, discussions on the topic of
mechanism versus vitalism, and that on both sides of the Atlantic
scientists and philosophers co-operated in these attempts to compare
their theories and points of view, and, if possible, make them meet.
To the " Symposium " of the Aristotelian Society on the question,
" Are Physical. Biological and Psychological Categories Irreducible ? ",
there contributed J. S. Haldane, D'Arcy W. Thompson, P. Chalmers
Mitchell, and L. T. Hobhouse. Their papers are to be found in the
Proceedings of the Society for 1917-18 (N. S., vol. xviii) ; they have
also been republished by Dr. Wildon Carr in *Life and Finite Individuality* (London: Williams and Norgate). The leaders of the discussion of the American Philosophical Association were L. J. Henderson
(Harvard), H. S. Jennings (Johns Hopkins), H. C. Warren (Prince-
ton), W. T. Marvin (Rutgers College), and myself. The present
essay is a reprint, with a few verbal changes, of my contribution
to the discussion, as originally published together with the papers
of the other four leaders, in the *Philosophical Review* (vol. xxvii,
No. 6, pp. 628-645). A select bibliography, compiled in connection
with the discussion, will be found in the *Journal of Philosophy,
Psychology and Scientific Methods* (vol. xv., no. 20, Sept. 1918).

special vital force? What is the nature of this force? What
is its mode of operation? Can any theory on this point
be tested and verified by experiment? If not, is such a vital
force anything more than a fiction, at least for a science
which seeks to be strictly empirical? Yet, without such a
factor, is there any way of accounting for the difference between the living and the non-living? What, again, is the
relation of biology to physics and chemistry? Is it a de-
partment of these latter sciences, or is it autonomous, with
a field of facts and with characteristic concepts of its own?
Suppose we decide for its autonomy, how does this affect
the ideal of a unified theory of nature? Does this ideal
commit us to seeking the explanation of all facts in terms of
the smallest possible number of concepts? And should
these concepts be taken exclusively from the physical
sciences?

These and similar questions have been interwoven in the
recent literature of our topic. They are obviously closely
connected with one another, yet no less obviously a discussion of each of them on its merits requires an expertness in
so many different fields of knowledge, that hardly any single
thinker nowadays can hope to handle with equal competence all sides of the problem. The best results, now as
in the past, may be expected from the sympathetic coöperation of scientists and philosophers. For we ought not to
forget that to the historical development of mechanism and
vitalism philosophers and scientists have equally contributed. It is enough to recall, prior to the nineteenth century, such names as Aristotle, Bacon, Galileo, Descartes,
Newton, Leibniz, Hume, Kant, in order to realise that our
topic has been one of the chief meeting-points of experimental research on the one side and philosophical speculation on the other. It is no mere accident that Hans Driesch,
in thinking out his vitalistic theory, found himself driven

into fundamental problems of logic, and that the advocate of a mechanistic theory, like Loeb, is much more of a " speculative " philosopher than he is himself aware of.

The thesis which we shall try to support, and the bearing of which on some of the problems above enumerated we shall try to draw out in the following pages, may be summed up in the formula: Not mechanism *or* vitalism, but mechanism *and* teleology. The " universe of discourse " of our discussion is best described, in Henderson's happy phrase, as " The Order of Nature ";[1] and biology is our best door of entry into it. For biology can hardly avoid the *larger issues of context* which are suggested by the appearance of living beings in nature, of organisms built upon and growing out of the inorganic. However much the worker in biology may seek to limit himself to the phenomena of life *as such,* to the problems of structure, growth, behaviour, without troubling himself about the larger questions of the origin and status of life in the system of nature as a whole, still even the most superficial acquaintance with biological literature shows that such isolation is largely artificial, and always on the point of breaking down under the pressure of the desire for fuller knowledge. It breaks down, first of all, because, whilst physicist and chemist can ignore the phenomena of life, the biologist cannot ignore the phenomena of physics and chemistry. The living beings which he studies, whether single cells or multicellular organisms, are far too obviously physico-chemical systems. Once the breach has thus been made, the whole tide of wider issues sweeps in. Beginning with the difference between the living and the non-living, there comes next into view the problem of the way in which the phenomena of life are conditioned by their occurrence in bodies, *i.e.,* in physico-

[1] See his book under this title.

chemical systems, and, again, by an environment, partly itself composed of living things, partly non-living. And once this point has been reached, the "order of nature" confronts us as the context within which the other questions must find their answers. Our argument will seek to confirm the view that there is both an order of objective phenomena, and a corresponding order of the sciences which give us the truth about these phenomena. It will thus attempt to do justice to the continuity of nature on the one side, and, on the other side, to the broad qualitative differences which we find within it, and which appear to demand an ascending, or, at least, a cumulative arrangement.

Within this universe of discourse, then, of biology expanded into the problem of the order of nature, the formula "not mechanism *or* vitalism, but mechanism *and* teleology" is to be interpreted. It means that we ought to replace the disjunction of mechanism and vitalism, as mutually exclusive alternatives, by the conjunction of mechanism and teleology. It demands that these concepts be treated as cumulative in the order of nature, and, therefore, teleology as *logically dominant* over mechanism in biology. It regards the arguments against vitalism as decisive, if by "vitalism" we mean the theory that in all the things called "living" there is present some non-mechanical, non-spatial, semi-psychical force or factor—whether biotic energy, or entelechy, or *élan vital*—which yet has the power to interfere by way of regulation or control with the physico-chemical processes in the body; which can suspend the second law of thermodynamics; which can select for realisation one of the physically open possibilities; which can create novelties, not only unpredictable in advance, but inexplicable after they have occurred. Vitalism in this sense we do not want to save, and this is the sort of vitalism between which and mechanism the choice for biology is usually said to lie. But whilst it is part of our thesis to reject vitalism on its merits, it is also part of it to reject the whole disjunction of vitalism and mechanism, acceptance of which would commit us to the affirmation of mechanism by the denial of vitalism. It is here that the second half of our thesis, " mechanism *and* teleology ", comes into play. This is intended to give full scope to mechanistic theory to carry us as far as it can, but it is also intended to maintain that there is a sound sense in which it is true to say, that the phenomena of life cannot be explained, or, better, formulated, in physico-chemical terms. Or, to put the positive side of the contention, teleological terms are required, not as substitutes for physico-chemical terms, but as fixing what we have called the " dominant " character of life-processes to which their physico-chemical aspect is subsidiary. The relation is easier to illustrate than to put into words. We find it wherever in nature there appears a new stratum or level, a new type of quality, or of structure. In the theory of colours, *e.g.*, or of sounds, the " dominant " concepts are derived from an analysis of colours and sounds themselves—colours as such, or as actually seen, sounds as such, or as actually heard—and it is only the ordering of these data in terms drawn from their own nature that gives relevance to the subsequent correlation of colour-differences or sound-differences with differences in the rate of vibration of some elastic medium. So, again, the dominant concepts of chemistry are patently derived from a study of the properties and states of elements and compounds in their relations to one another under varying conditions of temperature, presence of catalytic agents, *etc.* And it is not as a substitute for, but as a supplement, that we seek to correlate these facts and their laws with facts and laws of the physical structure and relations of atoms, or whatever the ultimate constituents of matter may be. So with the phenomena of life. The dominant concepts required for an adequate theory of them are, on the view here maintained, teleological, but this involves no denial of their physico-chemical aspect, or of the importance of discovering the physico-chemical arrangements and processes on which teleological characters and relationships are built. To fore-stall misapprehension, however, we ought to say at once that, when we speak of teleological concepts, we do not mean a design, or plan, or purpose, or desire consciously entertained by any mind, be it of God, of man, of animal, or of plant. We need teleological concepts freed of these implications; concepts so general that conscious designs or desires are but a special type falling under them. The way to such a view is opened by the concept of *value*, the introduction of which permits us to read relations of cause and effect as also relations of means to ends. The one reading belongs to mechanism, the other to teleology. The two readings do not exclude each other but are compatible, and, where the teleological reading is possible at all, cumula-tive. Life requires both readings, but the teleological read-ing must be dominant. This is our thesis.

One of the corollaries of this thesis is the " autonomy of life ", or to put the same point from a different side, the autonomy of biology. Now, in one sense this is, of course, a truism, which no one, when the point is put up to him, seriously wants to deny, and to insist upon which, there-fore, may seem a work of supererogation. Thus a convinced anti-vitalist, like Claude Bernard, is found writing: " Je serais d'accord avec les vitalistes s'ils voulaient simplement reconnaître que le êtres vivants présentent des phénomènes qui ne se retrouvent pas dans la nature brute, et qui, par conséquent, leur sont spéciaux. J'admets en effet que les manifestations vitales ne sauraient être élucidées par les seuls phénomènes physico-chimiques connu dans la matière brute . . . La biologie doit prendre aux sciences physico-chimiques la méthode expérimentale, mais garder ses phénomènes spéciaux et ses lois propres ".[1]

The same autonomy obviously can, and ought to, be claimed by every science for itself and for the field of phenomena which it studies. All the differences which experience reveals in the world are, in this sense, unique, specific, *sui generis*. Why, then, is it worth while insisting on such a truism? Because there is a noticeable tendency in many quarters to deny it, in effect, by the way in which the ideal of a " unified " theory of nature is interpreted. This interpretation constantly takes the form of claiming to " reduce " one type of phenomena to another, of treating one as *nothing but* another. Life, *e.g.*, we find it said, is " merely " a particular kind of physico-chemical process. Interpreted as a denial of vital force or entelechy, the statement is harmless enough. But it is harmful, or at least dangerous, in so far as the unique and distinctive character of life-processes is left completely unspecified and undetermined in this sweeping assimilation of them to physico-chemical processes in general. If we ask, *What particular kind* of physico-chemical process? it becomes clear at once that physico-chemical terms are not sufficiently specific and relevant for the answer required. In view of this situation, it is of the utmost importance to insist that the attempt to eliminate differences, to break down boundaries, to unify by the " nothing but " device, makes, not for orderly, but for disorderly thinking and does a disservice to science. The

[1] *Introduction à l'étude de la Médecine Expérimentale* (1865), p. 118. For a similar statement, see H. S. Jennings, *Am. Journal of Psychology*, 1910, pp. 349-370. For A. O. Lovejoy's comments see *Science*, N. S., vol. xxxiv, no. 864, pp. 75-80 (July 1911), and his paper on " The Unity of Science " in the *University of Missouri Bulletin* (1912), vol. i, no. 1, esp. pp. 22 ff.

phenomena of life require to be dealt with first and foremost in their own teleological terms, and this not as a mere convenience of provisional " description ", but as a necessity of adequate " explanation ", or, better, of *understanding*.

The principle of the autonomy of life, then, means the right to use in biology teleological concepts. That biologists constantly *do* use such concepts, is too familiar a fact to require illustration. Some frankly confess that they cannot help using them. Others are apologetic about them, as if they were a temporary makeshift pending the formulation of an " explanation " in physico-chemical terms. The thesis here maintained is that the use of teleological terms is not a symptom of relative ignorance. It is not a sign of the inferiority of biology to physics and chemistry. The principle of the autonomy of life should be for biologists a charter of emancipation from the false fashion which leads some thus to depreciate their science. It should be a watchword reminding them to have the courage of their practice, and to insist on their right to use the language demanded by the facts with which they deal. Those who are really consistent in eliminating all teleological concepts from their thought and from their language—and this is patently the ideal which some " mechanists " strive to realise—are compelled to misconceive and misdescribe the facts. The criticism which E. B. Holt directs against biologists who, in their anxiety not to compromise themselves with animal souls, analyse, *e.g.*, a bee's behaviour into successive responses to visual, auditory, olfactory, *etc.*, stimuli, and over it all lose sight of the *bee* and of the dominant fact that " the bee is carrying honey to its home ",[1] may serve to illustrate the point. It is noticeable that the analysis of Bethe's which Holt here criticises, is itself still far removed from using strictly physico-chemical terms. Suppose, then,

[1] *The Freudian Wish*, p. 77.

we push the issue back to the point to which a convinced
mechanist must want to push it. Is not, let us ask, the bee's
flight a case of the motion of a material body, and must it
not, as such, conform to the laws which physics has formulated for matter in motion? Of course it is, and we may
readily grant that, even though the flight of a bee, or the
antics of a monkey in his cage,[1] or the behaviour of any
other living thing have not yet been formulated in terms
of mechanism, yet " in theory " this can be done. The reason why it has not at present been done lies in the exceed-
ing complexity of the phenomena, not in any inapplicability
of the laws of matter in motion owing to their being sus-
pended, or interfered with, by some vital force. The important point is: supposing it were done, would it be relevant? Would it really explain, *i.e.*, give us a fuller insight
into, what the bee is doing and why, than the account in
teleological terms that it is laying by honey in its home?
The moral of these considerations is that biology not only
does, but may, not only may, but must, use teleological concepts, and use them, moreover, as logically dominant over
all other concepts which for subsidiary use it may borrow
from other sciences. That all living beings, or, better, living bodies, are physico-chemical systems is here conceded
and, indeed, insisted upon as much as the most whole-
hearted mechanist can desire. But what we also insist upon
is that, when we study living beings exclusively from the
physico-chemical point of view, their character as *living* does
not come within our field of study at all. From that point
of view the difference between living and non-living is
simply irrelevant. So far from being explained, it is rather
ignored. It is not part of the physicist's or chemist's universe of discourse. Witness the transformation of the
meaning of " organic " in the chemist's language. The term

[1] See A. O. Lovejoy, *Unity of Science, loc. cit.,* p. 16.

there has lost the exclusive reference to the living which it retains in the biologist's mouth, and applies for the chemist to all carbon-compounds whatsoever, regardless of whether they are found or produced in the living or in the non-living. This, surely, is instructive. And the moral of it is that the biologist who knows his business will not try to " reduce " himself to a species of chemist. Indeed, it is only on condition of his keeping his teleological categories dominant, that the investigation of the chemistry of vital processes becomes for him relevant and significant. He must first recognise a living thing or a living process *as such*, before the study of its chemical side or basis becomes important for him as throwing further light on his topic. In short, if our topic is carbon-compounds, life and the concepts it involves are irrelevant to us. But if our topic is life, then the laws of carbon-compounds, so far as these occur in vital structures and processes, are relevant, not because they reveal to us, as it is sometimes said, the " secret " of life, but because a knowledge of the chemical processes involved in life (or, put differently, of the chemical bases or conditions of life) is part, but not the whole, of an adequate knowledge of life. Nor is biology in any way inferior to chemistry and physics, because it uses them ("depends " upon them, as it is sometimes ambiguously expressed), so far as they are relevant for its purposes. Its cognitive interest is centred, first and last, upon the study of living beings, their structure, their growth, their behaviour. Their characteristic nature as *living* clamours for recognition in specific concepts. This is the situation to which the vitalist has the merit of calling attention, though he misinterprets it when he invokes entelechies or what not. This, again, is the situation which gives rise to the familiar assertion that " no physico-chemical explanation of life is possible ". Such an explanation is impossible, not because of the operation of a vital force, but because, however detailed and complete in itself, it would necessarily fail to touch the specific character of vital phenomena. To repeat: the principle of the autonomy of life, as here interpreted, means, not vitalism, but teleology—and teleology as compatible with, but logically dominant over, mechanism in biology.

This thesis may be challenged on the ground that it conflicts with the aspiration of science to achieve such an organisation of knowledge as shall enable it to *deduce* vital phenomena from physico-chemical phenomena. Very commonly in recent literature this ability to deduce is identified with an ability to *predict,* and neither is held to be possible except on the basis of a mechanistic theory of nature. In fact, the *reduction* of organic processes to inorganic processes is, according to this view, undertaken chiefly in the hope that it will enable us from purely physico-chemical data to *deduce, i.e.,* to predict, vital phenomena say the behaviour of an animal in a definite situation. Thus Wilhelm Roux, in his *Entwicklungsmechanik,* formulates the mechanistic programme in the words, "*Das organische Geschehen auf anorganische Wirkungsweisen zurückzuführen, es in solche Wirkungsweisen zu zerlegen, zu analysieren.*" So keen a student of mechanistic and vitalistic theories as A. O. Lovejoy expands this formula as follows: "In what would a *Zurückführung* of biology to chemistry or physics consist? It would consist in showing that a given organic process A can be subsumed under and *deduced from* a given generalisation B of the more "fundamental science."[1] In another paper this is further expanded as follows: "What the partisans of the doctrine of organic autonomy deny is that you conceivably ever can, from a study of the laws

[1] *Science,* N. S., vol. xxxiii, no. 851, p. 611.

of motion of inorganic particles, arrive at a law from which you can predict how any living body will behave, *even if you know the number, size, arrangement and composition of the particles composing that body."* [1]

Before passing to the particular issue of the predictability of organic phenomena, it may be as well to say something about prediction in general, to which an altogether exaggerated importance is assigned in modern theories of the function of science. Claude Bernard had a sounder view. *" Toute la philosophie naturelle,"* he writes, *se résume en cela: Connaître la loi des phénomènes. Tout le problème expérimental se réduit à ceci: Prévoir et diriger les phénomènes."* This distinction is surely well taken. It is a valuable corrective of the fashionable view which makes prediction the main interest and business of science, and treats the discovery of laws as nothing more than a means to prediction. Indeed, we may go even further here than Claude Bernard, and regard prediction, not as a co-ordinate aim of science, but as incidental to the experimental discovery of laws (in the process of verifying hypotheses), and as dominant only in the practical application of scientific knowledge in industry. From this point of view, it is a mistake when the typical formula for a scientific law:—If *A*, then *B*, is read off as essentially a prediction:—If *A* happens, then *B* will happen; or, If you do *A*, then you will get *B*. Fundamentally, a law is a statement of a functional correlation between variables. " If *A*, then *B* " means " *A* implies *B* ", and there is no exclusive or essential reference in this formula to the anticipation of future events. It would, moreover, be wholly false to restrict science to a preoccupation with the future. Science is as much interested in the past as in the future, and its problems as often take the form

[1] *Science*, N. S., vol. xxxiv, no. 864, p. 78. Lovejoy's italics.
[2] *Introduction à l'étude de la Médicine Expérimentale*, p. 100.

of discovering the causes of given effects, as of predicting the effects of given causes. And, lastly, the treatment of an implication as a prediction is false, not only to the character of an implication, but also to the character of a prediction. Prediction, in the proper sense, is not hypothetical, but *categorical*. You do not predict so long as you merely say, *If A*, then *B*. But you do predict when you say, Here is an *A*, and in virtue of the law, If *A*, then *B*, I infer that there will be a *B*. A law, in short, is not a prediction, but may make a prediction possible when applied to a particular case, or to put it differently, when a definite value is given for one of the correlated variables. And even then the correlation must be of the kind which involves temporal sequence or order.

Prediction, then, is by no means identical with deduction in general. It is a special case of deduction, possible only under special conditions. Moreover, it owes its prominence in the discussion of mechanism and vitalism to the fact that the relation of biology to physics and chemistry, or of organic to inorganic processes, is usually conceived, not merely as one of reduction, *i.e.*, of subsumption of particular under general, but as an *evolutionary* and, therefore, *temporal* sequence. In this context we get the problem of the origin of life, in the form whether from physico-chemical data alone a Laplacean calculator could have deduced, *i.e.*, predicted, the future appearance upon this earth of living beings. Or, more narrowly, could such a calculator, given an exhaustive knowledge of the particles and forces involved in the present position of a human body in its environment, predict the next movement of that body, *e.g.*, the words (articulatory movements) with which it is about to break silence? [1]

---

[1] I agree whole-heartedly with the remarks of H. S. Jennings concerning predictability in his paper "Life and Matter," originally

Let us make the question even more precise by restricting it to the law of falling bodies, and giving it the form of an imaginary experiment. Compare the fall, through the same distance of space and under the same atmospheric conditions, of two bodies which differ only in that the one is lifeless, the other living, whilst they are alike in weight, shape, surface-texture, and any other factors which affect the rate of fall. Do you, as physicist, expect to find any difference in the rate at which the falling body in each case traverses the distance to the ground? If you find no difference in this respect, is the difference between being lifeless and alive relevant to you, as a physicist, at all? It will not be part of the data which make the falling body a " case " of your laws. Hence your laws are indifferent, or neutral, to that difference. They hold equally in either case. A living cat does not infringe or violate them. It does not fall slower or faster than a dead one. Yet there is a difference, as we all know, not in the rate of fall, but in the turnings by which the live cat lands on its feet and breaks the fall, escaping injury and death, whereas the impact of the dead cat involves contusions of the body and broken bones. The point of the argument, if there is anything in it, is simply this, that the physicist's data and laws abstract from certain differences, which consequently can neither be subsumed under his laws nor predicted from them alone.[1]

written for the fifth International Congress of Philosophy which, owing to the war, was never held. The paper will be found in the *Johns Hopkins University Circular*, N. S., 1914, no. 10. The reference is to p. 11.

[1] Mention of " lifeless," in the sense of " dead," bodies suggests a curious point, about the exact bearing of which I am neither clear myself, nor are, so far as I can find, my biological authorities. If we dichotomise bodies into living and non-living, organic and inorganic, where do we put the bodies which are dead in the sense of having lost their life, of having been alive and having died? Does an animal or a plant by dying pass straightway into the same class with bodies that are lifeless in the sense that neither life nor death can be predicated of them? In short, death seems to fit awkwardly into the tidy classification of organic and inorganic. The point has

The conclusion which we would draw is that considerations of this sort support our previous contention. The biologist is interested in the study of living things, and hence finds it convenient to divide all things in nature into those which are living and those which are non-living.[1] The inclusion in his field of study of some things, the exclusion from it of others, depend upon the presence or absence of the distinctive quality or character which we call " life ", and which is empirically observable and recognisable. The physicist and the chemist are not interested in this character, and its presence or absence is irrelevant to them. Hence to them living bodies as much as lifeless bodies are physico-chemical systems. But the biologist's interest in life makes him interested also in the physico-chemical structures and processes without which life is not found in our world. Hence his point of view, in this respect, may be called synthetic or synoptic. In any case, if our universe is to be intellectually tidy and ordered, we need both points of view as cumulative and supplementary, *viz.*, the point of view

interesting ramifications. The biologist, in effect, ceases to be interested in an animal when it has died. It has ceased to "behave" and to "respond"; its organs have ceased to function; the phenomena of regulation, so important in the economy of life, no longer appear. Yet would a physiologist necessarily agree to draw the line there? I recall being shown as a student an elaborate and expensive apparatus in the Physiological Laboratory at Oxford, used for experiments upon eyes taken from dead frogs, the result being interpreted as bearing on the question whether black is a positive sensation. It seemed to me humorous, but mechanists may think the joke is on me.—If we look in another direction, we find in the economy of nature that dead organisms play an immensely important part as food for organisms which are alive. Is not breathing almost the only exception to the rule that, above the level of plants, living things absorb inorganic substances only indirectly, by inflicting death on other living things or living on things that have died? And to a large extent this is true even of plants.

[1] It is perhaps not an unnecessary reminder, at least to those of us who are unfamiliar with biology, but familiar with the history of philosophical terms, that when biologists use "animate" as a synonym of living or organic, and "inanimate" as a synonym of non-living or inorganic, they do not identify life with the presence of an *anima* or soul. They ring the changes on these terms simply to avoid monotony of style.

from which all bodies are physico-chemical systems, and
the point of view from which some are living and others
are not. There is, if we like to put it so, homogeneity and
continuity from one point of view, heterogeneity and discontinuity from the other. But nothing is gained by ignoring
one of these two sides.

But this, it may be said, is incompatible with the unity
of science, which requires a determinism in homogeneous
terms, such as can be supplied only by a mechanistic theory,
i.e., a theory by which all qualitative differences are reduced
to, and explained in, terms of one kind only, and these ultimately the terms of physics. The admission of non-
mechanistic concepts would destroy the determinism which
is essential to science in general and to experimentation in
particular.

The reply to this objection is, briefly, that our thesis not
only does not involve the surrender of determinism, rightly
interpreted, but meets all the logical requirements of the
situation. The main points may be summarised as follows.
(*a*) In the first place, we ought to distinguish between
determinism and mechanism. The determinism which is
identical with " reason " in science, and without which any
" rational " explanation of natural phenomena is rightly
said to be impossible, requires merely that every such phenomenon shall be " determined by " some other phenomenon,
i.e., correlated with it according to a law. A mechanistic
theory is but a special form of this general principle
of determinism, deriving its specific character partly from
the introduction of a temporal factor (cause preceding effect), but more characteristically from the exclusive use of
physico-chemical terms. (*b*) Every law is a statement of an
implication between universals, or, in mathematical terminology, of a functional correlation between variables. In the

natural sciences which deal with existences in time and space, presented or presentable in the form of sense-data, all universals have cases, or instances, or applications; all variables have definite values. (c) But a unified theory of nature does not require the reduction of all universals to one kind, or the restriction of all variables to one type of values. We have laws correlating geometrical, physical, chemical phenomena among themselves in each group, as well as laws correlating phenomena of one group with those of another. There will then result a scheme, or an order, in which differences are preserved and " saved ", instead of being " reduced ", and in which a unified theory is achieved by the correlation of different types, or groups, or levels, of phenomena which follow also among themselves each its own characteristic laws. (d) We shall thus expect to find what, indeed, we actually get in a large part of biological work, viz., a determinism in terms which are thoroughly teleological. Such a determinism will meet all the requirements of what H. S. Jennings pleads for under the names of " experimental determinism " or " radically experimental analysis ".[1] One might formulate the principle of determinism as " every difference makes a difference ". This is nothing but functional correlation expressed in other words. For, when two factors are correlated, a change in one must involve a corresponding change in the other—" corresponding ", whether or no the variations on both sides are measurable and quantitatively determinable. In scientific observation the rule of method is, given an observed difference A to search for some other observable difference B, such that A is present where B is present, absent when B is absent, and varies concomitantly with the varia-

---

[1] See his contribution to the discussion, *Philosophical Review*, Vol. xxvii, No. 6, pp. 592 ff; also his article on *Driesch's Vitalism and Experimental Determinism* in *Science*, vol. xxxvi, p. 434.

tions of *B*. This is the elementary ABC of induction. Experimentation applies the same principle by artificially introducing, removing, or varying *B* so as to study its correlation with *A*. As H. S. Jennings says—in complete accord with the teachings of logicians on this point—the whole " organisation " of experience by " discovery of correspondence in diversities " depends on this principle.[1] (*e*) The only point of refinement which we may, perhaps, claim to add to the above account is the insistence on what we have ventured to call the " logical dominance " of the characteristic concepts and laws of biology, on the ground that biology deals with structures and processes which have, indeed, their physico-chemical aspect, but cannot be reduced to exclusively physico-chemical terms without sacrificing precisely what makes them distinctive.

It remains to say a few words in defence of teleology and of the language of " purpose," by ridding the latter term of certain associations, the presence of which makes it unwelcome to scientists, and which are not required by the facts.

" Purpose " is objectionable, because it suggests the activity of a scheming or designing intelligence where no evidence of such is found. To talk of purposes in nature at once gives rise to the suspicion that their admission is to be exploited, as in the old Argument from Design, in the interests of an anthropomorphic deity; that intelligible law is to be replaced by an unintelligible will. But our plea here is that the terms can be freed from these implications and made scientifically useful. A transition can be made from " efficient " to " final " causes by the simple reminder, that a nexus of cause and effect can *also* be taken

[1] *Life and Matter*, p. 6 *et passim*. *Cf*. also the general position outlined there on pp. 10-11.

as a nexus of means and end, whenever the effect has *value*. A natural law neither demands nor forbids the introduction of the concept of value, and is, therefore, entirely compatible with it, if the empirical facts should demand it. Some modern writers, indeed, would limit the application of the concept of value to whatever is desired. Things, they say, become valuable, or acquire value, by being desired. But, again, it is not in this sense that the term " value " is to be employed here. When biological science speaks of conditions as " beneficial " or " harmful " for the organism; when it calls some chemical substances " foods," others " waste-products "; when it speaks of the " function " of an organ, or through the concept of " organisation " interprets the parts in the light of the whole; when, in dealing with " growth," " behaviour," " reproduction," *etc.*, it applies the concept of the maintenance or development of each characteristic type of living structure—its language is full of the kind of teleology which the term " value," or, if it be preferred, " objective value," is here intended to cover. Wherever, broadly speaking, the facts challenge us to say, not merely that B is the effect of A, but that B is the *reason why*, or *that for the sake of which*, A exists or occurs, there we have the *immanent purposiveness* of living things. To introduce here the analogy of human purposes, *i.e.*, to suppose the existence of these structures, the occurrence of these activities and functionings, to have been preceded by a desire for their existence or occurrence, or by a conscious design, plan, scheme, first thought out and then realised by the manipulation of means, would be misleading and irrelevant. No living thing begins by planning or desiring its own existence, its own form and function. No organism grows and lives according to a preconceived specification, building up its body like a builder working to a design, or like a tailor working to a pattern.

"No living thing", we said. And this covers not only plants and animals, but man. For, though we may claim each to be "master of his fate," yet for all the planning that we do, for all the efforts that we make to guide ourselves and our world towards desired results, we tend vastly to overrate the part that desiring and scheming play in making us and our world what they are. Conscious choice, intelligent control, art, mask but do not displace the immanent and unconscious purposiveness which the lives of individuals and societies exhibit, and which is discernible even through their misfits and failures.

When we ask what character in natural objects, or in nature as a whole, exhibits this immanent purposiveness, this "design," most clearly, the answer must surely be that it is *organisation*—not merely in the static sense of a systematic structure of differentiated parts, but in the dynamic sense of this structure at work and functioning as a whole, responding through its organs (which are very literally "instruments") to its environment, adapting that environment to itself and itself to it. A purposive structure, in Kant's famous phrase, is one in which parts and whole are reciprocally means and ends. The subordination of the parts to the whole lies precisely in that delicate mutual adjustment of the parts which, in respect of their functioning, we call *regulative*, and which in form as well as in function yields the characteristic individuality—one might almost say, using the word in the artistic sense, "the effect" —of each living thing. Aristotle went straight to the heart of the matter when he compared this organisation of each living thing to the order of a commonwealth. "And the animal organism must be conceived after the similitude of a well-governed commonwealth. When order is once established in it, there is no more need of a separate monarch to preside over each several task. The individuals each play their assigned part as it is ordered, and one thing follows another in its accustomed order. So in animals there is the same orderliness—nature taking the place of custom and each part naturally doing its work as nature has composed them." [1] We have here clearly what in the language of modern biology is expressed as " the conception of the living thing as an autonomous unit in which every part is functionally related to every other and exists as the servant of the whole ".[2]

And yet living beings are also constantly spoken of as " living machines " and their organs as " mechanisms " for doing this or that. Whence it is a short step to the demand for an exclusively " mechanical " explanation. But a brief reflection on the concept of a machine will both account for the plausibility of this language and yet lend support to our view. It is surely a startling paradox that machines, which, as human tools for human ends, are more patently purposive than anything else in the world, being artefacts of human design, should have furnished by analogy the concepts which are used to shut out from the purview of science, not merely conscious design, but the immanent purposiveness exhibited in organisation and regulation. Yet a machine is nothing if not organised, and frequently it is fitted with devices for regulating its own workings. It is, in fact, like an organism, a systematic structure of differentiated parts with differentiated functions. It was this uncanny likeness of machines to organisms which suggested Samuel Butler's brilliant fancy, in *Erewhon*, of a revolt of machines against man, their maker, the intelligence embodied in them making itself, as it were, independent. What

---

[1] Henderson has done a real service in reminding us of this passage in his *Order of Nature*, p. 16; Arist., *De Part. An.*, 645a, 20.
[2] Henderson, *ibid.*, p. 21. " Functionally related " in this context must be taken to bear both the mathematical and the teleological sense. The two senses correspond to cause-effect, means-end respectively.

is it that enables science to borrow from so purposeful and highly organised a thing as a machine the concepts for dealing with the non-purposive and inorganic? The answer would seem to be this. A machine, just because as a human tool it exists, not for its own sake, but for the sake of something other than itself, makes it easy to abstract from its purpose and to consider its organised structure as simply a system of particles and forces, undergoing transformations according to purely physical laws. A physicist, whom we will suppose ignorant of the purpose of a watch, might still be able to analyse it as a mechanism and to explain just why this intricate arrangement of toothed wheels and other devices, operated by a spring, must effect the rotation of two hands, each at its own uniform speed, but one twelve times as fast as the other. So far the mechanistic point of view, with its cause-effect principle, might carry him, nor need he know the end to which the whole arrangement is the means. Now, if it is easy to analyse a machine which has a purpose as if it had none, because its purpose is " external " to its own existence, it is even easier to ignore the immanent purposiveness of an organism, which is not obviously an instrument for anything. Thus, by a similar abstraction from their teleological character, organism and machine can be analysed, as if neither exhibited any characters except those of which we take account when we study them as physico-chemical systems.

CHAPTER VII

MECHANISM AND VITALISM: FURTHER PROBLEMS.

BROADLY speaking, the argument of the preceding essay has been built upon nothing more recondite than the two principles of the *autonomy* of each science within its own field, and of the *order* of sciences which results from the fact that one science may be, as we called it, " logically dominant " over another. The science which is higher in this sense makes a subsidiary use of the more general principles and theories of the lower, whilst maintaining throughout the characteristic concepts appropriate to its own more special and distinctive phenomena. In this way, so we had urged, the order of the sciences corresponds to, and reflects, the way in which in the " order of nature " phenomena of a higher level or type are, as it were, superimposed on phenomena of a lower type, whilst being at the same time conditioned by the latter, in the sense that without these latter the former are not found to occur. The relationships here involved seem peculiar, and none of the familiar metaphors or analogies appear to fit them. So far as the higher phenomena are conditioned by the lower—have in the lower their *sine qua non*—there is, if we like to say so, a " correlation." Yet this term, with its suggestion of a parallelism, or one-to-one correspondence, does not really hit off the way in which, *e.g.*, in breathing, the physical process of inflating and deflating the lungs, and the chemical process of oxidising the blood, are subservient to, are means for securing, an effect which is " beneficial " to the organism, or, in other words, a necessary element in its total self-maintenance. The teleological character which is dominant, and

is taken for granted when we talk of "breathing," instead
of talking merely of "oxidisation," or of sucking air into
a bag and expelling it again, depends on considering the
function of the process in the life-economy of the organism,
the *importance* of the part it plays in the creature's self-
maintenance; in short, its value. The recognition of this
situation, so we had argued, is required in order to "save,"
as elements in an inclusive world-view, both the appearances
which we call "mechanical," and those which we call
"teleological." For the lower science the phenomena of the
higher are merely another set of "cases" falling under its
general principles, but precisely for this reason the lower
science is completely incapable of dealing with what is
distinctive and unique in the phenomena of the higher.
This is why there is no *a priori* way of "deducing" the
higher phenomena from the principles of the lower. When
the higher phenomena are met with, they are always found,
not only to be consistent with the laws of the lower, but
also to require the existence of the lower phenomena for
their own existence. But no knowledge merely of the lower
phenomena would make possible a purely deductive "anticipation of nature"—a prevision of teleological structures
at a time when none had as yet made their appearance in
nature.

The present essay is to be devoted to a further examination of certain aspects of the problem—aspects which run, in
a tantalising way, through all the current discussions of
mechanism, vitalism, and teleology, without being, as a rule,
explicitly focused so that their bearing on the resulting
theory may be clearly perceived. We shall discuss these
aspects most conveniently under the following three head-
ings:

(1) The concept of machine in its relation to mechanical
theory.

(2) The " scientific " and the " romantic " points of view, with special reference to the ideal of " logical continuity."

(3) The empirical basis of teleology as applied to life.[1]

(1) First, then, we take up the concepts of machine and mechanism. " The living body in general, and the human body in particular, obviously acts in some respects like a mechanism, while in other respects it appears to act differently." With these words, Mr. L. T. Hobhouse, one of the Aristotelian symposiasts,[2] opens his contribution. Presently he goes on: " The characteristics of mechanism can be seen in a man-made machine," and after some discussion he sums them up in the formula, " A whole is mechanical when and in so far as its parts act uniformly in response to the forces operating in each of them, not varying in relation to the results of this action or to the state of other parts." The force of the negatives in this account will be appreciated by comparison with the formula for an " organic whole," *viz.*, " A whole acts organically when and in so far as the operation of any part is varied in accordance with the requirements of the whole as a self-maintaining structure." The crucial point of observation behind the contrasting formulae appears to lie in a comparison between what happens when a living organism and a man-made machine, respectively, get out of order. Supply motive power to a machine out of order and, so far as it works, or rather moves, at all, " each several part acts uniformly without relation to the rest in response to the forces operating upon it, whatever they may be." Disorder, in short, reveals the characteristic principle on which the working of a machine even in order depends, but which is there disguised by the

---

[1] See the *Note* at the end of this essay for a brief discussion of the problem of the origin of life, witn special reference to Bergson's *élan vital.*

[2] See note at the beginning of the preceding essay, p. 141.

fact that the human designer and maker has so arranged the parts and forces in their " normal " state, that, though " each acts uniformly without relation to the rest in response to the forces operating upon it," they yet together produce the result which the designer wants. A living organism out of order—short of the degree of disorder which results in death—struggles back to order and normal functioning, or as near to these as it can. Its structures are so arranged, and their functions so regulated, that it keeps itself in order and, when injured or disturbed, restores itself to order. A machine out of order loses the coöperation of its parts, nor can it, by itself, restore or recover that coöperation. It ceases to function as a " whole," where the character of wholeness consists in producing the result for which it is the instrument, in doing what it is designed to do and what, in good order, it actually does. An organism out of order, short of death, never ceases completely to function as a whole, though the character of wholeness here can be defined only as that self-maintenance, that performing of the characteristic cycle of activities, in which the life of each kind of creature consists. The coöperation of the parts, though disturbed, is not lost. Regulatory adjustments take place which enable as much of the normal life-economy to be carried on as possible, and which tend to restore it to full normality.

Something like this, in fact and theory, seems to be involved for Hobhouse in the difference between living organism and man-made machine.

With more elaborate scientific detail, the same contrast runs through the argument of another one of the symposiasts, Dr. J. S. Haldane, the well-known physiologist. " A living organism," he writes, " differs in this respect from any mechanism we can construct or conceive, that it forms itself and keeps itself in working order and activity." The moral which Haldane does not hesitate to draw, with a lengthy illustration from the stages in the development of the kinetic theory of gases, is that the scope of the mechanical theory is limited to what we can " construct and conceive," and that, even as applied to infra-organic, purely physical and chemical, entities and processes in nature, it is no more than a useful " short-cut," a convenient, but highly abstract, working-hypothesis, the formulae of which are " imperfect representations " even of the behaviour of molecules. " The abstract mechanical conception of a molecule is unreal." " We cannot sum up the properties of molecules in the conception of mass, extension, and central forces proportionate to mass, in accordance with the fundamental physical conceptions of Newton." The very progress of physical chemistry, he claims, is constantly sharpening and justifying the distinction between what is living and what is non-living. His main arguments [1] in support of this claim are the following two: (a) Physiological processes once thought capable of a simple and easy mechanical explanation, have for modern research turned out to be so complex, that the probability of a mechanical explanation sufficing is fast disappearing. " On the whole there is no evidence of real progress towards a mechanistic explanation of life." (b) " The idea of a mechanism which is constantly maintaining or reproducing its own structure is self-contradictory," for a mechanical explanation must assume, as given, a fixed system of interacting parts, and such a system can neither itself grow, nor out of a tiny speck of itself give rise to another system of the same sort. The growth of a crystal is no point to the contrary, no valid link between the living and the non-living, for " the arrange-

---

[1] We omit here his general philosophical argument that " the physical and biological worlds are only abstractions from the objective world," *i.e.,* " the world as interpreted in knowledge," or, in other words, that they represent degrees of approximation to a complete theory of reality.

ment of the molecules in the crystal is mere repetition, whereas in the organism there is individual variety of detail, and yet perfectly definite and specific unity of plan." This is clearly Haldane's version of Bergson's point that, for mechanism, " *tout est donné*," and of Driesch's distinction between mechanism and an " equipotential system." It may be recalled here to what an extent Driesch, in building up the concept of an equipotential system, relies on argument concerning what a machine can, or cannot, do.

The challenge of these views is taken up in the *Aristotelian symposium* by Professor Thompson who, adding to an equally sound scientific equipment the sure instinct of the practised debater, makes the following points in reply: (1) man-made machines have been equipped with devices, however crude, for self-regulation, such as, in infinitely greater variety, complexity, and delicacy, we find in natural machines. " In Nature herself, if we look at her larger handiwork, self-regulation and self-maintenance become paramount attributes and characteristics of her machines. The solar system, *quâ* mechanism, is the perfect specimen, the very type and norm, of a self-maintaining, self-regulating mechanism; and so also, grade after grade, are its dependent mechanisms, such as the world-wide currents of the atmosphere." This amounts to an assimilation of man-made machines and living organisms. The latter are viewed as more perfect machines—patterns, as it were, to the perfection of which human machines but remotely approximate. (2) The same assimilation, the same " community of principles in the two classes of machines," is supported by the actual and fruitful interchange of observations and ideas between the workers in ordinary physics and chemistry and those in biological chemistry and physiology. Physiologists, from their study of the " physiological machine," have helped to collect evidence for, and formulate, the principles of the conservation of energy. It was a botanist who introduced osmosis to the attention of physicists. (3) " Mechanism is not a stationary concept but a growing one ": its apparatus of concepts and principles is constantly expanding as further research reveals previously undreamt-of complexities. The concept of " matter " has recently undergone, and is still undergoing, profound modifications, but the new concept is still " commensurate with the old "—its fundamental character is still " mechanical." [1]

What emerges from this confrontation of witnesses on what a machine can or cannot do? The outcome of a judicial summing up would seem to be this:—

If by " mechanism " we mean the theory of " machines," the only question is, which among the objects in the world, and in respect of what properties and activities, are to be counted as machines? This, be it noted, is not a question to be answered by an *a priori* definition. The actual procedure of science is not now, and never has been, to inscribe first, as it were on a *tabula rasa*, a neat definition of what characters anything is to possess which is rightly to be called a " machine." The actual procedure is to compare and analyse objects, tracing affinities, noting differences, and thus collect, or, if we like to say so, construct, the concept or definition of a machine. Now the whole issue is, technically, whether certain affinities are to prevail over certain differences. If with Hobhouse and, on the whole, with Haldane, we collect our concept from man-made machines, the obvious differ-

---

[1] Here, as before, we omit Professor Thompson's general philosophical position, which is built on two principles, *viz.*, (*a*) a dualism of " matter " and " mind " (consciousness), biology being " the study of the forms, whether gross or molecular, assumed by matter in the fabric of living things, and all the changes, processes, activities associated therewith, so far . . . as we can study them apart from Consciousness, or 'conscious reactions'"; (*b*) a conviction that mechanism, though " but one aspect of the world," is a " glorious " aspect, and the study of it is one way of nourishing the " faith that the world is good."

ences between them and living creatures forbid, of course, the application of the machine-theory to the latter, for all that they are both "physical bodies." If with Thompson we start out by collecting our concept of machine from living creatures, we shall, of course, credit machines with the power to do whatever we find living creatures doing, and man-made machines will seem only poor caricatures of the marvels of Nature. Indeed, if it were not for Thompson's capricious retention of the dualism of matter and mind, there would be no reason why he should not acknowledge the existence of thinking and talking, empire-building, war-making, railroad-conducting, stockmarket-operating machines of Nature, as well as of self-reproducing and self-maintaining ones.[1] If a machine can do whatever a physical body does, then whatever human beings do, enlarges our concept of machine. La Mettrie's *L'homme machine,* like the *Mécanique humaine* with which Thompson would like to parallel the astronomer's *Mécanique céleste,* loses all its "materialistic" terrors if we credit the human machine, not only with physiological functions, but with art and science, religion and morality. Nothing but prejudice can put a stop to this extension of the machine-concept, though strangely enough the defenders of a mechanical theory of living bodies generally lose interest in their theory at this point. The reason is that, at bottom, the issue is not what a machine can or cannot do, but *what physics and chemistry can or cannot do* in the way of explaining the structure and behaviour of living beings. To this point we shall turn in a moment. Meanwhile, it is clear that the controversy about machines is bound to be indecisive, so long as the one party to the dispute tends to shrink the concept of machine to

[1] If self-reproducing, then marrying; if marrying, then, perhaps, loving; if self-maintaining, then eating; if eating, then, perhaps enjoying food and elaborating the arts of cookery. Why ignore these obvious glories of human machines?

structures which human beings have planned and made, whilst the other expands it to cover every natural body or system of bodies, from the solar system to the human frame.[1] Incidentally, there is a further ambiguity involved, when the difference between machines and organisms is treated as coinciding with the difference between the " non-living " (or " dead ") and the " living." The latter distinction corresponds properly to that between the inorganic and the organic in Nature, conceived *ad hoc* as exclusive of human artefacts.   The assimilation of Nature in her inorganic or non-living aspects—air, sea, mountains, or, more scientifically, the physicist's " matter " and the chemist's " elements "—to man-made machines is utterly inappropriate, for it looks only to the materials of which the machine is constructed and the forces which work it, not to its structure, *i.e.*, to the organisation of these materials and forces for a purpose.   In short, man-made machines are non-living, considered simply as material objects, but they are organic like organisms, considered in respect of their structure and function.   Strictly, they do not fit into any classification of natural bodies, unless we bring them in, by an extension of the concept of living body, as detached organs (so to say), or tools, fashioned by living bodies for the more efficient securing of their self-maintenance.

And so we come back to the point that " mechanism " puts us on a false track if it leads us to argue about what is, or is not, a machine.   The real issue is, as we said just now, what in Nature can, and what cannot, be explained in terms of the concepts of physics and chemistry.   Mechanism, or the mechanical theory means, in short, a physico-chemical theory.   And " explanation," as we need hardly

---

[1] *Cf.* Professor W. T. Marvin's examination of the argument that it is inconceivable that a machine should do what a living being does. *Philosophical Review*, vol. xxvii, no. 6, p. 624.

add after what has been said in the preceding essay, does not mean " deducing," in the sense of " predicting," particular phenomena, but the recognition of a phenomenon, when presented, as a case falling under the laws of physics and chemistry. Now if we are to call any object a " machine," and any process a " mechanical " process, so far as they can thus be treated as cases for the application of physico-chemical theory, then quite obviously man-made machines are only in part " mechanical." So far from violating, they conform to every physico-chemical law of which account has been taken in their construction, but this " taking account " of laws discovered by scientific research can as little be formulated in physico-chemical terms, as can the purpose which a machine embodies, or its usefulness in the economy of human life. And so, again, living beings in general, and human beings in particular, may be studied as " physico-chemical machines," to borrow the favourite phrase of Loeb and other enthusiastic mechanists, but our mechanists seem to think that when they have shown that, say, thinking cannot go on without physico-chemical processes in the brain, they have shown that it is identical with these processes, in the sense of being " nothing but " such processes and exhaustively describable in terms of them. Against these mistaken claims, those biologists cannot help being in the right who point out, that a theory based on actual observation of the behaviour of living beings in their natural environment, must yield a working concept of life not expressed in physico-chemical terms. Thompson, surely, hits off the actual position of the biological sciences happily and accurately when he writes: " For the ' ordinary naturalist ', the ordinary student of beast and bird, specific difference, if not all in all, is the cardinal concept; for all he cares, for all he sometimes knows, the tissue and the cell are concepts which might never have been devised. The comparative anatomist or the morphologist deal with larger units, and care little about the difference between a blackbird and a thrush, a robin and a wren. The physiologist deals with still larger groups: the cell and the tissue are his especial themes, and most (though of course not all) of the lessons which he learns are lessons common to and taught by the study of a very few 'types', such as man, the rabbit, and the frog. The working hypotheses of (say) the ornithologist are certainly not mechanical, they are very largely teleological; the ordinary working hypotheses of the physiologist are, in the great majority of cases, distinctly mechanical, and include and practically coincide with those of the physicist and the chemist." This corresponds to the position throughout maintained in these essays. The concepts of physics and chemistry, being abstract, are also general; hence, the living and the non-living alike present " cases " for their application. But the characteristic appearances of life in the structure and behaviour of living things are not adequately expressed by such concepts, not even though, like Loeb, one put the organism " as a whole " into the title of one's book.[1] Henderson hits the nail on the head so far as the characteristic " pattern," or " organisation," of living beings is concerned, when he points out that both in form and function organisms possess a pattern, that the study of patterns is ignored, in the main, by physics and chemistry, and therefore by the orthodox mechanistic philosophy built on them, and that " a mechanistic philosophy which leaves organisation out is meaningless." [2]   Why should we not be willing to recognise that, whilst all living bodies illustrate and verify physicochemical truths, many of which have been discovered only

[1] See Jacques Loeb, *The Organism as a Whole from a Physico-Chemical View-point.*
[2] See his contribution to the Mechanism and Vitalism discussion in *Philosophical Review*, Vol. xxvii, No. 6, pp. 571-76.

by the study of living bodies, yet there are also truths to be discovered about them which are not dreamt of by, nor expressible in the language of, physicist or chemist? Philosophy can render at least this service to science in this debate, that it justifies, in the interests of systematic knowledge, equally those who explore the physico-chemical principles which are common to both the non-living and the living, and those who, observing the differences between the non-living and the living, study the latter *as living* and build up an autonomous biological theory with characteristic concepts and laws of its own. We look for order in the universe, but why should that order consist exclusively in principles of one kind, and that kind " mechanical," in the sense of " physico-chemical " ?

(2) The question we have just asked cuts very deep into the contrast between two points of view, two methods of dealing theoretically with natural phenomena, which it has become fashionable in recent literature to label, respectively, " scientific " and " romantic." In part the contrast between them is described as one between two tempers of mind; in part it flows from two different concepts and ideals of logic. Let us consider each of them in turn.

(a) The scientific temper of mind is commonly identified with " naturalism " or " positivism ", the romantic with " supernaturalism " or " transcendentalism." Here is a typical utterance: " There have been, are, and always will be, dispositions reluctant to picture a Universe unsustained by creative will. ' Creative will ' assumes many phases, philosophically indifferent. It may be presented as God or gods, entelechy, or vital spark, but is something beyond prediction or control, the subject of observation, not of experiment. Belief in it is an expression at once of man's humility and of man's pride; an admission of the limits of our intelligence, and a soothing exaltation of what is beyond our intelligence "—thus Dr. P. Chalmers Mitchell, the fourth of the Aristotelian symposiasts. The same contrast between temperaments, dispositions, motives is insisted upon, among the leaders of the discussion of the American Philosophical Association, by Professor W. T. Marvin.[1]   He opposes "modern science" to "modern romanticism"; the belief that the Universe is "logically continuous" and, ultimately, "mathematical," to the belief that the universe is "alogical" and best described "in such pre-scientific language as that of the layman, the poet, and the animist."   The ideal of logical continuity requires, according to his analysis, as the main principles of scientific method, (1) determinism; (2) analysis of the complex into the simple; (3) the paucity, and (4) the mutual independence of the ultimate simples. The result is the ideal of a logical order of sciences amounting to one single deductive science, "in which all the special sciences or bodies of explanation follow from logically prior sciences and these ultimately from mathematical sciences."   Into such a scheme, a vitalistic theory after the manner of Driesch or Bergson will not fit.   The *élan vital*, the "entelechy," cannot be "explained," *i.e.*, deduced from physico-chemical premises.   They can only be "intuited." They are "indeterministic."   They are incurably "romantic" concepts.   They are the modern descendants of primitive magic and animism.   Indeed, their vice goes deeper still.   It is not merely intellectual, it is moral.   These theories offend, not merely by being unscientific, but by being demoralising.   They are symptoms of "weakness, fatigue, dependence, waywardness, and failure," whereas the scientific attitude is one of "vigour, independence, and mastery."   They are the creed of the "quitter" who wants peace and rest through reliance on non-human powers, in

---

[1] *Philosophical Review*, vol. xxvii, No. 6, pp. 616-627.

short, on a protecting deity, whereas science calls to man to be a master of his destiny, and preaches " the religion of effort, and of self-confidence." [1]

This reading of science as expressive of a particular intellectual and moral disposition which is to be contrasted with, and valued more highly than, the poetical, romantic, religious disposition, is still so common, and at the same time so at variance with the point of view maintained in these essays, that it is worth while to disentangle the truth from the bias in this whole estimate, especially in order to bring clearly into the focus of the discussion what is, at bottom, the one issue of genuine philosophical interest, *viz.*, what method of saving the appearances realises best the ideal of " logical continuity."

Now the antithesis of " naturalism " or " science ", and " supernaturalism " or " animism ", especially when considered in the context of the history of our civilisation, is justified up to a point, *viz.*, as a statement of the fact that physics and chemistry have achieved their " autonomy " (as we have called it) as sciences precisely by their emancipation from animistic and theological principles of ex-

---

[1] *Cf. loc cit.,* " If science wins, the world will prove to be one in which man is thrown entirely upon his own resources and skill, upon his self-control, courage, and strength, and perhaps upon his ability to be happy by adjusting himself to pitiless fact. If science fails, there is room for the childlike hope that unseen powers may come to the relief of human weakness. If science wins, the world is the necessary consequences of logically related facts, and man's enterprise, in Huxley's figure of speech, is the playing of a game of chess against an opponent who himself never errs and never overlooks our errors. If science fails, the world resembles fairyland, as matter of great anthropological and psychological importance; and man's enterprise either is no longer a task for skill and knowledge or is conditioned by the ' goodness ' of man's will or is in part a game of luck. Historically considered, the wish behind the belief in the victory of science is the motive prominently manifested in civilization in general, and in particular in vigorous, progressive, and youthful periods of history; whereas the wish behind the belief in the defeat of science is the motive markedly manifested in a people's childhood and old age, in general in savagedom and in periods of decadence or defeat."

planation. The " mechanical theory of nature " is nothing
but the triumphant declaration of this autonomy, its *magna
charta,* its bill of rights. The ramifications of this development in the history of European thought are as wide-spread
as they are often subtle and indirect. With almost theatrical
éclat it is advertised in Laplace's famous retort to Napoleon I, " Sir, I have no need of that hypothesis ", *viz.,* the
hypothesis of God for the explanation of the solar system.
More subtly it appears in the way in which the fundamental
concepts of the mechanical theory have been stripped of
all anthropomorphic colouring.   " Cause " no longer connotes " activity ", but only " invariable succession " or
" uniformity of correlation according to law ". *A fortiori,*
there has disappeared, along with " activity ", all reference
to " will ", and through will, to " purpose ", " design ", " intelligence ". Moreover, this tendency has operated, not only
in the direction of the extrusion of " God ", but, what is
perhaps more remarkable, it has deepened the dualistic
breach between body and soul, matter and consciousness.
Animal and human minds are, in themselves, far less objectionable to the mechanist than either an omnipotent
divine creator, or capricious spirits or demons which are
supposed to manifest themselves in all natural phenomena,
and are but precariously controllable by prayer, sacrifice,
and incantation. Compared with these, human " souls ", at
any rate, seem facts of normal, natural experience.   But
even they remain awkward appendages to the mechanistic
universe, and many are the devices for making that universe
immune against them, for sterilising them as it were, and
avoiding at all costs the necessity of admitting their efficiency as *verae causae.* The fear seems to be that, if consciousness is admitted to be effective anywhere, to be
among the causal antecedents of any physical changes, it
may, in principle, be effective everywhere.   Hence safety

is sought by excluding it root and branch. Thus we get Thompson's striking exclusion of " consciousness " from the field of biology. Thus arises the fashion, generally prevailing among all who approach biological problems from the physico-chemical side, of confessing incompetence to discuss consciousness, and then proceeding as if there were no such thing at all concerned in the phenomena under discussion. Thus we get the steam-whistle theory of consciousness,[1] more politely known as epiphenomenalism. Thus we get psycho-physical parallelism, combined in disorderly union with a belief in the " continuity " of evolution. Thus we get Loeb's thrilling programme of showing us—it is " only a question of time "—that sex with its poetry, mother-love with its felicity and suffering, the pride of good workmanship, the struggle for justice and truth, the enjoyment of human fellowship are, as instincts, akin to the tropisms of plants and animals, and open to a purely physico-chemical explanation.[2] The logical analyst chimes in from his own angle. " To the logical analyst souls seem round squares. They are complex yet simple. They have structure but remain unities. They are wholes without parts. They are creative agents but need no fuel . . ."[3] The net result is the curious one that, consciousness having been either denied outright, or ignored, or politely segregated, the remainder of the phenomena of life is handed

[1] See Huxley, *Collected Essays,* vol. i, p. 240. It does not seem to have been commonly noted that Huxley's inference to the epiphenomenal character of consciousness, from the fact that a decerebrated frog behaves as froggishly without consciousness as with it, proves much more obviously, not the superfluity of consciousness, but the superfluity of the cerebrum. It eliminates the function of the whistle-machinery far more conclusively than it eliminates the whistle-sound. The one thing which the experiments referred to by Huxley show quite clearly is that the cerebrum is not necessary for the performance of certain reflex-actions. On the relation of consciousness to the cerebrum they throw no light whatever.
[2] See *The Mechanistic Conception of Life,* pp. 30, 1.
[3] W. T. Marvin, *loc. cit.,* p. 621.

over, *sub voce* " body ", to physics and chemistry, and
biology as an autonomous science disappears.   It becomes
a special case of physics and chemistry.   This is bound to
be always the result of the application to biological phenomena of the rigid matter-mind dualism.   The mechanical sciences, in this division, claim the substantial body and
all its works; psychology gets the unsubstantial *anima* and
all its fire-works; and the human being, if enough of a
philosopher to remember the need for a synthesis, is left
to contemplate himself with amazement as a mysterious
conjunction of a soulless " machine "-body with a bodyless " ghost "-soul.

With the question of the proper way to " save " the appearances which we call souls, or minds, we shall be concerned in another essay.[1]   Here it is only necessary to
reduce these extravagances to their due bounds.   They overshoot anything that was necessary to check the unscientific
abuse of souls as principles of explanation—the *ignava
ratio* of regarding any given phenomenon as made sufficiently intelligible by saying that God, or man, or beast,
or devil, wanted it just so.   From " just so " stories of this
sort the progress of science continues to emancipate us,
though we should have more reason to be proud of the fact
that we are leaving off telling tales, if the sciences did not
occasionally produce myths of their own.

Reduced to its proper proportions, then, the mechanical
theory of Nature is nothing but the charter of autonomy for
the physico-chemical sciences.   But, emphatically, it does
not amount to the declaration that all phenomena in the
order of " Nature ", or in the wider order of the " Universe ", are exclusively physico-chemical in character.
Order demands the recognition of differences as much as the
recognition of identities.   " Mechanism " secures the right

[1] See the following Essay, Ch. viii.

of the physical sciences to eliminate from among their concepts, or working-hypotheses, all reference to will, purpose,
design, intelligence. As thus excluded, these may be called
" supernatural ", and even a human mind is, in this sense,
supernatural. But this device can, assuredly, not be interpreted as denying that there are other strata, higher orders
of phenomena, in the system of the universe, in the analysis
of which these, and other, terms may have their proper
place, supplementing and completing, not contradicting or
destroying, the account given by the mechanical sciences.
Mechanism, in short, is right as a protest against confusion
of categories, wrong in denying the legitimacy of all categories other than its own. Its advantages, and its justification, are that, within its own field of phenomena, it has
substituted, to put it briefly, the notion of " law " for that
of incalculable " will " or capricious " purpose ". As a
heuristic method of investigation this change has been of
incalculable value. It has opened the way to that observa-
tional and experimental procedure to which modern science
owes its triumphs. It has replaced the question " why? "
by the question " how? ". It has led to the formulation of
uniformities of correlation between phenomena, and to that
" experimental determinism " which demands that every
observed difference in phenomena be shown to be connected,
according to some general law, with other observed differences. It has led to measurement, and the statement of correlations in precise quantitative terms. It has supplied the
natural sciences with a programme of research, the inex-
haustibleness of which is brought home to us with every
fresh complexity which keener investigation reveals. All
this has its rightful place in the order of the universe and
the order of knowledge, and there is no need to say that
because this is right and good, every other point of view,
every other *ratio cogitandi* about the world, provided it does

not deny this mechanical *ratio* on its own ground, is wrong and bad.   We can smile at the kaffir-tribe, reported by Dudley Kidd, which, when drought threatened to destroy its fields and flocks, asked a neighbouring missionary to go forth with his umbrella, though even here we can perceive a crude attempt at correlating phenomena.   We are well rid of the belief, and the practices built on the belief, that by charms and sacrifices we can influence natural events, or rather avert the wrath or secure the good will of the spirits supposed to manifest themselves in natural events.   But it does not follow from this that religion is a superstitious survival of primitive animism.   All that follows is that we need another kind of theology, a better knowledge of God. It does not follow that there are not phenomena properly, and even scientifically, dealt with in terms of " life " or of " consciousness ", though it does follow that we need a better knowledge of these in their place in the articulate order of the universe.   There is nothing in the physico-chemical theory of " matter " which excludes, though it is equally true that there is nothing in that theory which positively supports, such speculative hypotheses as that of Bergson concerning the origin of matter through the slackening of the *élan vital*, or the theory mooted by thinkers as diverse as Charles Peirce and James Ward, that physico-chemical correlations, as uniformities, are analogous to " habits "— once plastic choices, now petrified routine.   The mechanical sciences have no use for such speculations, but are they therefore entitled to debar them by an intolerant censorship from the thinking of men in general?   Even a " personalistic " interpretation of Nature is not in conflict with the mechanical theory, unless that theory is illegitimately taken as claiming that nothing can possibly be true except what it says.

With these remarks we may leave the more extravagant

manifestations of the bias against "romanticism" and "supernaturalism". For, after all, they but avert attention from the really important problem of method, *viz.*, how to reconcile the demand for "logical continuity" with the recognition of unique differences in the order of nature.

(b) This issue is a technical, a "logical", one. Continuity means, at bottom, identity. Identity is commonly taken as requiring that all phenomena, however different at first sight, shall to a deeper understanding reveal themselves as being of the *same* sort, or, to put it differently, cases of the *same* principle. They shall differ, in the last resort, only as sets of values for the variables of a mathematical formula differ, which all "satisfy" the formula. The differences between the sets of values have no significance beyond making it possible to discriminate any one from any other one. Beyond that, the only thing which matters is that they should alike be cases of the *same* functional correlation. The carrying-out of such a programme as Professor Marvin, among many others, advocates [1] appears to depend wholly on whether the differences between the phenomena in the universe are differences simply of this mathematical sort. *If* they are not, some other method of holding differences within the grip of an identity will have to be sought; *that* they are not, appears to be shown clearly by the difficulty which mathematicians find when they try to apply their logical apparatus to empirical data. In one way or another, they are compelled to acknowledge a gap, an incommensurability, between *a priori* and *a posteriori* knowledge. The identification of empirical data as "values", or "cases", of functions laid down *a priori* has about it something precarious and arbitrary. All-too-frequently, the empirical shows itself to be "alogical", by

[1] See above, p. 175.

refusing to fit into the neat patterns prepared for its reception. Whence, according to the thinker's mood and disposition, result disparagements of the intellect (*vide* Bergson) or of the world of experience (*vide* Russell). In any case, in the face of this gap, who can genuinely hope to be able to " deduce " empirical details from abstract *a priori* generalities?

But quite apart from such unsubstantiated dreams of deductions, is even an *ex-post-facto* unification of science along these lines possible? Can we conceive the sciences which we actually have, as allowing themselves to be ordered in a single comprehensive scheme on the principle of logical " priority " and " posteriority "—such that the prior science furnishes the premises from which the posterior sciences " follow "? Until some more definite and convincing progress towards carrying out this ambitious aspiration has been made than can, so far, be exhibited for inspection, it must remain an open question whether we are here dealing with a legitimate ideal or a will-o'-the-wisp. And, if there is any value in our concept of the " autonomy " of each science, and any truth in the account given in the preceding essay, of the super-ordination of phenomena, the evidence would seem to be against the possibility of the unification dreamt of by the " logical analyst ".

But, apart from this debatable possibility of exhibiting all sciences as branches of a single stem of deductive theory, there is in the proposed " reduction " of biology to physics and chemistry, and in the " explanation " of the phenomena of life in terms of, *i.e.*, as cases of, physico-chemical laws, another point of great logical interest which more positively supports the view taken in these pages.

To " understand " anything—what is this but to perceive, or appreciate, the " universal " in it? It is only to the mind which grasps the " universal " that the particular be-

comes " intelligible ". Hence the importance for knowledge
of " generalisation ". A general " rule ", a scientific " law ",
furnish us with the most obvious and familiar instances of
this power of universals to make large, and in their sensuous
detail often widely diverse, masses of facts intelligible.
They draw attention to the common character of the many
diverse particulars. They unify; they very literally identify differences. Hence the intellectual achievement, the
advance in knowledge, involved in every discovery of a law,
and even more in the extension of it to a fresh field. To
recognise some group of phenomena which are, *prima facie*,
very different from those of another group, as cases of the
same sort, permitting the application of the same principles,
is a contribution of the first order to the unification of
knowledge. No wonder that, pressing along this line, the
ideal of achieving the maximum of generalisation should
have been set up and pursued. It is a legitimate ideal, but
the method of research to which it gives rise is subject to
strict limitations, and, used by itself, it leads to " abstraction ", *i.e.*, to a levelling, or assimilating, of differences
which ought to be recognised in their characteristic uniqueness and retained in an order of super-imposed " levels " or
" strata ". This is precisely the point involved in the argument of the preceding essay, that the physico-chemical
analysis of living things must, perforce, ignore precisely what
is characteristically " living " about them. In short, the saving of appearances requires chiefly a saving of differences
from being completely swallowed up by the " another-case-
of-the-same-sort " or the " nothing-but-so-and-so " method.
In the language of the logicians, commonly called " ideal-
ist ", we require not only universals of the " abstract " type
of the general law applicable to a range of cases which, for
all their differences from each other, count as being all of
the same sort, but we require also universals of the " con-

crete " type of the individual " system ", or " world ", to
be analysed on the homely principle that it " takes *all* sorts
to make a world ".[1]   To follow the track of universals is
always to recognise identity in difference, but we may do so
either by forming " classes " of " cases " of the " same
sort ", or by discerning " systems ", " wholes ", " structures " (or whatever else we may call them) into which
elements of diverse sorts enter as constituents, and in which
they acquire new functions and often exhibit new properties.[2]   The universe, or cosmos, is obviously such a system,
and the differences in it must be preserved by showing how
the higher are conditioned by the lower, without being therefore reducible to, *i.e.*, identifiable with, the lower in the way
we call " being of the same sort ".   Once we enter upon
this path, we must, of course, expect intellectual adventures,
and some philosophers hold back because they do not like
the adventures that await them.   For the working methods
of the logical analyst will no longer prove wholly adequate.
New levels of phenomena will have to be recognised and
dealt with in their own terms.   Synthesis as well as analysis
will be required—a synoptic insight such as, innocent of
any deep philosophical issues, we all currently rely on
in perceiving the identity of a person, or of a people, in
their many-sided interests and activities.   In general, it
may be said that the emphasis on " law " is the characteristic of " abstract " science, and, more widely, of the spirit
of generalisation by the ignoring, or levelling, of differences,
whilst emphasis on " system " as an actual " whole " func-

[1] *Cf.*, on this whole distinction, B. Bosanquet, *The Principle of Individuality and Value,* especially Lectures II and III ; and *Logic,* 2nd
edition, *passim.*
[2] The concepts of "integration" or "organisation". as employed.
e.g., by E. B. Holt, in *Response and Cognition* (*The Freudian Wish,*
pp.153 ff.), appear to meet this requirement.   The critical point is the
admission that the " whole" formed by the organisation of the parts
"now does things which the isolated parts never did or could do"
(p. 154).

tioning through differentiated " parts ", is the characteristic of " concrete " philosophy, of the spirit of unification by " saving " differences whilst acknowledging the conditions necessary to their existence.

In short, the former, " scientific," method, seeks logical continuity by the way of " abstract " identity; the latter, " philosophical ", method does so by the way of " concrete " or systematic identity. And, on the technical side, *this* rather than the antithesis of positivism and romanticism constitutes the philosophically important divergence between the two methods.

(3) The third problem on our list, that of the empirical evidence for teleology, as applied to the facts of life, may be stated in a way which presents a genuine difficulty for the view here advocated. Intellectual honesty compels equally a frank formulation of the difficulty and a frank confession, that the solution here adopted is not one to which mere argument can compel those to assent who do not see their way to it. We are face to face, in short, with one of those ultimate problems on which human beings seem bound to differ in their interpretations, making instinctively or reflectively one of those fundamental choices, which lead some to characterise the position adopted as an " article of faith ", or a " postulate ", or an " assumption ", or an " affirmation of the will ", and which lend colour to the view that differences in philosophical theories spring from differences of " temperament " and " disposition ". But, as we have seen in a previous essay,[1] to admit all this is not to admit that such choices are unreasoned or unreasonable. Though argument may not produce agreement on these ultimate issues, still they are arguable, or at least comparable with each other by argument. And such

[1] See Chapter III.

argument helps each thinker to make clear to himself and others the grounds of his choice, and to realise, from the very difference between his choice and that of others, that there is some limitation or idiosyncrasy in his own. As philosophers we *reason* to the best of our power on these issues, but in reasoning we must have something to reason with. It is because philosophers differ in these materials of their vision, that the resulting theory or interpretation is for each the view he must reasonably take, and yet different from the views to which others are as reasonably led.

The relation of mechanism and teleology presents precisely such a problem in which ultimate choices come into play—choices in which thinkers sum up the *total* impressions gathered from their acquaintance with the world and their efforts to trace the order, and read the meaning, of its infinitely varied spectacle. Teleology, as we argued in the preceding essay, introduces the concept of *value*. From the point of view of mechanism all value-predicates are out of place: only *facts*, and the causal correlations of facts, engage our interest. But, as we put it, a causal nexus can sometimes also be read as a nexus of means and end. Where B requires A as the condition of its own existence, there, provided B has value, we can reasonably say that B is that for the sake of which A exists.

If this theory of the relation of teleology to mechanism is not to lead us seriously astray, two qualifications would seem to be required as safeguards. The concept of value is a dangerous thing and easily misused. Hence it is well to remind ourselves, (a) that it should not be used as an argument against determinism. The suspicion with which teleology often meets, springs from the fear that it is the thin end of the wedge of indeterminism. It is thought that when once we begin to value facts as good or bad, we shall presently slip into saying that they would have been better, had they been different, and end by arguing that, because they *would* have been better otherwise, therefore they *could* have been otherwise. Whereas, for determinism, every fact is " necessary ", *i.e.*, it could *not* have been otherwise than it is in its actual context. The teleological point of view, as understood in these pages, implies no such retrospective indeterminism. And (b) it does not set up the untenable claim that we can show of any and every particular detail, picked at random out of the system, just how and why it is good, either as a means or as an end. It bases its appeal, so to speak, on broader effects. Its position is, perhaps, best appreciated by putting to oneself the question, whether, as one surveys the order of appearances—matter, life, mind; or, more concretely, the inorganic world, the world of plants and animals, the human world with its achievements not only in material civilisation, but in art, science, social organisation, friendship, and love—one does not appreciate and recognise, going up the scale, a value which the lower levels lack, or in which they share only as necessary conditions of the things which are worthwhile for their own sakes.[1]

Now it is precisely here that we must admit that the making of this experiment does not yield the same result for everybody. It calls for a comparison of total impressions which an infinite variety of detail has gone to form in each thinker's personal experience, and the resulting estimates are bound to differ. The most we can do is to consider a few of the most typical, in order to make sure that we have not wholly omitted or ignored the facts on which they rest.

[1] The reader would do well to compare my inadequate statement of this argument with the fuller presentation of it by B. Bosanquet, *Logic*, 2nd edit., vol. ii, pp. 218-223.

There are, at least, three chief ways in which our teleological argument may be met. (1) It may be denied outright that there is anything of value in the existence of either life or mind. Or (2) whilst life and mind are admitted to be values, it may be denied that nature can be interpreted as existing for their sake. Or (3) values may be regarded as purely " subjective ", as, so to speak, the mere shadows cast by natural instincts, hence as offering no basis for an objective teleology in the interpretation of the world.

(1) Those who take the first position commonly accept the current standards of value, but maintain that, as measured by them, the overwhelming impression to be gathered from experience is one of disvalue. Life, they say, is ugly, brutal, cruel, ruthless. Hunger and lust are its driving-forces. Struggle is its key-note—a struggle for food; a struggle for mates; a struggle against the forces of the inorganic universe ever threatening it with extinction; a struggle against rival forms of life, parasites and enemies, large and small; a struggle even against living fellows of the same kind. To live is to prey on other life: its law is the law of the jungle, " kill or be killed ". The general verdict on life must be that which Hobbes passed on men's existence in the supposed state of nature:—" nasty, short, and brutish ". And when this sort of critic turns from plant-life and animal-life to human-life, where his moralising judgment is more obviously in place, he finds abundant material in every direction for painting a picture in dark colours. The selfishness, the stupidity, the viciousness, meanness, perversity of human beings, whether taken individually or collectively, in all their ramifications and remoter consequences, may well furnish a theme for pessimistic eloquence, and justify the conclusion that, if this is the crowning achievement of the universe by which above all else it is to

be judged, nothing but indignant condemnation deserves to be its portion.[1]

(2) From this extreme denial of any value, not only to life in general, but even to the manifestations of the human spirit, we turn to the second position which admits that there are things of great and intrinsic value, especially in the endeavours and creations of men, but denies that in the context of the universe they are anything but happy accidents destined, after a transient bloom, to total extinction. It is the familiar argument from the prospective annihilation, not only of human civilisation, but of all organic life on this earth. With various expressions of this point of view, and various reactions to it, we have already met in a preceding essay.[2] Here we may illustrate it by another utterance: " It is conceivable that man and his works and all the higher forms of animal life should be utterly destroyed; that mountain-regions should be converted into ocean depths; the floors of oceans raised into mountains; and the earth become a scene of horror which even the lurid fancy of the writer of the Apocalypse would fail to portray. And yet, to the eye of science, there would be no more disorder here than in the sabbatical peace of a summer sea." [3]

(3) The third position is perhaps the one most insidiously and plausibly antagonistic to our view. It is to be found in that ethical naturalism, for which calling a thing " good " is only a way of saying that it is being desired, for which values are functions of instinctive needs. All living things cling to life; hence the theory that life is worth living is but the mirage of value with which reflection justifies the primitive instinct of self-preservation. That mind, surveying itself, should find itself good, and extend its

[1] For a vivid and impressive presentation of the dysteleological argument, see H. G. Wells, *The Undying Fire*.
[2] See Chapter III.
[3] Huxley, quoted by Bosanquet, *Logic*, 2nd edit., vol. ii, pp. 216-7.

approval to the world which has made it possible for minds to exist, seems still more plausible, but the value to which this self-bestowed testimonial bears witness, is none the less an illusion.   There are, on this view, no objective values which minds help to sustain, and the participation in which, or the enjoyment of which, makes human existence worthwhile.   There are only needs and instincts conferring a passing worth, *i.e.*, the character of being desired, on the objects needed for their own satisfaction.   "Of course it is a fact that devotion may breed the illusion that the object of devotion is intrinsically precious; but it is perverse to explain the devotion by the illusion rather than the illusion by the devotion." [1]   This puts the antithesis of the conflicting theories of value in a nutshell.   The "apprehension of values ceases to be, then, any possession of or participation in an objective good by the mind; it becomes rather the utterance and projection of the basic exigencies of our existence.   Values become intelligible only from below.   Devotion to an object comes to signify no apprehension of any inherent worth residing in the object, in that which the desire faces and which it may hope to possess.   If we still think that our desires, our loyalties, and our devotions look ahead to their objects whose worth shall justify them, we suffer from the old illusion.   In truth, we are told, these activities and propensities, the objects of all our strivings are but mirrors in which are reflected the real forces, the brute and basic necessities of our existence which lie behind them." [2]   These are the words of a critic of this view, but they are a fair statement of the view criticised.

To those for whom any one of these three views expresses the plain and obvious truth, there is nothing more

[1] E. M. McGilvary, *The Warfare of Ideals*, in the *Hibbert Journal*, October, 1915, p. 46.

[2] G. P. Adams, *Idealsm and The Modern Age*, p. 107, and also chs. v and vi, *passim*.

to be said. All one can do is to think oneself fully and sympathetically into each of them, and then judge whether it squares with the total impression which one's own experience yields. If it does not square, the way is opened for seeking another interpretation more consistent with one's own gathered vision. Whichever view we adopt, there is no escaping the responsibility involved in every judgment concerning the nature of the universe as a whole in its bearing on those values which make human life, at its best, a thing of spiritual grace and beauty, and not merely an instinctive effort to keep alive an animal body and perpetuate an animal species.[1] At any rate, the choice we have made is in favour of the affirmations that the higher we go in the order of appearances, the more undeniably do they exhibit the character of values; that these values are not merely "contingent," or accidental, in the total scheme of things; and that they are not merely subjective or merely illusory. A complete presentation of the empirical data which have gone to form the total impression summed up in these propositions would be the modern equivalent of a theodicy. It would not be possible without calling in the evidence of religion, especially in its bearing on the problem of evil.[2]

Meanwhile, even in the present scientific context, something of the dialectic of teleology may be exhibited. There is a useful lesson to be learned from L. J. Henderson's recent attempt to show, mainly from bio-chemical evidence, that there is a teleological "pattern" in nature, and from the criticism with which this attempt has met. In his books on *The Fitness of the Environment* and on

---

[1] *Cf.* B. Bosanquet, *Logic*, 2nd edit., vol. ii, p. 220, note: "If you believe that the world-system is wholly indifferent to the interests of civilization, you shoulder just as heavy a logical responsibility as if you believe the opposite."
[2] For Religion, see below, Ch. x. On the problem of Evil I hope to say something in the second volume of *Studies*.

The Order of Nature, Henderson argues that when the physico-chemical system is viewed, not in abstraction by itself, but in its bearing on life, the manifold forms of which it conditions and makes possible, it becomes startlingly clear that the fundamental properties of the three common elements, carbon, hydrogen, and oxygen, and of some of their compounds, and the wide distribution of these elements and compounds, exhibit a maximum of fitness for the needs of precisely such living forms as we actually find upon earth. This " fitness of the environment," is, from the purely physico-chemical point of view, a happy chance. Countless other distributions, countless other conjunctions of properties would have been just as possible. The fact that the actual distributions and conjunctions have this fitness for life is for physics and chemistry irrelevant, and their principles afford no specific explanation for it. It becomes intelligible only if we read it as a teleological pattern, as a " preparation " for life.[1] The antithetic reading of the situation is supplied by Professor Warren. " We may raise at least two objections to Professor Henderson's argument. In the first place it is *ex post facto*. The evolutionist holds that organic life has grown up *as it has* as a result of conditions which *actually exist*. If carbon were absent or rare, possibly another type of organism would have evolved, based upon silica compounds. If the properties of elements had been otherwise, we might expect to find different types of organisms, exhibiting different characteristics. If the earth's surface were mainly land, possibly fresh-water or aerial organisms would have arisen earlier than marine types. In other words, evolution is a process of adaptation to the *given* environment. Whatever environment is present is presumably *fit* for the types of organism which evolve within

[1] See for details, esp. *The Order of Nature,* Chs. viii-x, and *The Fitness of the Environment*, Chs. vii, viii.

its limits."[1] We may legitimately wonder how Warren can be so very sure that, if the environment had been fundamentally other than it is in its chemical constitution, other types of organisms would have evolved within it at all. There are in his argument two strains which ought to be kept apart. One is the appeal to the perfectly sound principle that "every difference makes a difference." We cannot consistently conceive that the same organisms should have evolved, or be able to live, under conditions fundamentally different from those under which we find them. But it does not follow that other organisms would have evolved instead. Ought we not rather to say that under other conditions no life might be possible at all? "Only life as we know it would have been impossible," it may be retorted; "how can you deny that other forms of life are possible than those with which we are acquainted." But how can our opponent affirm it? We are approaching the point where it becomes a question what our *ignorance* does, or does not, permit us to conceive as "possible." In a nutshell, the situation is this. We both know the given forms of life in the given environment. This is our actual world. We both believe that in this environment only these forms of life are possible. This is the principle of determinism, and if we are thorough with it, we shall say further that the actual forms of life are also necessary. The issue which divides us is, whether from the supposition of an entirely different environment we are to infer forms of life unlike any we know, or treat this suggestion as scientifically illegitimate—as a speculation which, in the absence of positive grounds, hangs in the air.

The lesson which may patently be learned from this example, will help us to clarify the issue. Teleological concepts, we shall all agree, are out of place except where something

[1] H. C. Warren in *Philosophical Review,* vol. xxvii, no. 6, p. 613.

which is an actual fact is also an actual value—where something which exists is also intrinsically good. If now it be granted that life and mind are intrinsic values, then we have before us a world in which these values are facts, and necessary facts. For they are conditioned or determined to be just what they are. Formally, the world is a " deterministic " one, *i.e.*, subject to the " law of sufficient reason." And nothing but this deterministic point of view prevails in the abstract sciences of physics and chemistry which supply the frame-work of " mechanism." Yet this mechanical world is such as to evolve life and mind. If we are not willing to say that this is a fortunate coincidence, nor, with Leibniz, that God in his wisdom and goodness chose to create out of an infinite number of possible worlds the " best possible," *i.e.*, the one in which the maximum of value could be actually embodied, there is no alternative open but to say that the total scheme of the universe is not indifferent to the values to which it gives rise and which it sustains; that the existence of values in it as necessary facts reflects value on the whole; that the elimination of teleological concepts from the mechanical sciences, the divorce of fact from value, is the result of an abstraction which a more synthetic or synoptic point of view corrects.

The empirical basis of the teleological point of view, thus, is precisely this, that values, like life and mind, are not only facts which " happen " to occur, but necessary facts, *i.e.*, facts which, so far as our positive evidence goes, must occur under determinate mechanical conditions and cannot occur without them, though it does not follow that, therefore, they are themselves of the mechanical order and analysable in purely physico-chemical terms. The appeal to the *actual* nexus of necessary fact and value makes us secure against the bogey of other possible worlds, such as Huxley suggests, in which for science there should be no disorder, and yet in which there should be nothing of value. When thrown into the scale against the actual nexus of fact and value these unmotived possibilities weigh as nothing.

A Note on Bergson and The Origin of Life

It is but meet that a philosopher, having stated his view, should offer a sacrifice at the altar of the unknown god in the shape of confessing "ultimate doubts." In this case, having tried to save both necessity and value in our theory of the universe, we cannot do better than throw our ultimate doubts into the form of a consideration of "novelty" and "creation" in their relation to necessity and value, with special reference to Bergson's theory of "creative evolution" and the *élan vital*. So far as vitalism offers points of philosophical interest, it is in Bergson's theory rather than in Driesch's that they are to be found. For, although Driesch's concept of "entelechy" involves "experimental indeterminism," it does not, like Bergson's *élan vital*, involve absolute indeterminism. The entelechy is introduced as explaining what from the mechanical point of view would be inexplicable novelty and creation. The argument rests on the principle, well-known to the school-men, that there cannot be more in the effect than there is in the cause. If any structure, at the end of a process of growth or evolution, exhibits perceptibly a higher degree of complexity than was perceptibly discernible in it at the start, there must, so Driesch infers, have been present throughout an imperceptible, semi-psychical factor, to account for the appearance of more out of less. This additional factor which restores the balance is the "entelechy." [1] Of course, the entelechy is endowed by Driesch with the power of getting results out of a given constellation of physical and chemical elements (*e.g.*, out of a cell) which could not have been got out of it on purely "mechanical" principles. Conversely, its own *modus operandi* is not analysable, or calculable, in physico-chemical terms. Thence results experimental indeterminism: "Two systems absolutely identical in every physico-chemical [*i.e.*, perceptible] respect may behave differently under absolutely identical conditions, in case that the systems are living

[1] See *e.g.*, *History and Theory of Vitalism*, pp. 195 ff. and *The Problem of Individuality*, pp. 47 ff.

systems." [1]   But in that the difference in behaviour is attributed to the entelechy, Driesch's view is deterministic in the absolute sense. In fact, the entelechy does not belong in any sense to another level or order of phenomena: it is simply an additional, though imperceptible, factor operating to modify, and even suspend, physico-chemical laws.

Quite otherwise is the position of Bergson. For him, the creativity of the *élan vital* does manifest itself in a continual production of more out of less. In Bosanquet's sympathetic phrase, " The stream rises higher than its source." Determinism and mechanism are powerless to make intelligible the spontaneous and inexhaustible fertility of the life-impulse in the creating of novel forms of structure and behaviour. Their " laws " express only the uniformities and routines which the life-impulse assumes when it slackens and relaxes, but which are melted into plasticity where the spear-point of life pushes through to novel achievements. No wonder that Bergson declares that only by " intuition " from within, not by analytic " intelligence " from without, can this life-impulse in ourselves and in the world around us be apprehended.

Now, whether we can share this intuition or not, there is at least one point in Bergson's critique of " mechanism " which deserves consideration.

(a) This point may be expressed bluntly by saying that mechanism is incompatible with evolution. This is the real point in Bergson's theory of *durée* or " real time ", as distinct from the " spatialised " time of physics. The mechanical point of view is non-evolutionary, *non-historical*. A mechanical system is a closed system. The changes which, as a given configuration of elements and forces, it can undergo, are strictly predetermined. *Tout est donné.* In such a system no novelties can appear: all is repetition of the same. Routine, not creation; uniformity, not variability, are its dominant characteristics. The theory that Nature is a mechanical system is in flat contradiction to the theory that there is a historical process of evolution, in the course of which there came a point at which life first appeared in a hitherto lifeless world. " Mechanism " analyses on its " formal " side into determinism, on its " material " side into physics and

[1] Quoted from correspondence with Driesch by H. S. Jennings in *Philosophical Review,* Vol. xxvii, No. 6, p. 581.

chemistry. The general formula of determinism is, " If A, then B ", and *also*, " If not B, then not A ". If the world was once without life, the conditions which now, when there is life, we perceive to be necessary for its existence, cannot themselves have as yet existed. Why not? Because their conditions, in turn, did not yet exist. Thus the novelty of the origin of life is thrown back on the novelty, at some point in history, of the conditions of life, and so forth *in infinitum*. But for mechanism there can be no novelties, except by the accident of our ignorance. Mechanical theory finds life existing under determinate conditions and formulates the law. It finds these conditions in turn determined by conditions, and once more formulates the law. It goes on finding: *tout est donné*. But the historical process of evolution sifts somehow through the meshes of the mechanist's intellectual net and escapes.

The difficulty may be crystallised into the dilemma: either life must have been there always, or it could not have got in at all. And if we choose to take the first horn, it is clearly more plausible to think of life as " being there always ", not in the form of particular sorts of living beings, but as a metaphysical ultimate, be it as Schopenhauerian " will ", or as *élan vital* depositing " matter " in its downward, embodying itself in living forms in its upward, movement. The inorganic world is, so to speak, the death, the organic world the eternal youth, of the cosmic life-impulse. Poetical metaphors seem almost unavoidable in the attempt to render Bergson's theory.

But that the dilemma is genuine, and not merely fanciful, may be easily shown by the shifts to which scientific theory is driven when it honestly faces the problem of the " origin " of life, which is, of course, but a special case of the problem of the origin of anything new in kind in a universe so conceived that it does not provide for the emergence of what is new in kind. It is hard to say which is more remarkable:—the profound insensibility of many " mechanistic " writers to this problem, or their wild guesses when they become sensible of its awkwardness. Typical of the wild guesses are the speculations of Arrhenius on the possibility of life having got into our planet by the immigration of microscopic living particles from interstellar space. This, surely, if accepted, would amount to a confession of the bankruptcy of the physico-chemical theory of life. It admits, by implication, that it is not in virtue of some physico-chemical character that these microscopic particles are called "living". Moreover, the suitability of the physico-chemical constitution of the earth for the maintenance and development of these living particles is, of course, not "explained", but assumed as a piece of good luck.

Good luck, or, in other words, chance, coincidence, is what, in fact, all scientific theories on the origin of life take for granted at the crucial point. Of course, they are none of them so naive as to call it good luck, but that is what it comes to when the camouflage of a learned terminology is stripped off. The commonest device is to say "let but such-and-such things happen, and behold you have the first bit of living substance". Exactly: you take for granted what is required to get life, and, of course, life results. Nothing could be simpler. Here is a typical instance:—"A little reflection will serve to show that if we are not diffident in our application of the conception of catalysis it will provide us with an explanation of life from the very start. Let us suppose that at a certain moment in earth-history, when the ocean waters are yet warm, there suddenly appears at a definite point within the oceanic body a small amount of a certain catalyzer or enzyme. Let us, moreover, imagine that the sea-water contains in solution a number of substances which react very slowly to produce an oily liquid, immiscible with water. A reaction of this character based upon probable solutes of the early seas might easily be specified. Now in the third place, we must imagine that our enzyme is related with this reaction in such a way as greatly to reduce the chemical friction which it encounters, and hence markedly to increase its rate. What will be the outcome? Why, obviously the particle of enzyme will become enveloped in the oily material resulting from the reaction, and if it happens that the original substances which enter into combination are soluble in the oil as well as in the sea-water, the little oil drop will wax greater until it is split up into smaller globules by the natural currents of the ocean. It is clear that that developing oil drop is intended to represent the origin of the first and simplest life-substance . . . The most fundamental objection which can be raised against the theory has reference to the source of the original enzyme. This enzyme is a very special sort of a body, and consequently its fortuitous formation in the primeval oceans may be regarded as an improbable event. However, this is not equivalent to saying that it was an impossible occurrence, and since only one event of this specific kind is re-

200 CONTEMPORARY METAPHYSICS [Ch. VII

quired by the theory during a period of time covering many millions of years, objections based upon general considerations of probability have practically no force. Chemistry must answer the question as to whether our first enzyme is possible. A very great number of different compounds must have been formed as a result of the multitudinous chemical reactions which undoubtedly took place in the primordial oceans, and there is no reason why one of these compounds should not have been just the body required to mediate the origin of living matter. The striking fact that the enzymic theory of life's origin, as we have outlined it, necessitates the spontaneous production of only *a single molecule* of the original catalyst, renders the objection of improbability almost absurd ".[1] Of course, if you imagine the right conditions you have a right to imagine the right results, but we want more than imaginations concerning how it *might* have happened; we want evidence that it *did* so happen. It is not enough to say: there is no reason why it should not have happened as imagined. We want to know whether there is any reason to think that it actually did happen. Happy chance is the *deus ex machina* which helps these theories across the gap between the "possible" and the "actual". It would be just as logical to argue that because one among the theoretically possible combinations of cards in a pack is that which, on dealing, will yield four hands each consisting of a complete suit, therefore that distribution *will actually* result, if only some one goes on long enough shuffling and dealing. Unless we are prepared to say that *every* combination which is "possible", *i.e.*, conceivable, is also actual, or must necessarily at some time become actual, the actuality of the *right* combination, *i.e.*, the combination to which alone some special interest, or some consequence of value, attaches, requires always a specific reason for its explanation. Indeed, the becoming actual of *any* one of the alternatives permitted by the system requires a positive reason. A "possibility" can become an actuality only when it is a "necessity". There is no escaping this logical principle. For the actual is, by the very principle of determinism, not only possible but also necessary. If this is true of the actualisation of *any* possibility, it is even more eminently true of the actualisation of those possibilities

[1] L. T. Troland, *The Chemical Origin and Regulation of Life*, reprinted from the *Monist*, January, 1914, by the Open Court Publishing Co.

which yield life and mind. We are brought back to the familiar parting of the ways:—Was it luck? Did it just happen so? Or is the realisation of the right possibility when, for all we know, it might have remained unrealised, somehow connected with the value of the result? In some such form as this the concept of objective value is bound to return upon us in these speculations.[1]

We may be accused here of ignoring a third alternative—the "cunning" which Samuel Butler opposed to Darwin's lucky accidental variations.[2] But to attribute cunning, and with it consciousness, be it to life in general, be it to individual cells, or even merely to germ-cells, outruns all empirical evidence, and even Butler's fascinating and skillful argument does not make the suggestion plausible. It throws too large a burden on slender analogies.

In any case, neither luck nor cunning play any part in the creative activity of Bergson's *élan vital*. As a metaphysical principle it does not need luck, and, on the other hand, it does not hamper itself with plans. It aims at no ends. It just creates in abundant profusion unpredictable novelties. Mechanism does not give the clue to its riddle, neither does "finalism", which is but mechanism upside down. For once the end is fixed and the plan thought out, the whole process of realisation is determined. There is no creativeness in it any more. That will all have gone into the thinking out of the plan, which is a process to be understood only from within by intuition, by living through it oneself, not to be dissected from without by analytic intelligence.

There can be no doubt that Bergson's philosophy is the completest antithesis, and the sharpest challenge, to the positions advocated in the preceding essays.[3] There is no room within his metaphysics of creative evolution for the hierarchy of appearances for which we have tried to argue as characteristic of the order of the universe. There is no room for our view of the nexus of fact and value. It will stand as a possible alternative, unless,

---

[1] It should be noted that the "mechanism *and* teleology" theory of the preceding essay is an attempt to state the relation of life to its physico-chemical conditions as actually found. It does not pretend to be a theory of the historical origin of life. And all that is suggested here is that, if we speculate on origins at all, the fact that the result has value, cannot be ignored as *a priori* irrelevant.

[2] See especially Butler's *Luck or Cunning?*

[3] The same has to be said of Charles Peirce's *Tychism*, many of the doctrines of which resemble those of Bergson.

and until, it can be shown that creative activity is a *logical* process, and accessible in this its logical character to a reflective analysis which will not simply " mechanise " it and " spatialise " it after the manner of Bergson's *intelligence*.   But the examination of Bergson's free-will argument (in *Les Données Immédiates de la Conscience*), which would be necessary for this purpose, lies beyond the scope of these essays.

CHAPTER VIII

HAVING been engaged, in the preceding two essays, in an attempt to save the appearances in biology, with much incidental discussion of the philosophical problems which that attempt raises, we are now to make an attempt to save the nominal object of psychology, *viz.*, the soul, or, as we shall say, the mind. Our argument, welcoming in the interests of *concrete* analysis the present-day movement towards a *functional* theory of mind, will plead for a synthesis of the Aristotelian and Descartian, the biological and introspective, points of view. This requires that we should frankly face the difficulty, too often ignored, that the terms mind, soul, consciousness, are used in very different contexts and hence with widely different meanings. The lines between these contexts are not easy to draw; indeed they are more or less fluctuating. This situation is reflected in the fact that modern psychology strikes the observer hardly as a single science, but rather as several sciences going under one name. It is certainly true, that in no science is there so much controversy about fundamental concepts or about methods. No other science is in the paradoxical position of offering descriptions of its subject-matter as widely divergent from each other as are " mental processes " and " behaviour." No other science offers a parallel to the startling phenomenon of a leading psychologist solemnly propounding the question: " Does Consciousness Exist? " [1] Moreover, a great deal of what, in a broad sense of the term, might be set down under " mental life," is not included in current psychology

[1] William James, in *Essays in Radical Empiricism.*

at all. Social Psychology has, indeed, of recent years begun
to correct the abstractness of the over-individualistic point
of view of classical psychology. A book like James's *Varieties of Religious Experience* has shown the way from
excessive generalities to a study of a concrete type of experience in its specific modifications. Behaviourism has
broken down the artificial isolation of a mind from its body
and its environment. Freud has furnished an integrating
principle which, with necessary qualifications, E. B. Holt,
for example, is beginning to use to such excellent effect,
that he even re-discovers, with due psychological authority,
the commonsense of Socrates' moral teaching.[1] There is, in
short, noticeable a distinct movement from the abstract to
the concrete. But it is still true that psychological theory
hovers uneasily between physiology on the one side and
" philosophy of mind " on the other. Too many psychologists, when they become conscious of these depths, seek
safety in confining themselves to the purely experimental
side of their subject, content to gather facts and let theory
take care of itself. But the policy of the ostrich works no
better here than elsewhere, and fundamental questions are
not disposed of by being ignored.[2] At any rate, unless we
are greatly mistaken, there is in present-day psychology,
so far as it dares to speculate, a noticeable movement
towards a more concrete concept of mind. Mind is coming
again to be looked on as a dynamic and effective factor in
the world, precisely because it is again being looked on as
functionally related to its bodily basis, and through its
body to the wider world. Something of this development
we shall try to trace, but before we can do so profitably,

---

[1] *The Freudian Wish*, p. 141 ; see also the whole of ch. iv.
[2] Münsterberg's distinction between causal and purposive psychology is, of course, an example of the recognition that there are
different points of view yielding widely different concepts of mind,
but his distinction between them is too sharply dualistic to be
satisfactory.

we must work our way past certain difficulties which threaten to make all theory of mind impossible.

The saving of mind, like the saving of any other appearance, is effected, as we know from preceding essays, by devising a theory which accepts the appearance in question and exhibits it in its place in the order of the universe. And accepting an appearance is itself a matter of theory concerning what the true, or real, nature of that appearance is.

There was a time, not so very long ago, when the most conspicuous obstacle to a saving of mind would have been the theory known as " materialism." There is no need to stir once more the ashes of this burnt-out controversy. At the present day the obstacles to the framing of an adequate theory of what a mind is, spring from sources far other than the bogey of a purely material universe. One obstacle is to be found in the denial that data for a theory of mind are available. This denial is based sometimes on the alleged difficulty of self-observation or introspection, but more frequently on the alleged impossibility of any mind directly observing any other. Another obstacle arises from the abstract concept of mind which is still being defended, or perhaps we should rather say being wrestled with, in some quarters, as a supposed requirement of the theory of knowledge.

Of this latter obstacle we can dispose without much ado. If the problem of knowledge is, first, conceived in terms of a " cognitive relation " between a " subject " or " knower " and an " object " or " known "; if the subject, next, is defined as " mind " and as different in nature from everything that is object or known; and if, lastly, to give a final twist to the tangle, the distinction of subject and object is identified with the distinction of soul and body,

then, of course, a situation is created which is well-nigh
desperate. For all these distinctions result in, so to speak,
isolating a mind alike from its body and from the objects
which it is supposed to know. They burden us with the
problem of the relation of body to soul, conceived as two
distinct substances. They burden us with the even more
awkward problem of the relation of intra-mental " ideas "
to extra-mental " objects." Many and ingenious are the attempts to escape from these predicaments, especially the
latter one. Sometimes it is done by a declaration *ad hoc*.
Thus Bertrand Russell assures us that " the faculty of being
acquainted with things other than itself is the main characteristic of a mind," [1] and this is about the beginning and
end of what this distinguished thinker has to say about the
nature of a mind. Similarly, Professor S. Alexander tells
us that minds " enjoy " themselves and " contemplate "
other things, though he, to be sure, makes a valiant attempt
to build a psychology on this basis.[2] Some of the American
Neo-realists propound a " relational theory of consciousness " in order to fill the mind with real things and save real
things from being engulfed by the subjectivity of ideas.
But—if the bull be permitted—the best way to get out of
these coils is never to get into them. In other words, the
all-important thing is to refrain, first and last, from mixing
up theory of mind with theory of knowledge, especially in
that sense of the latter in which it is devoted to solving the
insoluble conundrum how a mind shut up with its own
ideas knows that there are objects outside to which its ideas
correspond.[3] The problem of the theory of mind, like the
problem of the theory of any other phenomenon in the

[1] *The Problems of Philosophy*, p. 66.
[2] See especially *Foundations and Sketch-plan of a Conational
Psychology*, in the *British Journal of Psychology*, vol. iv (1911).
[3] For the genuine problem of the theory of knowledge, see the *Note*
at the end of this essay.

world, is concerned with data and their interpretation—
with learning to recognise the data and interpret them
rightly.

This is, of course, exactly the attitude of any psychology
which is not false to its name. The two working-assump-
tions of every psychologist are: (a) that minds [1] of all
sorts exist for him to study—he takes minds for granted
exactly as every other scientist takes his subject-matter for
granted; (b) that minds can be known, i.e., that true
propositions concerning minds can be formulated on properly tested evidence. Thus the psychologist proceeds—
naïvely, if we like to say so—with his business of finding
out as much as he can about what minds are and what they
do. Nor does he make much difference between evidence
drawn from his observation of his own mind and evidence
drawn from his observation of others. Certainly the theory
which he aims at is a theory of mind as such, not of his
own mind in particular, still less of his own mind exclusively.

But it is just here that the other obstacle threatens to
bar the way to a theory of mind. It challenges introspection: How is it possible for a mind to observe and analyse
itself whilst carrying on simultaneously the activities to be
studied? Can a mind become wholly object to itself, or
is the object always a part, a fragment focused by attention, the subject remaining a surd, a background of non-
objectified immediate feeling? It challenges no less completely and vigorously all observation of other minds: only
bodies and their movements are open to public observation;
minds are inward and private and observable each only by
itself. A mind can know other minds only by analogical
inference, whence it seems to follow that a psychologist

[1] The term is here used without any prejudice to the position of
the behaviourists.

erects an amazingly audacious superstructure of generalisations on a slender basis of self-observation.

The fact that psychology in practice successfully ignores these misgivings may reassure us, but even a pragmatically-minded philosopher will want to know, not merely that a procedure is successful, but why it is so. It behooves us, therefore, to satisfy ourselves that the above objections to the very possibility of a theory of mind do not hold.

This task we may conveniently accomplish in two stages, considering, first, the general problem of acquaintance with minds, and, secondly, the various theories concerning a mind's acquaintance with itself and with other minds.

(1) The question, What is a mind? is equivalent to the question, What does the term " mind " mean? The approach to our first problem by way of meaning has this advantage: it reminds us that when we are engaged in the study of appearances for which we have empirical data, terms are both denotative and connotative or descriptive, *i.e.*, experience both furnishes points for their application and materials for the development of the description, or theory, of the nature of what we are dealing with. The meaning of every descriptive term is a concept, a universal, a theory—drawn from experience by that ordering and interpreting of data of which synthesis and discrimination are the correlative sides, and which is open both to verification and to expansion and correction by fresh experience. Thus "psychology without a soul" merely proclaims, in epigrammatic form, that a certain theory of what a soul is, is false. It does not deny that there are phenomena to which, with a different connotation, the term is applicable. Again, when James puts the question, " Does consciousness exist? " and answers at first, " There is no such thing ",

the sting of his answer lies in the " such ". For his second answer is another theory of consciousness.

But how are we to set about getting and verifying the true theory, the correct meaning, of mind?

Bluntly put, the answer is, of course, " Study actual minds, get at the thing behind the word." But do we not need the description, or theory, for the correct identification of the instances? Put bluntly again, How shall we know a mind when we meet one? The question may seem absurd, when applied to the particular case of minds, familiarity with which we are all ready to assume. But the principle it raises is important to note, if only because it gives us an opportunity to reinforce the position we have taken up in these essays concerning the place of " experience ", or " data ", or " particulars ", in knowledge. This position is that even the minimal datum is never less than a this-such. There is always some degree of acquaintance with the *nature* of a thing whenever we meet with the thing at all. With this clue to guide us we have to solve the problem of making ourselves acquainted with its nature more completely, the ideal goal being to know its whole nature. Theory thus rests on acquaintance, and, more than that, on cumulative acquaintance, which, as it progresses, involves much discrimination and ordering of diverse data. But the nature of a thing is always " universal," and the progress towards a completer theory is controlled by this universal character.

Applying this general view to our present problem, how the meaning of " mind ", *i.e.*, the theory of the nature of mind, is built up by the study of actual minds, we see that we have to *realise,* and keep realising, by acquaintance with minds what the nature of mind is. Minds *exhibit* themselves, and we have to study their exhibitions so as to gather gradually an impression of their complete nature. There are

various ways of such exhibition. An animal exhibits its
mind by behaving as it is its nature to behave. But for a
psychologist to perceive its mind correctly, depends on what
he attends to, and with what insight into the meaning of
what he perceives. For him, in turn, to exhibit what he perceives to another psychologist, so that the other sees what he
sees, may need much argument and common technical terms,
mutual understanding of which presupposes that both have
previously learned to synthesise the same sort of data in
the same sort of way. Psychological laboratory-technique
refines the ways in which human beings exhibit their minds
to each other for purposes of study, but it is artificial and
restricted compared with the infinite diversity of ways in
which by speech, gesture, conduct, men in their dealings
with each other exhibit their minds to each other. Self-
observation is the study of the exhibitions of one's own
mind, and it may, of course, take experimental form. Every
one is acquainted with what it is to be a mind by being one,
though being a mind and exhibiting one's mind are not the
same thing as noticing, or reflecting on, the exhibitions with
theoretical interest. Certainly self-observation is wider
than introspection, at any rate when the latter term, as
" looking into one's own mind ", is so restricted that observation of one's body and one's behaviour towards surrounding objects and other human beings is excluded. But to
exclude these is precisely to cut off the most illuminating
exhibitions of one's mind. The difficulties urged against
introspection do not touch this side of the evidence, and,
again, on this view of the evidence, the alleged inaccessi-
bility of other minds loses most of its terrors.

Of course, it is true that no one can simply point with his
finger at a mind, either his own or his neighbour's, as he can
point at a coloured patch. But argument, or theory, is an
indirect way of pointing. It teaches to identify by descrip-

tion. It directs the attention so that the desired effect or impression may be got.

The upshot of all this is that the meaning of " mind " must be derived from acquaintance with minds, it being the systematic account of the universal nature of mind as exhibited in particular minds. Even the first acquaintance with a particular mind is already, so far as it goes, an acquaintance with the universal nature of mind, though it takes further acquaintance with fresh data to develop this knowledge of the universal at which the theory of mind aims.

(2) We are now in a position for the second part of our task which consists in reviewing, in their connection with each other, the various theories concerning a mind's acquaintance with itself and with other minds.

We may begin with the familiar view that the only mind which any one can become acquainted with is his own mind.[1] We may call this, briefly, the principle of the privacy of mind. To adopt it as the basis of psychology seems fatal, for strictly taken it would limit the psychologist to self-observation and autobiography. Intercourse by language hides the difficulty in human psychology: in animal psychology it becomes inevitably glaring. We cannot wonder that, in protest, a demand for an " objective " psychology should have sprung up, refusing to concern itself with the inaccessible " inside " of other creatures' minds, and studying instead the well accessible " outside " of their behaviour. But even more interesting is the development of this protest

[1] This view, though verbally similar, is, of course, to be strictly distinguished from such a view as that of Leibniz's *Monadology*. The privacy of minds of which we are here speaking, is compatible with the beliefs that there are bodies or physical objects, that these are radically different from minds, that a mind can know by acquaintance both its own body and the bodies associated with other minds. All it denies is that any mind can be acquainted with any other mind.

in the direction of a rival theory of minds as open to one another's inspection, as in fact " overlapping," [1] The possibility of the knowledge of other minds, of getting judgments concerning them which not only are *de facto* true, but which we can see to be true, has been attracting an increasing amount of attention in recent philosophical literature. It will repay us to study the situation in some detail.

At one extreme, we have the familiar view that only bodies are perceptible by the senses, whilst minds, from their very nature, are imperceptible. It follows that whilst, by sight and touch, I can observe another's body, I cannot observe his mind. His mind is not a datum for me. I know it, if it can be called " knowing ", only by inference, and by a dubious inference at that. Among recent writers, Mr. Russell has been most prominent in pressing this view and elaborating its consequences. For him the belief that there are other minds, and that they are so-and-so, is " psychologically derivative." It is based on the observation of other peoples' bodies plus the analogical inference that when other people's behaviour resembles mine, they have thoughts and feelings like those which I have when I behave as they do. This is, in fact, the most commonly accepted theory, but few of those who have accepted it have drawn out its consequences with the same ruthless intellectual honesty as Russell. He recognises that the belief in other minds, thus founded, is " soft," *i.e.*, open to doubt; that the evidence for it is inconclusive; that it is an " instinctive belief " for which the best we can say is that it is a reasonable working hypothesis, because " it systematises a vast body of facts and never leads to any consequences which there is reason

---

[1] " We often know something of both the contents and the limitations of another's mind. And this is at least to say that somehow one consciousness may overlap another." E. B. Holt, *Concept of Consciousness*, p. xii.

to think false. "[1] At the same time he would, clearly, like something speculatively " harder " than this pragmatic argument, for he realises that trying to do without this belief has devastating consequences. At once the testimony of others becomes mere " noises and shapes ", and my world, resting now on a purely solipsistic basis, shrinks into a miserable fragment of what it is when I allow the experiences of others to supplement my own.[2] And thus Russell leaves us in the amusing position of holding a belief which is at once instinctive (we " cannot help " it), logically unjustifiable, and so eminently useful that as reasonable men, if not as philosophers, we do well to stick to it. Is this not a little perverse? Meanwhile, we can but regret that Russell has not paid more attention to what must underlie the analogical and pragmatic attribution of mind to others, viz., a mind's acquaintance with itself, and the conditions of its possibility.

It is, in fact, characteristic of the attitude of most of those who hold knowledge of other minds to be purely inferential, that whilst denying knowledge by acquaintance of other minds, they take self-knowledge for granted as if it raised no problems; and then place a burden upon the analogical and pragmatic arguments which they are quite incapable of bearing.

Russell condemns the analogical argument chiefly on the ground that phantasms in dreams appear to have minds, and that there the inference is held to be mistaken. But there are stronger reasons than this. The " animism " of primi-

---

[1] *Our Knowledge of the External World,* Lecture III, p. 96.
[2] When in the mood to eschew the luxury of soft beliefs, Russell boldly sets up the ideal of building all knowledge, including physics, on a solipsistic basis, though when, in the search for hard data, he turns his annihilating analysis on the " self ", it can hardly be said that any " ipse " remains. At least, there are hints that the belief in the identity of one's own self from moment to moment, from experience to experience, is distinctly soft.

tive peoples means an extension of the belief in souls, spirits, or demons, far beyond what our sciences endorse. The suggestion that similarity to human behaviour is the basis of the extension is surely stretched to the breaking-point when river, rain and sea, wind, storm, stars and stones are regarded as animate. Is it not rather that the primitive thinker fails to discriminate living and non-living, animate and inanimate than that he hypothetically endows with conscious life, akin to his own, objects *prima facie* given to him as non-living and inanimate? Moreover, if our knowledge of other minds really rested on analogy alone, it would be very much more limited than it is, and this not merely because the clue of similarity soon fails face to face with strange forms of life, but chiefly because each person's acquaintance with his own expressive looks and gestures is exceedingly limited, and what we have of it is as much mediated by perception of others (*i.e.*, by inverse analogy) as by self-perception. The principle that "we do not see ourselves as others see us" covers a very large range of our expressive behaviour, and even frequent use of a mirror would but partially remove this handicap. In so far as each of us is limited in his knowledge of how he looks and behaves under the influence of certain experiences, whereas he is very familar with the corresponding looks and gestures of others, the situation assumed by the analogical argument is non-existent. Our criticisms do not, of course, amount to the contention that analogy gives no help at all. On the contrary, for the detailed extension of our knowledge of the minds of others it is of great value. But we do contend, that it cannot well be either the only, or even the chief, source of the hypothesis that other bodies have minds.

The case is not much better with the pragmatic argument. An " idea " (= an hypothesis), we are told, is true

if it "works". Most plausibly this means that in order
to verify an hypothesis I must act on it, and judge by the
congruity of the results with my anticipations. Suppose
the other body has a mind like my own, it will behave, on
being treated by me in a certain way, as I should myself
behave if treated in that way. I make the experiment,
and if the response agrees with my anticipation, my hypothesis "works". I kick a stone and address insulting language to it: it does not kick or answer back—hence it does
not "feel", it has no "mind." It is easy to see that it
depends entirely on the nature of my hypothesis whether
the evidence I obtain is positive or negative. What would
be confirmatory evidence for one theory of mind, might well
be negative evidence for another. A fetishist who fears that
his stone idol will revenge itself on him for having been
treated abusively, may regard an illness into which he falls
as verification of his fears. Thus the evidence is bound
to be ambiguous so long as a change in my hypothesis may
turn unfavourable into favourable evidence and *vice versa.*
Am I to make belief in God dependent on the issue of a
prayer experiment:—if this wish of mine is fulfilled, I shall
know there is a God; if it is disappointed, I shall know
there is none? People do argue like that, but it is not
obviously a good argument. In short, we may make our
pragmatic experiment with entirely false notions of what a
mind is or does, and, consequently of what would, or would
not, be evidence of mind. Moreover, as in the analogy
theory, the experimenter, *ex hypothesi,* is familiar only with
his own mind; hence he could recognise evidence only of a
similar type of mind. Evidence of types of mind widely
different from his would necessarily be for him negative
evidence.

A somewhat different version of pragmatic " working " is
to be found in James's famous " automatic sweetheart "

argument.[1]   James asks us to suppose " a soulless body which should be absolutely indistinguishable from a spiritually animated maiden, laughing, talking, blushing, nursing us and performing all feminine offices as tactfully and sweetly as if a soul were in her ", and then goes on, " Would any one regard her as a full equivalent? Certainly not, and why? Because, framed as we are, our egoism craves above all things inward sympathy and recognition, love and admiration. The outward treatment is valued mainly as an expression, as a manifestation of the accompanying consciousness believed in. Pragmatically, then, the belief in the automatic sweetheart would not *work* . . ." [2] The use which James proceeds to make of this argument throws a revealing light on it. With regard to the universe it is absolutely indistinguishable whether it is the product of blind forces or the work of a benevolent God. But the belief that it is the work of God is emotionally more satisfactory, hence it works, hence God exists. Does not this give the argument away? In the absence of differential evidence, emotional preference is to tip the scale. It is the old " will-to-believe " argument cropping up. If, *per impossibile*, an automaton were to be so cunningly contrived as to be really " absolutely indistinguishable from a spiritually animated maiden ", our pragmatist lover, proceeding happily on the hypothesis soothing to his vanity, would get from his automatic sweetheart all the love and sympathy he could possibly want in the only way he could possibly get them, *viz.*, in the look of her eyes, the tone of her voice, the caressing touch, the tender embrace. Nor would he ever discover his mistake: the " absolutely indistinguishable " saves him from

---

[1] *The Meaning of Truth,* p. 189, *note.*
[2] There is a good example of the automatic sweetheart in Offenbach's *Tales from Hoffmann.* There the automaton is discovered when her mechanism goes wrong and her behaviour becomes unpleasantly distinguishable from that of a living maiden.

that awful fate. Never, surely, did philosopher invent an argument which more securely entrenched sentimental illusions. If the presence of mind in a human body is not differentially evident, the game is up. The hypothesis that there is a mind must be capable of verification by a recognisable difference between facts which corroborate it and facts which refute it. In the absence of such a difference, emotional preference is no better than instinctive belief, and philosophy becomes the gentle art of mistaking pleasing make-believe for truth. Of course, the pragmatic method of verification by experiment presupposes the possibility of getting differential evidence, and as such it has a legitimate place in our dealings with other minds. But, like the analogy-argument, it helps rather to add detail and precision to our knowledge of others, than to mediate the initial step from the existence of one's own mind as a datum to the existence of other minds as an inference.

Its main fault, however, is that it does not examine the principle of the privacy of each mind, of its isolation from every other. So long as each mind is supposed to be imprisoned in its own inwardness, no intellectual acrobatics will help it to burst the walls of its prison and have intercourse with its fellows.

A half-way stage on the way to the principle of overlapping minds is represented by the theory of empathy (*Einfühlung*) in its various forms. Broadly speaking, this theory appeals to the feelings we experience in contact with other minds. Expressive gestures still play their part, but they are used no longer by way of comparison and analogy. Instead we are bidden to note the feelings which they evoke in us, and to find in these feelings our evidence for our knowledge of other minds.

Perhaps the best approach to the theory of *Einfühlung,*

as applied to the knowledge of other minds [1] is through a consideration of sympathy, in the literal sense of " sharing ", as we say, another's feeling. What exactly does this " sharing " mean? " I am as pleased about your success as you are ". " I feel your sorrow as much as you do." " Your joy is also mine ". Let us note the precise point of this sympathy. In order to share another's feeling I must not merely be pleased at his pleasure or be sorry that anything should grieve him, for in order to experience these secondary or response emotions about the other's emotions, I must somehow know what these emotions of his are. It is precisely the method of this " knowing " which is in question. Clearly, unless we are to invoke telepathy, he must somehow show me what he feels. But how can he show me his feelings except by means of outward signs such as sounds and gestures? Here the empathy theory seeks to open a way for direct experience. The other's words and actions, it holds, evoke in me not merely the same emotion as his, but an emotion *which I feel at once as his and not as mine*. For this emotion fuses with, is felt by me as inseparably part of, or one with, the gestures I see, the words I hear; and these, though seen and heard by me, are not my gestures and my sounds. A cry of terror and I tremble, not because, in the first instance, I am afraid for myself, but because I " hear ", *i.e.*, immediately feel, the terror expressed in that cry. I " see " a look of pride in another's eye. But such " seeing " is precisely *Einfühlung*. For what I see, strictly, is not pride, but the colour, shape and movements of the eye. The pride is " expressed " and as such is *felt* by me, but I feel it, not as my pride, but precisely as the pride of that other whose eye I am looking

---

[1] Theodor Lipps, the father of the empathy theory, developed it in the first instance as an instrument for the analysis of æsthetic experience. Its application to our problem is of secondary interest for him, and not beyond doubt in its details.

at. I feel pride, but I do not feel proud myself in the sense in which to feel proud is to *be* proud. The pride I feel is *his*, not mine. Even if he looks at me superciliously, I feel his contempt in his look, whilst at the same time I may feel, on my own behalf, resentful or humiliated.[1] Perhaps the most challenging way of putting the empathy theory is to say that, for it, a feeling which may be called "mine" in the sense that I feel it, is yet felt by me not as mine, but as another's, and this not by way of inference from data, but as a genuine character of the data themselves. Its merit is to draw attention to experiences to which the rigid distinction of mine and yours is but awkwardly applicable. It leads us to question the almost legalistic attitude of the privacy-principle, which bids us say, in effect, "Here is my mind, there is yours; my mind has its own thoughts and feelings, your mind has yours; and it is impossible for what is mine to be yours."

To the perspectives which are opened up by questioning this principle we shall return. Meanwhile, we can learn something further from a different form of the empathy theory which Professor S. Alexander has developed.[2] Whilst still clinging to the view that it is of the very essence of consciousness not to be shareable, Alexander holds that each mind must have a clue to the other mind in some direct feeling, or modification of feeling, of its own. "The clue would seem to be found in those elementary experiences, on the level of instinct, where coöperation, reciprocation, or rivalry is necessary in order that the experience should have its full flavour. . . . Thus it (tenderness) is felt more towards an affectionate than towards a cold child, and it is felt more and differently to a child and to a puppy. . . . We may press a yielding object

---

[1] Cf. Lipps, *Æsthetik*, pp. 106, 140.
[2] See his article on *Collective Willing and Truth*, in *Mind*, N. S., No. 85, pp. 17.

and become aware of its soft firmness and have besides the experience of our own effort of grasping. But there is all the difference between this and the experience of a hand which in any degree returns the pressure of ours. . . . The experience of another man's trying to get the same thing as yourself is a direct suggestion that he is *wanting* it, and is a different experience from seeking the object and being merely obstructed. . . . Thus the immediate basis of our experience that another person exists is a direct ingredient in certain feelings, which ingredient is not present if that other being were inanimate or unconscious." On this basis Alexander disposes of the automaton. " An automaton might look and even act like a child, but if it did not participate in our behaviour to it, we should miss the flavour of tenderness." Clearly, for Alexander, no automaton could be " absolutely indistinguishable " from a conscious person, for there is a difference of behaviour which we directly feel. A conscious person " responds to our action and fulfils it." From this point on, the recognition of something common in the experiences of different minds becomes increasingly manifest. For there is at least a common situation which the several minds are experiencing and with which they are dealing. " It is not because under similar circumstances foreign bodies exhibit behaviour like our own that we believe them to be minds like ourselves, by an act of inference; but because in one and the same situation they take part with ourselves in a joint action in which their part may or *may not* be like our own, and because without such response on their side our own experience is incomplete." It is clear here that in this appeal to social experience, or " intersubjective intercourse ", the common situation makes possible the experience of the other mind's response or opposition, coöperation or competition. For Alexander this " instinctive " experience of other minds is open to animals in their relation to other animals and to men. Among men, dealing with one another, the experience becomes " reflective " and is vastly extended by speech, and by " combination of wills in practical affairs or of intellects in the pursuit of knowledge." Notwithstanding these admissions, however, Alexander reasserts that assurance of another mind's existence is gained only by an " act of faith ", and that knowledge of its nature remains wholly symbolic. " We transfer the contents (of our own consciousness) to this foreign being, and give indefinite scope to our sympathetic imagination in this construction ". This transference, however, is based, for Alexander, on empathy, not into the expressive movements of another, but into the objective situation in which the other acts. By imagination I put myself into the other's place and thus experience how it feels to be in such a situation. " I do not feel your feeling, but I read my feeling into your imagined position."

Alexander's view is particularly instructive because his very attempt to effect a synthesis of privacy plus inference (or " transference ") with social intercourse plus the sharing of a common world, exhibits very clearly under the pressure of what considerations the former view is brought to its breaking-point.

This brings us, finally, to theories which take their stand either on social intercourse or on the common world.

The former, with a good deal of difference in detail, appeal, one and all, to the principles: (a) that self-knowledge is possible only in a social medium; (b) that most of the purposes of an individual mind are social, involving not only coöperation with other minds, but functional differentiation of members in a social system; (c) that the individual owes his knowledge of the universe far more to communication from others than to his private efforts.

Thus all these theories are innocent of any flirtation with solipsism. They point out that the very facts which are commonly quoted as supporting the privacy, or mutual isolation, of minds—*e.g.*, that I cannot feel my neighbour's toothache, nor he mine; that no one can know what goes on inside my mind unless I give outward signs, and that by posing, pretending, lying, I can not only conceal my mind, but mislead the inferences of others—have point only in a medium of social relations. They argue that we first learn about ourselves from and through our fellows; that each of us gets to know his own mind because he is treated by others as having a mind of his own, long before he is able to discover that fact for himself; that it is only through the minds of one's fellows that one's own fragmentary glimpses of the universe are completed.[1]   Or, again, it has been argued that each of us, as an actively willing subject, or ego, directly acknowledges other subjects, each with a will of his own. Will meets will, in conflict or coöperation, and demands to be acknowledged. Social life is a tissue of such mutual acknowledgments, and in these we must look for the basis of our knowledge of each other's minds. Even the minds of animals are known to us only by such an act of acknowledgment.[2]   Or, lastly, it may be bluntly asserted that " it is a pure blunder of subjectivist psychology to assume that somehow the fact of my own existence as a centre of experience is a primitive revelation. . . . Self-knowledge, apart from the knowledge of myself as a being with aims and purposes conditioned by those of like beings in social relations with myself, is an empty and senseless word." [3]

As is clear from the very language employed by these writers, they are thinking of self-knowledge, rather than

[1] See *e.g.*, Royce, *The World and the Individual*, vol. ii, ch. iv.
[2] *Cf.* Münsterberg, *Grundzüge der Psychologie*, ch. ii.
[3] A. E. Taylor, *Elements of Metaphysics*, p. 205.

of mind-knowledge. But the very fact that the language of " self " and " other " comes so readily to our lips when we are talking about minds helps to emphasise that the social relations of mind to mind are the medium in which mind-knowledge arises. This suggests that the individualistic standpoint of traditional psychology, basing itself simply on the existence of a multitude of individual minds, and thus led to study mind as a class-character, involves an abstraction similar to that of considering human beings merely as specimens repeating the type of an animal species, instead of as differentiated and organized in social systems. The student who comes to the study of mind from the side of biology is easily tempted to think of mind merely as a class-character repeated, no doubt with variations of degree and kind, in all the members of an animal species. He cannot learn too soon that, from this point of view, social relations, and the higher forms of mental life generally, tend to be either ignored, or not to be treated on their merits.

A second important lesson which the social theories of mind bring to light is the ambiguity of the word " mine ". It is due to this ambiguity that theories so diametrically opposite as the " privacy " view and the " social " view are in the field. We must seriously consider the possibility that when the upholders of the privacy view say that my own mind is a datum, yours an inference, they are using " my " in a different sense from that in which the upholders of the social view maintain that " I " and " you ", myself and yourself, my mind and other minds, are correlates; that the distinction between them is developed *pari passu;* that both are equally inferential, equally concepts or " ideal constructions ". The familiar criticism of the privacy view —" If I am acquainted only with my own mind as a datum, how do I know it as ' mine '? What right have I to call it mine? 'Mine' has meaning only by contrast with 'not-mine' ('yours' or an 'other's') "—turns wholly on the ambiguity of the personal pronoun. The fact is that "mine" may be used either in a social sense, or else like "this", "here", "now", as a mere linguistic synonym for "immediate experience", or "datum". The advocate of the privacy view, when he talks of "his" mind as a datum, is talking tautologically. He really means *these* present feelings and thoughts here and now. If calling them "his" is anything but another way of saying, "these . . . here and now," if it means *his-not-another's*, he is, of course, at once guilty of the fallacy with which the advocate of the social view charges him.[1]

The point comes out more clearly in Russell's statement of the privacy view than in that of any other writer. With our clue, it is easy to see that the inference to other minds from the datum of my own is but a special case of what is, for Russell, perhaps the most crucial problem of philosophy, *viz.*, how to justify quite generally the inference to the existence of non-data from the existence of data. In short, it is the problem of "transcendence". But, of course, the full meaning of "my mind" or "my self" transcends any datum as emphatically as does "your mind" or "another self."[2] The minds which the psychologist studies cannot be saved by eschewing transcendence and inference, and falling back on bare data. They can be saved only by that synthetic and cumulative organisation of data which Russell himself calls "logical construction". Indeed Russell has made an ingenious attempt to construct a world which, in his own words, "can, with a certain amount of trouble, be used to interpret the crude facts of sense, the

---

[1] A fuller statement of this ambiguity will be found in the article on *Solipsism* which the writer has contributed to Hastings's *Encyclopædia of Ethics and Religion*.

[2] *Cf.* above, p. 23, footnote.

facts of physics, and the facts of psychology." [1] More than that—in suggesting that the physicists' construct of a material thing and the psychologists' construct of a mind differ only in that both classify the same appearances from different points of view, he comes very near to the view that a mind is, in E. B. Holt's language, a " cross-section " of the universe." [2]

This brings us to the second group of social theories, if for convenience we may so label them, *viz.*, the theories for which minds are objects of observation to each other through the medium of a common world.

To the " objective " and " behaviouristic " motives in present-day psychology, and to the " realistic " motives in present-day philosophy, which reinforce theories of this type, we have already alluded. Their common principle is to analyse a mind in terms of its " contents ", which contents are at the same time regarded as being, and remaining, constituents of the object-world, capable of becoming simultaneously objects of other minds. There are three converging arguments which make theories of this type exceedingly plausible, notwithstanding an effect of paradox which they almost invariably produce on first acquaintance.

(a) The first argument appeals quite frankly to the method of observation of behaviour, which is the chief method of animal pschology, and plays no small part in human intercourse and in the psychological laboratory, though outweighed among human beings by communication through language. For the success of this method it is essential that the question, " What is a creature conscious

---

[1] *Our Knowledge of the External World,* p. 93. The text has " physiology " but the context shows, I think, that this must be a slip for " psychology ".

[2] The main difference is that Russell's mind-classes do not overlap, do not have members in common, whereas Holt's cross-sections do.

of? " should be answerable, not by inference about the creature's imperceptible mind, but by observation of its perceptible actions. It must be interpreted to mean, not " What goes on in the privacy of the creature's inner consciousness? " but " What is the creature looking at, listening to, sniffing at, digging for, watching for, *etc.*—in short, what is it doing? " In order that the question in this form may be answerable, the object which the creature under observation is responding to, or interested in, must be perceptible to the observer, too. He must be able to identify it among the objects which he is himself perceiving. It must be an item in the environment within which he is watching the creature's behaviour.[1]   The " world " as the observer is aware of it, may be much more comprehensive and varied than the " world " as the creature under observation is aware of it. But the important point is that the creature's world is contained within the observer's—that, to this ex-

---

[1] The argument, *e.g.*, of von Uexkuell's *Die Umwelt und die Innenwelt der Tiere*, rests throughout on the above principle; and so, of course, do the explicit contributions to "behaviourism", like John Watson's *Behaviour*. For an elaborately worked-out example from the observation of human behaviour, see E. B. Holt, *The Freudian Wish*, esp. pp. 85 ff. Its application to language may be illustrated by the following quotation from R. B. Perry's *Present Philosophical Tendencies*, Part V, Ch. xii, § 8, p. 291: "Language does not arise as the external manifestation of an internal idea, but as the means of fixing and identifying abstract aspects of experience. If I wish to direct your attention to the ring on my finger, it is sufficient for me to point to it or hand it to you. In seeing me thus deal with the ring, you know that it engages my attention, and there occurs a moment of communication in which our minds unite on the object. The ring figures in your mind even as it does in mine; indeed the fact that the ring does so figure in my mind will probably occur to you when it does not to me. If, however, I wish to call your attention to the yellowness of the ring, it will not do simply to handle it. The whole object will not suffice as a means of identifying its element. Hence the need of a system of symbols complex enough to keep pace with the subtlety of discrimination. Now the important thing to bear in mind is the fact, that as a certain practical dealing with bodies constitutes gross communication, so language constitutes refined communication. In the one case as in the other, mind is open to mind, making possible a coalescence of content and the convergence of action on a common object."

tent, the two worlds coincide, or " overlap ", or, at least, can be made to coincide.   Instead of speaking of " two worlds coinciding ", we might equally well speak of a " common " world for both, in fact of " one " world present to two minds.   And the principle is, obviously, capable of extension to any number of minds.   When I watch a cat lying in wait for its prey near a mousehole, do I not know what she is thinking of?   When I see people in the street turning their heads, and, on looking around myself, perceive a trolley-car off the rails, do I not know what they have in mind?   The whole issue may be reduced just to this: should such everyday experiences as these be interpreted on the principle of a common world, in which situations constantly arise such that each can say that he perceives what others perceive, and that what things mean to him they mean to others?   Or should he " introject ", *i.e.*, treat what he perceives and what others perceive as so many " private ", " inaccessible ", " mutually exclusive " contents of consciousness?   The alternatives are private, or " subjective ", sensations and ideas, which, being mine, cannot be yours, being yours, cannot be mine, *versus* common and public objects, which we—you and I—not only share but know that we share.

(b) The second argument tries to bring even introspection to the support of the second of these alternatives.   To introspect is to take stock of the contents of one's mind.   But an enumeration of these brings to light nothing but objects belonging to the universe at large, and actually, or potentially, open to other minds.   The things I see are, or may be, seen by others; the sounds I hear—as when a crowd listens to a speech—are not debarred from reaching other ears by the fact that they reach mine.   Any object in the world which is, or may become, a content of my mind, is, or may become, an object also of other minds.   And, in any case, it remains always just the object it is in the world. The particular selection, or grouping, of items in my mind may be peculiar to me and private, but the items themselves are not. " In so far as I divide them into elements, the contents of my mind exhibit *no* generic character. I find the quality " blue ", but this I ascribe also to the book which lies before me on the table; I find " hardness ", but this I ascribe also to the physical adamant; or I find number, which my neighbour finds also in his mind. In other words, the elements of the introspective manifold are in themselves neither peculiarly mental nor peculiarly mine: they are *neutral and interchangeable*. It is only with respect to their grouping and interrelations that the elements of mental content exhibit any peculiarity." [1]

(c) The third argument seeks to meet the plausible objection that an analysis of mind cannot be given in terms only of contents or objects, but must recognise, over and above all objects, the existence of *acts* of mind, or else of an indefinable entity or quality of " awareness ", in virtue of which alone an object can be said " to be presented to " a mind, or " to be its content ". English realists, from G. E. Moore and Bertrand Russell to S. Alexander, have been unanimous in holding to this analysis of experience into act and object (sensing and sense-datum, thinking and concept, *etc.*), identifying the act or awareness as the peculiarly *mental* or *conscious* factor in the situation. They take this analysis for granted as self-evident. Alexander explicitly defends it as an " intuition ".[2] American realists and behaviourists deny this whole analysis; they refuse to recognise any distinctive mental act. What activity there is belongs to the body, or more specifically to the central nervous system (including the sense-organs). The

[1] Perry, *loc. cit.*, p. 277.
[2] *The Basis of Realism,* p. 7 (*Proceedings of the British Academy,* vol. vi).

verbs naming mental acts, looking, hearing, thinking, *etc.*, are all to be interpreted as referring to specific responses, or "motor sets" in operation, analysable in physiological terms. The alleged evidence of introspection in favour of a peculiar mental activity is flatly denied. The supposed "feeling" of activity is shown to consist of movement sensations (or rather "sense-data"), thus confirming the view that what activity there is, is bodily activity. The body is the *principium individuationis*. Its position in the universe is always unique, and so is the history of the nervous system of each of us, which determines so largely what each of us perceives, thinks, desires, is interested in. This is the germ of truth which the "privacy" theory tries to preserve by setting up imperceptible, inward consciousnesses, isolated from each other and from the world of objects; hence, in principle, incapable of coöperation in knowledge or in conduct.[1]

[1] See Perry, *loc. cit.*, Ch. xii, § 6, pp. 254, 5 (against W. James); Ch. xiii, § 9, pp. 321-3 (against G. E. Moore). It is interesting to add an argument, which without any influence from realism and behaviourism, reaches a similar conclusion with an effect of fresh observation. "I have sometimes sat looking at a comrade, speculating on this mysterious isolation of self from self. Why are we so made that I gaze and see of thee only thy wall, and never thee? This wall of thee is but a movable part of the wall of my world; and I also am a wall to thee: we look out at one another from behind masks. How would it seem if my mind could but once be *within* thine; and we could meet and without barrier be with each other? And then it has fallen upon me like a shock—as when one thinking himself alone has felt a presence—But I *am* in thy soul. These things around me are in thy experience. They are thy own; When I touch them and move them I change *thee*. When I look on them, I see what thou seest; and I experience thy very experience. For *where art thou?* Not there, behind those eyes, within that head, in darkness, fraternizing with chemical processes. Of these, in my own case, I know nothing, and will know nothing; for my existence is spent not behind my wall, but in front of it. . . . And there art thou, also. This world in which I live, is the world of thy soul: and being within that, I am within thee. I can imagine no contact more real and thrilling than this; that we should meet and share identity, not through ineffable inner depths (alone), but here through the foregrounds of common experience; and that thou shouldst be—not behind that mask—but *here*, pressing with all thy consciousness upon me, *containing* me, and these things of mine. This is reality: and having seen it thus, I can

The dispute about mental activity between the English and American realists illuminates just what it is in the " relational theory of consciousness "—to use R. B. Perry's term for it—that produces the effect of paradox alluded to above. In three ways, chiefly, is this paradox felt.

(1) This theory of consciousness seems to leave out " consciousness ". The English thinkers' emphasis on acts and awareness seems much more like what we mean, or think we mean, when we talk of " being conscious " of something. A theory of consciousness, like that of S. Alexander, who regards it as a new *quality* arising, in the course of evolution, when the organism has developed the requisite nervous system, seems to give the body its due and still save the mind as a non-physical something, wholly *sui generis*, endowed with the function of " enjoying " itself, and " contemplating " the object-world within which it has arisen.[1] Its weakness is that, when we have acknowledged that there is this indefinable awareness, we have exhausted all that there is of interest in it.[2] The philosopher's interest turns at once to the concrete universe—the field of knowledge and action. Provided that universe is saved, it may well seem a small matter whether, in addition to the physiological responses, which are common ground to both sides, there is, or there is not, an indefinable something to be called " awareness ". The whole dispute is one of the most curious in the history of psychology, and it is hard to see how it is to be settled, if treated as a question of evidence, or, at least, of mere introspecting or intuiting. Thus treated,

---

never again be frightened into monadism by reflections which have strayed from this guiding insight" (W. E. Hocking, *The Meaning of God in Human Experience*, pp. 265, 6).

[1] A similar concept of consciousness, as a " mental light" revealing the universe, has been advocated among American thinkers by Professor J. E. Boodin in *A Realistic Universe*.

[2] The above remark requires to be qualified by acknowledging that, for S. Alexander, at least, beauty requires the co-operation of mind and object (*The Basis of Realism*, in *Proceedings of the British Academy*, vol. vi).

it looks as if what is unanimously by realists on one side of the Atlantic is nearly as unanimously not found by realists on the other side. Reality, clearly, is having its little joke with the realists. Introspection does not settle the question, because introspection cannot be kept clear of theory. To report findings in descriptive terms is at once to theorise. There is no getting away from that. Hence the real moral of the dispute is that " meanings ", *i.e.*, theories, of consciousness are at variance. We shall suggest below what may be the correct solution.

(2) The theory of minds overlapping in a common world may be accused of pressing identity in two directions to points where obvious differences begin to be ignored. (a) It requires restatement at least to the extent of making room within its general frame-work for all the facts commonly summed up in the principle of the " relativity of sensations ". However right it is in insisting on the fundamental truth that two persons can perceive, and recognise that they perceive, literally the *same* real thing, it must also be made to include the fact that, owing to differences of position, distance, angle of vision, condition of sense-organs, past history of the nervous system, there are differences in what each perceives of the identical object. To develop, because of these differences, a new monadology, as Russell does in effect, is as one-sided as to insist on complete identity. Appearances are not to be saved by any such extremes of short-cuts. (b) And the theory requires also a fuller recognition of other ways in which minds may fail to overlap and, hence, will be limited in knowledge of one another. The field of perception supplies an illustration. Those of us who enjoy the full possession of our senses find it easy to say what a blind or a deaf person must miss. Our common world is definitely poorer for them by so much as it lacks all colour and light and sound. We can confidently say that,

because in the darkness and silence of the night we have a clue to what the world of the blind-deaf person lacks compared with our daylight world of colour and sound. But it is not so easy for us to realise, how varied and interesting the world may be to a blind-deaf person, who has learnt to make the most of the data of the remaining senses which we comparatively neglect. His world, in short, is not only poorer, but also richer, and it is just where it is richer that our understanding begins to fail. Descriptions such as Helen Keller and others have furnished, do not wholly fill the gap. Better would be experiments like that of the heroine of *The Rosary*. How far, again, can we share the world of animals which, like dogs, live by differences of smells that we are unable to perceive? That we are as insensible to most of the odours of the universe as we are to the "music of the spheres" may be a blessing in disguise, but it is none the less a definite limitation. Perhaps, as F. H. Bradley suggests, a dog's philosophy would run: What smells is real, what does not smell is nothing. But even the profoundest human philosopher is inevitably an outcast from the dog's paradise of smells.[1]

(3) Lastly, on any interpretation of the behaviouristic view, it is to be remembered that behaviour may be intentionally deceptive. Language, as Talleyrand remarked, is intended to conceal rather than reveal thought. But the lie in words is not so potent a source of misunderstanding as the lie in deeds. And this, in turn, suggests sham, make-believe, pretence, with all their ramifications. Some animals lie to their pursuers by shamming death. In human intercourse the problem becomes ethical, not only in the crude form, Is it ever right to tell a lie? but in the subtler forms of pretence

---

[1] It is worth remarking also on the differences in the means of expression. Whatever advantage over animals language gives to men, the lack of a tail is a real handicap in the expression of emotions by gesture.

and make-believe which social convention exacts as part of " good manners ". Our ideals of tact, etiquette, politeness exact a certain amount of make-believe as a moral duty. More than that, the self-control, or self-repression, necessary in the building of a moral character, involve something closely akin to pretence in the effort not to betray certain feelings, not to express certain thoughts, not to indulge certain desires. No doubt, it is one thing to suffer from certain thoughts and desires; another, to encourage and entertain them, though not to the point of overt action. It is one thing to repress a feeling in order to deceive others concerning its presence, another, in order to be rid of it oneself. To regulate one's behaviour in an effort at self-purification is different from regulating it so as to mislead others into thinking one is better than one is. A *suppressio mali* in conduct need not be a *suggestio falsi* to others. Still, the suppression of the visible act is common alike to the effort to emancipate oneself, and to the effort to deceive. Hence the dividing line between them is always dangerously thin. Too frequently the moral struggle stops with the make-believe in outward conduct that satisfies the social demand. Hence the sins of thought, the vicarious indulgences in imagination, which may make a man's life a lie not only to others, but even to himself.

The privacy view, on the one side, the " over-lapping-minds " view, on the other, seem both in their extreme forms too rigid for facts, such as these, to be comfortably fitted in. Indeed, they were not devised with a view to facts such as these. But by just so much do they fail to save the appearances completely.

We have fetched a wide compass, and it is time that we gathered in our results and applied them to the purpose in hand, to the saving of the mind.

Saving the mind, we have found, means acknowledging the existence of minds as genuine phenomena in the order of the universe. But such acknowledgment is possible only in terms of a theory of what a mind is, or of what it is to be a mind. We have sought to remove the difficulties which are alleged as standing in the way of such a theory, on the grounds that no mind can fully know itself, still less be known by any other mind. In trying to free the theory of mind from these embarrassments, we were compelled to notice other difficulties arising from the fact that theories of what a mind is may be framed in very different contexts. The biologist and animal psychologist needs a theory of mind which will allow him to observe minds as functions of living bodies in their environment, and this spectator point of view is applicable also to human minds. Yet when the psychologist takes minds at the human level proper, he runs up against two facts which cannot be kept from profoundly modifying the purely " objective " or spectator attitude. One of these facts is self-consciousness, making possible self-analysis and introspection. The other is the social relations of men: their mental life in social form. The psychologist's own mind comes into the picture as an object of study, and in coöperation and conflict, in the fluctuating relations of self and other self, the thoroughly social character of his own life is brought home to him. The former fact, taken by itself, leads to an extreme individualism, if not solipsism—a retirement of " mind " or " consciousness " upon what is " mine ", in the sense of immediate, unique, unshareable feeling. The other fact may lead to an opposite extreme of emphasising what is actually or potentially common to many minds. The problem is, somehow to get all these floating bits of theory into some coherent scheme—the common character of minds as such and also their diversity of type; their conjunction with living bodies and their function in the economy of life; their uniqueness as individuals; their sharing of a common world; their social relations pregnant with consciousness of the play of self versus other self. All these have their place: the trouble is to find that place.

This is the situation which we had in mind when, at the beginning of this essay, we threw out the suggestion that the present-day movement in psychology pointed towards a synthesis of the Aristotelian and Descartian, the biological and introspective, theories of mind—a synthesis which must needs be both polemical and constructive, holding fast what is of value in each of these two points of view, but going definitely beyond either where the saving of the appearances makes this necessary. It remains to substantiate this suggestion.

To any one surveying the road which the theory of the mind has travelled since the days of Hume and Kant, such a suggestion may seem unpromising. Without being guilty of mere caricature, he might recapitulate the history of modern theories of mind somewhat as follows. Hume and Kant, he might say, found in the field a " metaphysical " theory of the soul as an immaterial, spiritual substance, indivisible, self-identical, immortal.[1] For this sort of soul they denied all empirical evidence or warrant. In its place Kant put the " empirical ego ", Hume the " bundle of ideas ", rebaptised by James and other empirical psychologists the " stream of consciousness ". Thus they inaugurated the era of the " psychology without a soul ", for which there is no soul or self which " has " experiences; which feels, thinks, wills. The experiences themselves, the feelings, thoughts, volitions, as they come and go, are all the soul there is. And when it comes to the self, James is, in

---

[1] *Cf.* Descartes' *res cogitans,* Berkeley's " spirit which is active in perceiving ".

certain moods, even more annihilating. "The inner nucleus of the spiritual self" the "self of selves", so James declares, consists, when carefully examined, mainly of "peculiar motions in the head, or between the head and throat". The ordinary man may glibly say "I think", but introspection, so James tells him, shows nothing but "I breathe".[1] At the same time, whilst the self thus seems to shrink into the bare experience of certain bodily processes, the stream of consciousness threatens to make up for losing a soul by appropriating the whole universe. "What is the subject matter of psychology?" asks Yerkes, and replies: "It is consciousness, or the world of objects and events viewed as consciousness . . . Upon reflection we discover that the whole world may be viewed either as consciousness or as objects and events existing apart from consciousness".[2] Here at last the ordinary man may think (or breathe) is something substantial to lay hold of. But just as he stretches out his hand, the prize is snatched from his grasp by the behaviourists. Whilst most psychologists assure him that there is such a thing as consciousness, and that by introspection he can perceive that it is there and what it is like, the strict behaviourist denies both consciousness and introspection. He does not think it possible to find out what goes on inside a creature's mind. Hence he proposes to study the creature's behaviour in response to definite features of its environment. You say the creature has a mind? Well, there it is, patently exhibited before you in its behaviour. What is the creature conscious of? What does it perceive or think? Look what it does and to what objects in the environment it responds. Its consciousness is the cross-section of the environment composed of the things to which the creature's central nervous system

[1] *Essays in Radical Empiricism*, p. 37; *Principles of Psychology*, vol. i, pp. 299-305.
[2] *Introduction to Psychology*, ch. ii, p. 13.

specifically reacts. Do you ask for a self, a knower? There is the body. It is the knower, and its specific response is the knowing. Thus, with the passing of the spiritual substance, we first got "a psychology without a soul", and now we are getting a psychology even without consciousness. From spiritual substance to stream of consciousness, from stream of consciousness to cross-section of the universe defined by behaviour—such are the vicissitudes which the mind has suffered at the hands of its students.

But if, with the programme of a synthesis of Aristotelian and Descartian theories to guide us, we take a more comprehensive view, this whole development appears in a somewhat different light.[1] We can then see that it is a steady effort to work back from empty abstractions to a more concrete point of view. It is surely significant that E. B. Holt should explicitly present his behaviouristic or functional concept of consciousness as a modern statement of Aristotle's theory of the soul.[2]

For Aristotle, a living body, an organism, is "besouled" (ἔμψυχος), when it is actively exercising its proper function. What actual seeing is to the eye, that having a soul is to the organism as a whole. The soul of a plant consists in that it lives a typical plant-life according to its kind, carrying on the cycle of activities of growth and generation in the manner characteristic of that sort of plant. Similarly, the soul of an animal consists in its using its body to carry on effectively the sort of activities proper to that kind of animal. In this sense the soul is the "actualisation" of

---

[1] Our programme has obvious affinities with the three stages in the growth of psychology, according as the fundamental concept is life, mind, or experience, which Professor James Ward distinguishes in his recently published *Psychological Principles*. There are some differences between the view set forth in Ward's first chapter and the view of this essay, but they are probably differences of language rather than of doctrine.

[2] *The Freudian Wish*, pp. 49 and 95 ff.

the body's " potentiality ". It is like the difference between a machine at work, performing the function for which it was built, and the same machine standing still, except that a machine, unlike a living body, neither builds itself (*i.e.*, grows) nor performs its functions of its own initiative. So a human soul consists in a human body actually doing all the things which make a normal human life, from the nutritive and generative activities which it shares with plant souls, through sensation, appetition, locomotion, which it shares with animal souls, to the characteristically " rational " activities which are specifically human.[1] A soul, then, for Aristotle, is the " form " or " entelechy " of a body, *i.e.*, the actual functioning of a body according, as we might say, to its immanent design; and obviously a functioning body implies a setting or environment to which its functioning is related. Thus out of the fundamental concepts of a living body as a system of organs; the functions or uses of these organs as subsidiary to the function of the system as a whole; and the actual functioning ($\varepsilon\nu\varepsilon\rho\gamma\varepsilon\iota\alpha$) of the whole in its setting, Aristotle builds a theory of the soul according to its three kinds, plant-soul, animal-soul, man-soul. Dropping all technical terminology, we might simply say that, for Aristotle, to be, or have, a human soul is to do whatever things a human body can do, and preferably to do them well, *i.e.*, with that excellence which comes from grasp of principle grounded in sound habituation.

His standpoint is, of course, " objective ". His " energeia " is " behaviour ", especially when behaviour is extended to cover, as it ought to cover, " working or playing, reading, writing, or talking, making money or spending it, constructing or destroying, curing disease, alleviating poverty, comforting the oppressed, and promoting one or an-

[1] That Aristotle, unable to find an organ for the intellect ($\nu o \tilde{v} \varsigma$), should have got into a difficulty at this point in carrying through his view does not affect the argument.

other sort of orderliness." [1] This is, of course, the reason why Aristotle has no difficulty in using his theory of the soul as a basis for theories of perception, of moral training, of citizenship. It is a theory drawn to the proportions of the actual, as well as of the " good ", life for human beings, concretely taken in a concrete world. But compared with traditional modern psychology, other than behaviourism of the Holtian kind, Aristotle's theory strikes us as almost alien for two reasons. One is that it is wholly free from the obsession of the problem of the relation of body to soul, conceived as two disparate " substances ". The other is that it lacks the individualistic note of introspection, and has no term equivalent to " consciousness ".

Consciousness and the body-soul dualism owe their central position in so much of modern thought chiefly to Descartes. This is not to deny that Descartes, in his concept of mind as a *res cogitans,* substantially distinct from body as a *res extensa,* was the heir of centuries of scholastic thought. But it would be irrelevant here to trace how, through the influence of Christianity, carrying on and gathering up kindred tendencies in Greek and Eastern thought, the dualism of " flesh " and " spirit " was developed into a metaphysics of two substances, or how the religious individual's preoccupation with the state of his soul, in respect of sin and salvation, gave rise to that inwardness and self-analysis which prepared the way for the attitude of introspection.[2] Suffice it to say, that when Descartes laid down his famous *cogito ergo sum;* defined the soul as the substance which is conscious; and which, moreover, is conscious, in the first instance, only of itself and its " ideas " but not of any real thing, be it its own body or God, he definitely established the " subjective " point of view, and

---

[1] E. B. Holt, *loc. cit.,* p. 58 (slightly abbreviated in quotation).
[2] St. Augustine's influence on this development is especially marked.

fixed that gulf between a mind and its body, as well as between a mind and the real world " outside ", which it has taken centuries of philosophical argument to break down again. Indeed, what Descartes did was even more fundamental than this. For actually, his appeal to *cogitatio* or consciousness, was an appeal to *self-consciousness,* but, owing to the exclusion, not only of the body and the corporeal world generally, but also of the social world of other selves, it was an empty and abstract self-consciousness to which he appealed—a self-consciousness reduced to bare immediacy. Descartes' method of doubt, together with his desperate shifts for justifying the belief in the existence of " real " things corresponding to the " ideas " in our minds, shows that it is really he to whom modern philosophy owes the recognition of immediate experience, or data, and the problem of " transcendence ".[1] The self, or ego, existence of which is assured by the *cogito ergo sum,* is not the concrete self, conscious of itself as a member of a physical and social world, but a mere synonym for immediate experience, for *this present* feeling, *this present* thought, *etc.* So far those critics are right who urge that Descartes was entitled to say, not *cogito,* but only *cogitatur.* The personal pronoun here covers the ambiguity pointed out above.[2]

This is not to deny the value of Descartes' influence on philosophy in that he emancipated natural science from the animism with which in scholastic speculation it was still infected. But in treating living bodies, even the human body, physically regarded as mere machines, he set the fashion of reducing biology to physics; he bequeathed to psychology

[1] Hume deepened both the recognition and the problem in the ultra-empirical setting of his own analysis. It is characteristic that modern thinkers occupied with the same problem, like Bertrand Russell, have affinities with both Hume and Descartes. The deeper affiliations cut across the current superficial classifications into Empiricist and Rationalist.
[2] See pp. 223, 4.

and philosophy the body-soul problem; he burdened theory of knowledge with the dualism of intra-mental ideas and extra-mental things; he divorced and isolated each individual mind alike from other minds and from the common world; he destroyed for psychology all chance of a concrete analysis of human minds by dividing the living man not only between a soulless body and a bodyless soul, but by dividing the soul further between a metaphysical, non-empirical " substance ", and an abstract self-consciousness whittled down to the bare data of immediate experience. As far as any single thinker can be called so, he is the father of all evil in modern philosophy.

Fortunately, these errors acted as challenges and stimuli to thought and thus prepared the way for most of the constructive philosophy and psychology of modern times. On its logical or epistemological side, Descartes' concept of consciousness, through the problem of transcendence, led, *via* Hume, to Kant's re-discovery of *judgment* (instead of *idea*) as the clue to the analysis of knowledge. On its psychological side, his concept of consciousness made possible the contributions of introspective psychology, though these were loaded, from the pressure of their initial setting, with three defects: (a) a tendency to sensationalistic associationism; (b) a complete ignoring of the motor or behaviour aspect of mind; (c) a leaning towards either epiphenomenalism or parallelism as the relation of soul to body, with the result that consciousness, whether as thought or will, ceases to be an effective factor in conduct or evolution.

The inevitable reaction to these fictions is represented, partly by McDougall's return to an animistic (*i.e.*, spiritual substance) theory of mind and an interactionist theory of the relation of mind and body, partly by Bergson's theory of the *élan vital* and his peculiar theory of the relation of mind and body in *Matter and Memory*.

But the real saving of mind requires neither an *anima* nor an *élan vital*. What it does require is that we should undo Descartes' abstractions without surrendering that advance in inwardness and self-analysis, which has come to character- ise modern men in direct proportion to the increasing com- plexity of modern life, with its increasing stress and conflict of spiritual values. Descartes' *cogito,* so far as it does stand for a human being's consciousness of himself, is but the highly attenuated reflection in theory of the characteristi- cally modern feeling for personality, *i.e.,* of the individual's sense of his own value; of his uniqueness; of his " rights ", not only as a human being but as the person he is; of his moral autonomy as a rational being; of a world open to his self-expression, in science, in art, in industry. But a human mind, thus conceived, can neither be divorced from the body in which it is very literally " embodied ", and through which alone it is actual and effective, nor from the natural or social environment from which it draws its " contents " and which, by its responses, it modifies and helps to make or mar. The modern Aristotelianism of the behaviourists carries us a long way in this desired direction, and so does the concept of consciousness as, in respect of its contents, a " cross- section of the universe ". But to the element of truth in the emphasis on inwardness and subjectivity this " objective " view hardly does full justice. What seems required is a concept of mind, not so much merely as a " cross-section " of the universe, but as a *focus,* or *centre,* of experiences of the universe—a " subject " (in Hegel's sense of the term), not a substance; a new power, one might almost say, evolved in the world, endowed with the function of bringing past ex- perience to bear on the interpretation of present data, of planning and guiding action in proportion to knowledge, of controlling desire and seeking new truth, of enjoying beauty, of loving and hating, of serving and fighting, of coöperating with its fellows and of persecuting them, of ascending, in short, to all the heights and falling to all the depths which men and women know to lie within the compass of human nature.

The crucial facts which our modern Aristotelians do not yet cover with such meanings as they have been able to give to their terms " behaviour " and " cross-section of the universe ", are precisely those for which, on the whole Aristotle's νοῦς stands. No doubt, the principle holds that the central nervous system provides for all the achievements of νοῦς, but this is not equivalent to a behaviouristic analysis of, say, the logical operations which result in the formulation of a scientific theory—say of behaviourism it-self—or the creative thinking of an artist, or constructive statesmanship, or great administrative and organising achievements in business. No doubt the body is concerned and the environment to which the body, or rather the nerv-ous system, selectively responds; no doubt, too, past re-sponses have their influence. But with all this, we are still far from having rendered in " objective " terminology the secret of inventiveness, creativeness, and all manner of con-structive thinking and doing. It seems as if, in the main, this could only be done, as many philosophers have tried, and are trying, to do it, by direct analysis of these activities and achievements in their *logical* character. In fact, do not all considerations point towards the need of acknowledg-ing minds or souls as unique concentrations of elements of the universe, infinitely diverse in range and variety of elements concentrated, and fluctuating in power of dealing with them, but, at their best, able to elicit from the materials focused perhaps a new scientific theory, perhaps a plan for an adventure, a business enterprise, a social reform, per-haps a new thrill of beauty to be enjoyed and communicated through a work of art?

The " saving of the mind " means, at its fullest, the saving of appearances such as these.   The extent to which these familiar facts are ignored by much current theory is the measure of its failure to be equal to its opportunities.

Note on the Theory of Knowledge

(See p. 206)

The name of epistemology has not unjustly become a by-word for all that is least reputable in philosophy, for all the arid dialectics and idle hair-splitting over fictitious problems which are, proverbially, the philosopher's besetting temptation.   Even after we have successfully disentangled ourselves from the old dualism of ideas and objects, intra-mental thoughts and extra-mental things, we are still confronted by a perplexing variety of analyses of the " knowing-process " or the " knowledge-situation ".   But what is not always clearly seen is that this variety of analyses, with all the impatient argument at cross-purposes to which it gives rise, is here, as always, a symptom of logical instability of concepts, of the criss-crossing of inconsistent points of view.   In fact, problems may be put under the same heading of " knowledge ", and yet be discussed from widely different points of view, i.e., in contexts, and on the basis of assumptions, utterly disparate.

We shall do something towards threading our way through the maze, if we distinguish at least two angles from which, in recent philosophical literature, the problem of knowledge has been formulated and discussed.

(1) We may start out by saying that knowing is a specific activity of certain kinds of animals (including the human animal), and that, like other activities, such as eating or walking or talking, it must be observed and studied by taking typical cases of it.   This way of approach is often called " empirical " and " scientific ".   It certainly takes for granted the point of view of biology.   It places knowing in a biological context, interprets it as one phase of the living creature's commerce with its environment.   The " cognitive relation " is similarly interpreted.   The creature, through its mind, is the knower; the environment, with more or less selection, is the object, or known.

Alternatively, with less explicit emphasis on the biological setting, but still fundamentally with the same orientation, we may ask what a given mind knows, where " knowing " means simply " being aware of ", in the widest sense. It means asking, What is in X's mind? What is X perceiving, thinking, imagining? To say that this question is largely answerable by observation, by watching the " responses " of the " knower " to his environment, is, granting the biological setting, plausible enough. And if, in addition to observing the knower, the observer understands the knower's language, the limits of the observer's own mind are the only limits to his finding out what the other knows. In short, if by something being known we mean merely its being " in ", or " present to " somebody's mind—very literally some body's mind, for the " body " is the " subject " on this view [1]— the problem of knowledge admits, in this form, of a solution in terms of the knower's behaviour (including his language) towards his environment. His mind, his consciousness, his knowledge will be a " cross-section " of the universe, consisting of those elements of the universe to which the knower's nervous system specifically responds. Throughout this way of putting, and solving, the problem of knowledge, nothing more is, clearly, in question than a stock-taking, so to speak, of the contents of a knower's mind, considered as a selection from the contents of the universe at large. With the virtues of such a view, as providing a delightfully " realistic " escape from the toils of " subjective idealism ", we are not here concerned. All that interests us is to distinguish this type of theory of knowledge from another one which is quite differently oriented.

To this second theory we are led, not by seeking to distinguish what, out of the total universe, is and what is not object for a given mind, but by seeking to distinguish between " opinion " and " knowledge ", or, better still, between truth and error. The problem here is not one of stock-taking; of noting, or inferring, a given person's awareness of this, or failure to be aware of that. It is a problem of evaluation: is what he [2] is aware of " really " or " truly " so? Is it what he believes it to be? Even this way of putting it is still misleading, at any rate for any

---

[1] E. B. Holt, *Response and Cognition,* in *The Freudian Wish,* p. 174. See also above, pp. 237, 8.

[2] The " he ", of course, of this question may be " I ". Do I *know?*= Is it *really* so, where " so "=as I perceive and judge it to be.

one who should throughout keep the emphasis on " he ", on some
" particular " mind. For the real point of this second kind of
theory of knowledge is, not to find a general formula defining
the conditions under which independent reals become objects of
somebody's apprehension or contents of some mind, but to discuss the character (or " what ") of the real world from the angle
of the question, whether it truly is what it is judged, or believed,
or assumed, to be. Our topic of investigation is not what is
de facto " in ", or " before ", a given mind. Our topic is judgments, theories, beliefs, and the grounds on which their claim
to be true, and to constitute " knowledge " because they are true,
may be justified. We are to deal, not with " ideas ", as distinct
from " real things ", but with real things as they are perceived
and conceived to be. A theory of knowledge of this sort will find
its " typical cases " of knowledge in any systematic body of judgments such as the natural sciences, and it will be entirely indifferent to the question whether a particular scientist happens, at
the moment, to be noticing a particular fact, or to be thinking
of a particular theory. It will examine the logical structure of
the sciences, point out their dominant concepts, evaluate their
success as attempts at the systematisation and interpretation of
empirical data, estimate their degree of abstractness, and so forth.
With individual minds, as properties or activities of animals or
human beings, taken biologically in their environment, it is not
concerned. Rather is it concerned with the nature of the universe or of " reality ",[1] approached from the only possible angle
of the logical adequacy, or truth, of the judgments or beliefs
which in systematic form sum up what the data, synthetically
used, reveal of its constitution and character. It is concerned
with knowledge, not with knowers, with science, not with scientists. And when it says " knowledge ", or " science " it means
the world as known, *i.e.*, the world as it is judged to be in judgments which, like scientific theories, have within certain fields
made good their claim to be true. Of course, we can, if we
please, be interested in scientific theories, or discoveries, as incidents in the personal history of great scientists, just as we rightly
honour such men for having " added to knowledge ". But to
the main problem of theory of knowledge this is irrelevant. What
matters is not the fact that somebody accepts a theory but

[1] See the argument of Essay IV.

whether that theory is true. And, again, it is not the details of theory which matter, but the fundamental, or, in our language, " dominant " concepts. Theory of knowledge, somewhat like Kant's *Critique of Pure Reason*, but without the latter's entanglement with " consciousness-as-such ", asks whether the general character and logical framework of the world are what scientific, moral, religious judgments declare it to be. This situation is obscured by the necessity which none of us can escape of relying on some one else's authority in matters in which we cannot get knowledge at first hand. Then the fact that so-and-so, believed to be an authority, thinks so, is important as evidence for its being so. But the authority may err, not only in detail—other workers in the same field will sooner or later correct his mistakes—but by extending the fundamental concepts of his field of knowledge beyond the boundaries within which they are valid. And then arises precisely that problem of the systematic order of the universe as a whole [1] which has to be faced, whether we call the attempt to solve it " theory of knowledge " or " metaphysics ".

Let us push this contrast a little further. The verb " to know " is ambiguous, in that its uses range from the mere affirmation of awareness to the emphatic affirmation of truth. When I say, in common intercourse, that I " know " a thing, I may mean no more than that I am aware of it, in the sense that I have witnessed it, read it, been told it, *etc.* Or it may mean that emphatically the thing *is* so, that my judgment or belief that it is so *is true*, not because it is " mine ", but because there is good evidence to show that it is so and not otherwise. Of course, I can appeal to these grounds only so far as I am aware of them. Still my claim that I " know ", *i.e.*, that what I think is true,

[1] Is it still necessary, at this time of day, to remind critics of the phrases " as a whole " or " point of view of the whole ", that they miss the point if they keep interpreting these phrases in terms of their own contrast between the illimitable universe and the narrow human mind? Every educated man, including the critics, thinks of the universe partly in terms of the fundamental concepts of the various natural sciences, partly in terms of moral, religious, æsthetic concepts. Every judgment he accepts as true introduces, or implies, some one or more of these concepts, and claims that reality, in one of its aspects at any rate, is so. Here, surely are enough materials out of which to try to form a " whole ". How? is no doubt a matter of experiment. But those who have never tried have no right to say " it can't be done ": and those who have tried and failed, should not stand in the way of those who want to try again.

rests not on the mere fact that I happen to be aware of both grounds and conclusion, but on the fact that the grounds logically support the conclusion, that there is an "objective" relation between them which would be equally authoritative for any other thinker. This is the factor of "objective control" so much emphasised by many writers on logic and theory of knowledge. Obviously to the study of it the fact that it appears in individual minds is irrelevant, though such appearance is the *sine qua non* of its being accessible to study at all.[1]

Another way of putting the contrast between the two types of theory of knowledge is to say that the concept of the "cognitive relation", as a relation between knowing mind and object known, belongs essentially to the former type, and *not* to the latter at all. So far as the second type of theory can be said to have any concern at all with any sort of relation which might be called "cognitive", such concern would be either with the relation, if any, between datum" or "fact", and "judgment" or "theory"; or else, after the manner of F. H. Bradley, with the adequacy of "discursive thought", *i.e.*, of all relational concepts whatsoever.

At any rate, the present chaos in epistemology will not disappear, until it is clearly recognised that some such sorting out of problems, as we have above suggested, is absolutely necessary.[2] We can take human beings as known to psychology and physiology, bring them as an animal species within the field known to zoölogy and biology, place them in an environment as known

---

[1] The fact that the meaning of "knowledge" ranges from awareness at one end, which if we like to say so, is "subjective", to truth or fact, at the other, which are "objective", has many curious consequences. It accounts, for example, for the oft-felt difficulty of distinguishing between truthfulness and truth. "Many people cannot see the difference between impeaching their argument and impeaching their veracity" (Bosanquet, *Essentials of Logic*, p. 25). Again, in debate, it is not easy to attack a theory without seeming to attack those who hold it. However objective and impersonal the criticism may be in tone, there is but a thin line between the imputation of error and the imputation of stupidity, or of bias amounting to intellectual dishonesty. At best, though the dispute be all about objective truth between two lovers of it, it is a measuring of minds and personalities against each other; and "personalities" are apt to result where the fate of reputations trembles in the balance—a good example, we must suppose, of what Hegel calls "die List der Vernunft".

[2] An essay in the second volume of *Studies* will give a fuller exposition and defence of the above view, especially in its historical context.

to physics, chemistry and the rest of the natural sciences. Between a human being thus known and an environment thus known we can, then, to our hearts' content construct a " cognitive relation ", in terms of which we, onlooker-wise, can say just what of the environment our human knower perceives, remembers, *etc.* It is a harmless amusement, and even an addition to knowledge. But what it is not is a theory of knowledge in the sense in which such a theory should seek to answer the question, how far all this apparatus of sciences which provides the setting for the cognitive relation can claim to be knowledge, *i.e.*, what grounds there are for thinking that the universe is really, or truly, such as the sciences, between them, declare it to be, and what is to be done with the evidence of all the modes of experience which the sciences ignore—with all the bricks which the scientific builders reject as not fitting into their pattern.

It is only fair to acknowledge that the doctrines of the various neo-realistic schools of thought, however much they may differ from each other or from the position maintained above, may certainly claim one great and undeniable merit, *viz.*, that in their polemics against epistemology and " idealism " (or what they take to be idealism), and in their efforts to disentangle objective reality from the " accident " of being known by someone, they are at least clearing the way for themselves to a *Gegenstandstheorie* which bears unmistakably all the marks of a return to metaphysics.[1] Are we venturing on an unsafe prophecy when we say that their metaphysical interests will compel them, sooner or later, to take up the considerations which yield theory of knowledge in our second sense?

[1] The most recent example is E. G. Spaulding's *The New Rationalism* which has come to my notice too late for detailed reference in the course of these essays.

CHAPTER IX

THE SELF IN SELF-CONSCIOUSNESS

THROUGHOUT the preceding essay, it will have been noticed how often problems of " mind " touched so closely on problems of " self " as to be almost inseparable. It will help us to open up our present topic, if we recapitulate these contacts.

The most obvious of them is incidental to the familiar view that each mind is certainly conscious of itself, whether or no it be conscious of anything beyond itself. The upholders of this view might even, if it were put to them, be found willing to make this the defining characteristic of a mind. Self-knowledge, in the sense of self-awareness, they might say, is the essential prerogative of a mind: only a mind has this unique relation to itself.

But the exact meaning of this view is far from obvious, however plausible the language may sound. It appears to identify being a mind with being a self, being conscious with being self-conscious. This identification, however, may well make us pause. We shall hardly accept it in the sense that to be conscious is the same as to be conscious of being conscious; *i.e.*, it is not " consciousness ", as an abstract *quale*, of which it can be intended to say that it is aware of itself and of nothing else. But if we turn from consciousness in the abstract to the objects of which we are conscious, the suggestion that whatever any mind is conscious of is a piece, so to speak, of itself, comes to all our ordinary habits of thinking with the effect of violent paradox. This paradox is but intensified when it is defended, along the

traditional lines, by turning every object into a complex of
"mental" sensations or ideas. For this defence cuts clear
across all the ordinary classifications of the objects we are
conscious of, as "minds" and "bodies", or "particulars"
and "universals", and so forth. It cuts across—indeed, it
threatens to make meaningless—even the familiar distinction between me and you, what is my self and what is your
self. If it is of the essence of a mind to be aware of itself,
and of nothing but itself, the whole status of the "other"
becomes exceedingly problematical. Not only what is other
than mind (non-mental), *i.e.*, the physical world, is affected,
but, even more sweepingly, what is other than *this* mind,
i.e., other *minds*, other *selves*. This situation led us to
recognise as one of the chief sources of trouble in the theory
of mind, consciousness, self, the fact that these terms, and
especially the pronouns of the first person singular, are used,
at one end of the pole, as pure demonstratives referring to
immediate experience or feeling, and, at the other end, in
a social context in which each mind or self not only is, but
also recognises itself to be, surrounded by, and related to,
other minds and selves, as well as non-mental objects. Psychology, like every other science, is a *social* phenomenon.
The knowledge, *i.e.*, true theory of what mind is, which it
seeks to offer, is attained by the coöperation of different
minds, communicating to each other, in fact pooling and
even correcting, their observations and theories. For this
to be possible, minds must be capable of becoming "common" and "public" objects to each other, and "objective"
psychology has here its justification. At the same time,
each mind has an individuality of its own, which not
only enables it to be discriminated as one "object" from
others of the same sort, but which enables it also to make
its own distinctive contribution to the social intercourse of
minds in general, and in particular to the coöperation of

minds in the building up of knowledge, whether of minds or of anything else. Here lies the value of introspection; here, too, the relative justification of the "privacy" view.

In short, to sum up, the dialectical difficulties which we had found surrounding the theory of mind, derive, so we now see, from the intensified difficulties surrounding the theory of self. Psychology, as a social phenomenon, is possible only for minds individually capable of self-consciousness. And self-consciousness, as we may now put it, is *double-edged*. It has its basis, on the one hand, in immediate feeling, this-here-now. But it requires no less, and is sustained and developed only by, the varying relations of each self, not only to the "not-self" in general, but to specific *other* selves in social intercourse. If we try to whittle down the self to mere immediate feeling, the very distinction between self and not-self, or other self, disappears, and nothing is left but the general contrast between datum and nondatum. If, on the other hand, we go for the concrete self, as known to itself *and* to others, we not only find that data are transcended,[1] but that this transcending is a social or coöperative process. Moreover, it is social or coöperative at, broadly, two levels. One is the level of ordinary social intercourse in all its diverse practical sides: the rubbing of mind against mind, the various mutual influences and contacts, the actions and reactions which are constantly forming each of us, the play of self against others, friendly or hostile. The other is the level of reflective theory, at which minds who have at the former level learned to recognise themselves, and each other, as selves, take stock of this whole situation and try to work out a systematic and comprehensive theory of it.

---

[1] Whether we describe this transcending as inference, or construction, or interpretation, or synthesis, makes no difference.

Not the least of the difficulties which stand in the way of such an attempt arises from the elusive and shifting meanings of " self-consciousness ". Abstractly, it is tempting to argue that self-hood (being a self) must precede self-consciousness (being conscious of one's self). There must be a self, it may be said, before there can be consciousness of one, but experience appears to show that one's self is not simply a datum, but grows and develops, one might almost say lives, in all the nuances and oscillations of self-consciousness. Yet, on the other hand, we want to distinguish being conscious from being self-conscious. Merely to have experiences is not the same thing as to have experiences into the pattern of which the difference between self and not-self enters.

This last point, perhaps, gives us the clue which leads to the solution. Is it not best to say that a mind is not a " self " in the pregnant sense, until its experiences take on the characteristic structure of a distinction between self and not-self? To be merely conscious, then, will mean to have experiences into which, for all that they are mine, no trace of a contrast between me and not-me enters. To be self-conscious will be to have experiences marked by this contrast. And only when, and in so far as, this contrast is felt, or is capable of being felt, will it be safe to say that there is a self to be conscious of.

Selfhood and self-consciousness thus hang very closely together and both, at the same time, imply a social medium, *i.e.*, effective relationship to other selves. Moreover, on this view we can further distinguish between self-consciousness and self-knowledge. The latter belongs definitely to the level of reflective theory. It consists of one's own judgments about one's self. It implies that one makes of one's self an object of attention and study. The judgments of explicit self-knowledge require to be distinguished from all the countless judgments which are mere expressions of self-consciousness. Most of the judgments of current conversation in which " I " figures as subject, are spontaneous self-revelations rather than critical self-judgments. They belong to the give-and-take of social intercourse. They are not made with scientific interest in the effort after self-knowledge. Relatively to self-knowledge, they are data—materials for a study of self. It is clear from this that self-knowledge enjoys no special prerogative of infallibility. The theoretical judgments I make about myself, do not, as a class, exhibit any marked superiority in respect of freedom from error. And, apart from self-deception, it is a far from easy task to make the whole of one's self effectively an object of study. This is not only because in some respects others are in a better position to know me as I really am, than I am myself, but even more because it is hard for reflection to comprehend and order the endless ramifications and fluctuations of self-consciousness. For the line between Self and Not-Self, or Other Self, is not a fixed, but a shifting, one; and elements which in one context fall on the side of the self, may be excluded from it in another. There are even experiences in which the distinction between self and other, whilst still felt, is yet transcended in a union of self and other, an identification of self with other. It was, we may suppose, the thought of these fluctuations of self-consciousness, and the consequent difficulty of " giving an account " of one's self, which moved Mr. Bradley to write: " We are all sure that we exist, but in what sense and what character—as to that we are most of us in helpless uncertainty and in blind confusion. And so far is the self from being clearer than things outside us that, to speak generally, we never know what we mean when we talk of it ".[1] The difficulty is akin to that which, by common consent, be-

[1] *Appearance and Reality*, ch. ix, p. 76.

sets all attempts at an " objective " history of contemporary events.

Our argument sums up to this: Self-consciousness is the name for all forms of experience the structure of which exhibits the characteristic distinction of Self and Other. Such experiences are the source of, and furnish the data for, explicit self-knowledge. They bear witness to the existence of self in a world other than it, and containing other selves in various relations to it. More particularly, self-consciousness is the general form of experience for a self in social intercourse with other selves. If there is a level of mental life at which experiences are not characterised by any sense of distinction between self and not-self, it is better not to speak of a " self " at that stage, though once the distinction has come to be felt and the self come to be recognised as against the other, these un-self-conscious experiences can be constructively affiliated to those marked by self-consciousness.

A last source of difficulty demands to be briefly dealt with. Just as psychology is not concerned with a particular mind for its own sake, least of all with the psychologist's own mind, but studies minds of all sorts as furnishing the materials for a knowledge of the nature of mind as such, in its different forms under different conditions, so our interest here is in " the " self. So far as each of us supplies data for such a study from his own self, the accounts of particular selves have to be stripped of their autobiographical character and generalised. Here, as elsewhere, every particular is a " this-such ", an instance of a universal; and it is as an instance bringing new knowledge of the universal, that the particular, even in extreme and abnormal cases, has its value for science. We come here upon yet another way in which self and self-consciousness turn out to be double-edged. For the terms point, on the one hand, to the extreme of individual uniqueness, " self-identity ", differentiation from all that is " other " and " not-me ". Yet, on the other, within varying limits, what is true of one self is true of others. And more than that: selves do not merely form a class of similars, but as members of communities supplement and, as it were, complete one another in every coöperative enterprise or achievement which it is beyond the power of any single self to plan or achieve by itself. The very uniqueness of each self and their differences from each other become positively significant through membership in a common life, so far at least as differentiation of function corresponds to the differentiation in character and ability of the constituent selves. In a very curious and striking way this is illustrated by the meaning of the personal pronoun, in the first person singular and plural. The speech of ordinary intercourse is " personal " and self-revealing, or self-communicating, to a high degree. No other word, we can safely say, is used with such frequency as the personal pronoun, I, and its derivatives. This fact bears witness to the centrality of the " self-other " structure of experience. This does not mean, of course, that we are always " thinking of ourselves " in a reprehensible sense, or that there is no such thing as disinterested interest in the " Other ", be it the physical world, or fellow-men. But it does mean that the self-not-self form is dominant in most of human experience. Thence results the curious ambiguity in the meaning of " I ", which is unlike the ambiguity of any other word in the language. " I " is, of course, in the first instance a denotative or demonstrative term, a label for self-reference, a signal for directing the attention of others to oneself. But it differs from other demonstratives in that it has meaning only as applied by each speaker exclusively to himself. Other demonstratives may mean the same object in application for different speakers, as, *e.g.*, when you and I both refer to " this page." But when I say " I ", and when you say " I ", the same word means a different self to each of us. " I " is as exclusive a symbol in application as a proper name, but with this difference that it is " proper " only in each person's application of it by himself to himself. I is a *common* device for *exclusive* self-reference by *individual* selves. But just because it is a common device, just because each self refers to itself as " I ", differentiates itself from " you ", recognises community with others in " we ", this common function can be studied as a universal, under the name, or description, of " the self " (the " Ego ", or, as James has it, the " Me "). At the same time, our whole argument makes it clear how one-sided and fragmentary any account of the self is bound to be which ignores the experiences expressed by each individual self in the " we " form of language. The plural of the personal pronoun is standing testimony, too often neglected by philosophers as well as by psychologists, to the fact that the identity of individual selves is compatible with their functioning as constituents of identities (wholes, systems) of a higher order, and that these relationships are recognised, and expressed in language, as characteristic of what are perhaps the most important forms of self-conscious experience.

The " saving of the self " calls, not so much for a definition of the self, as for a theory exhibiting the self, enabling it to be appreciated, we might almost say perceived, within its proper context and in the typical range of its manifestations. This task we can best attempt by dealing, first, with the " constituents " of the self; next, with personal identity; and, lastly, with the fluctuations of self-consciousness. Throughout, our task demands the synthesis of two points of view. Just as in dealing with " mind ", we found it necessary to combine an "objective" with a "subjective" approach, the evidence of the spectator with the evidence of introspection, so in dealing with the self there are two sources of judgments. One consists of the utterances, naïve or reflective, which every one makes about himself; the other of the judgments uttered by others, or implicit in their attitude and behaviour.[1]

(1) In order to appreciate the movement from an abstract to a concrete theory, we cannot do better than begin our discussion of the constituents of the Self with the crude body-soul metaphysics which still do duty for a theory of the self in popular thought.

Dr. J. McT. E. McTaggart, in his discussion of immortality,[2] calls attention to the awkwardness of the current phrase, I "have" a soul, suggesting, as it does, that "my" soul is something I own, a piece of property almost, which is no part, or constituent of me, its owner. His point is

---

[1] It need hardly be said that the two sets of judgments which we are here distinguishing in respect of their source and point of view, do not fall apart as they do in the following passage which is typical of a theory, the prevalence of which has done much to retard the development of a concrete study of both mind and self. "Suppose, then, I could remove the brain-cap of one of you, and expose the brain in active work,—as it doubtless is at this moment. Suppose, further, that my senses were absolutely perfect, so that I could see everything that was going on there. What would I see? Only decompositions and recompositions, molecular agitations and vibrations; in a word, *physical* phenomena, and nothing else. There is absolutely nothing else there to see. But *you*, the subject of this experiment, what do *you* perceive? You perceive an entirely different set of phenomena; viz., consciousness,—thought, emotion, will; *psychical* phenomena; in a word, a self, a *person*. From the *outside* we see only physical, from the *inside* only psychical phenomena."—Quoted from Professor Joseph LeConte's comments on Royce's *Conception of God* (1895), pp. 43, 4. It need hardly be pointed out that, even from the "outside" there is more to be seen of a person's mind and self than is here conceded. And as for the "inside", let this experiment decide. Suppose, while Professor Le Conte was exposing the brain of some one, a third person removed the Professor's skull-cap and studied his brain, would the things which the Professor is seeing, the "molecular agitations" and the rest, thereby suddenly be transformed from "physical" into "psychical" phenomena?

[2] *Some Dogmas of Religion,* Ch. iii, p. 78.

that the immortality of my soul, if it really were thus different and separable from me, would be worthless. What interests us is the immortality of that which, saying " I ", means itself. The important question is not, Is my soul immortal? but, Am I immortal? Or, to put it differently, if my soul's immortality is the same thing as my immortality, then my soul is not something which I *have*, but something which I *am*. I am my soul: but to affirm this is, very obviously, to affirm a theory, to give an account of the nature of my " self "; and it is such a theory quite regardless of whether my soul, *i.e.*, myself, does or does not survive death.

Should the same conclusion be extended to the body? The phrase, I have a body, seems parallel to the phrase, I have a soul. Should it, too, be interpreted to mean, I *am* my body? This is, clearly, what is intended ordinarily by popular thought. " I am my body and my soul ", or, " my self consists of body and soul ", would fairly sum up its position. For even when it is said that I " have " body and soul, the " having " is intended to convey a relationship much more close and essential than mere ownership of things which I can acquire or lose, possess and use or give away and use up. A man, it will be urged, can be stripped of all his possessions, and still be himself. He can be divorced from all his associations to other human beings, to his home, his country, his church, and still retain his identity. But if, in fact or in hypothesis, you take his body from him or his soul, in either case is he destroyed. The remaining fragment, supposing anything to remain after the mutilation, is no longer what he, or any one else, would call his " self ". His body and his soul are the irreducible constituents of his " self ".

The above statement represents an attempt to set down in explicit terms the implicit metaphysics of current views concerning what a human being is essentially made of. If the statement strikes any reader as obvious and familiar, then this is so far testimony to the success of our attempt. But current thought is not so simple or self-consistent, as we have here made it out to be. Moral and religious teachings, to say nothing of metaphysical theories quite differently oriented, have passed as fragments, and streaks of tradition, and allusions in literature, at least into the average thought of educated people, and a very brief reflection will suggest questions to which the above statement can supply no answer, and theories which are inconsistent with it. If we try to hold to the view that a self consists of a body and a soul, such questions as: What is a body? What is a soul? How are they connected and related? cannot be put aside. On the other hand, there are plenty of theories which, whilst distinguishing no less sharply between body and soul, insist that the self is identical only with the soul, and that the body is not genuinely part of it at all. Most of these theories are inspired mainly by moral or religious motives, connected with beliefs in survival of death, pre-existence, re-incarnation. But recently the same position has been defended, in a purely scientific spirit on grounds of introspective analysis by Professor John Laird in his *Problems of the Self*.[1] And there are theories combining both motives, with much variation in detail, like Professor W. Mc-Dougall's " animistic " theory in *Body and Mind*, or Miss May Sinclair's vivacious argument, ranging from Samuel Butler and Freud to the mysticism of East and West, in *A Defence of Idealism*.

An exhaustive examination of all these experiments in speculation lies beyond the scope of this essay. But a few salient points require to be touched on, if we are

[1] For a review of this book by the writer, see *Philosophical Review*, vol. xxvii, no. 3, pp. 296-303.

to exhibit the contrast between abstract and concrete theories.

The best preparation for a critical appreciation of the body-and-soul theory of the self is to realise, not only how fully and adequately all that one feels, thinks, wills, does, can be expressed in terms which do not introduce the distinction of body and soul at all, but even more to what an extent the attempt to classify the elements of one's being under these two mutually exclusive heads cuts across the *felt unity* of the self. A trivial example may serve to bring out the point. Is it really satisfactory to analyse the experience of being bitten by a mosquito, by assigning the bite to the body and the itch to the soul? Emotions, again, resist equally the attempt to set them down exclusively either to the body or to the soul, and the attempt to divide their felt unity between the two. This, surely, is the plain moral of the James-Lange theory of emotion, which shows that what we feel are the physical disturbances, the beating of the heart, the sudden flush in the face, the shiver down the spine. Is it really possible to analyse voluntary activity, *e.g.*, the doing of one's work, on the scheme of a material body and an immaterial soul, mysteriously conjoined, somehow coöperating in the production of an intelligent, purposeful act? Take a man in a fight and split him up, if you can, with your body-soul theory, so as to show that his body does this and his soul does that. Take any desire, more especially a so-called "physical" desire; take hunger or sex and, once more, try your analysis honestly on the facts. If the body-and-soul theory holds, such a phrase as "bodily desire" is a contradiction in terms. For the desire will have to be assigned to the mind, and nothing strictly physical will enter into it, whilst the bodily state, correspondingly, must be taken as divorced from all consciousness. In being hungry, where is the line between body and mind? This point is not countered by the reminder that there is a hunger of the soul for righteousness as well as a hunger of the body for food. This merely shows that the self, being many-sided, hungers for many different things. It does not show that it is a compound of a material and an immaterial " substance ", somehow conjoined.

Our suggestion, then, is that the two-substance theory of the self is an artificial rendering of the ways in which a self actually experiences itself. But we ought not, for this reason, simply to condemn it without considering on their merits either the grounds which make the two-substance theory plausible, or recent attempts to reformulate and defend it.

The grounds which favour a dualistic theory of the self may be grouped as being either moral and religious, or else scientific.

There can be little doubt that the experience of moral conflict—of the self divided between, and torn by, desires, not only incompatible in execution, but opposed in moral value—has done much to confirm the antithesis of body and soul in popular thought. It would go beyond the evidence to say that in this conflict we have one of the original roots of the theory. But we can say that the conflict lends itself to formulation in terms of the theory, and thus in turn lends plausibility to the theory. More particularly when the conflict takes the form of an effort to resist a " temptation ", to prevent strong excitement or intense craving from passing into overt action, to maintain the supremacy of " will " or " reason " over " impulse " or " passion ", the antithesis of " flesh " and " spirit " springs readily to our lips. The task being primarily to restrain bodily movement, to repress a physical disturbance lest it burst into action, the power to control and oppose the body is naturally ascribed to something other than the body, though still part of the self. To interpret a conflict within the self as due to distinct substances, or forces, or, in the most attenuated version, faculties, is the natural procedure of primitive metaphysics. The experience is that I am trying to control myself, to do this rather than that, to refrain from doing what I know I ought not to do. The theory turns this into a struggle between my " spirit " and my " flesh ", ascribing failure to the " weakness " of the latter despite the " willingness " of the former. And it ends by differentiating body and soul so completely, that it becomes a wellnigh impossible task to explain how the one can influence or control the other at all. A genuine fact of moral experience has been translated into an abstract metaphysical scheme.

Moreover, it is not merely the experience of moral conflict which has exercised its influence on this development. There are also all the experiences which lead to the familiar estimates of the body as both the indispensable instrument of, and also a handicap to, the soul. Without it, the soul can effect nothing, yet with it, it can effect nothing perfectly. If we go behind the metaphors of instrument and handicap to the experiences crystallised in them, we see at once that education and self-education, training and learning, the acquisition and the practice of the skill to do something, characterise, in greater or less degree, every human life. From the infant's efforts to learn to walk, feed itself, clean itself, clothe itself; to talk, write, read, up to the mastery, later on, of special forms of manual skill, of special expertness in, and aptitude for, conducting industrial and commercial undertakings, or scientific researches, or any other human enterprise—the general task is to learn to do something and to do it well. Moreover, these doings have to be regulated and ordered, if room is to be found for them in life, compatibly with their relative urgency on the one side, and the resources of strength and time on the other. And, lastly, some of these activities not only stand higher in the scale of values than others, but are possible only if other activities are managed with strict economy. " Dissipation " not only disorganises life, but consumes the time and strength which ought to be given to doing more important things as excellently as one can. Now in all activities, from the manual to the most intellectual, the body is involved. There is no " doing " without it, there is no excellence of achievement attainable without training one's body, or without disciplining and ordering the needs and impulses which have their basis in its organisation. One might almost sum up the task of education, moral and intellectual, in the phrase " learning to make the most of one's body." Along this line we are led to the suggestion, which is in harmony with the conclusions of the preceding essay, that one of the best clues to the nature of soul or spirit is to think of them in terms of the activities which we have learned to perform, the excellence with which we habitually perform them, and the worth which belongs to them in an objective scale of values. From this angle we can understand how the body comes to be looked on as the instrument of the soul. And from this angle, too, we can understand why it should seem a handicap or obstacle. For training involves fatigue and pain which make it hard to persist. The needs of the organism, especially hunger and sex, with the enjoyment attendant upon their satisfaction, have legitimate claims, and yet make the ordering of life in subordination to higher values more difficult. Through the limitations of physical endowment, accomplishment tends to fall short of aspiration. If often we do less well than our best, and if the best we can do does not measure up to the ideally best we can conceive, the body tends to receive the blame. The "flesh" is either too weak to respond to the call of the "spirit", or else obstructs with rebellious desires of its own. Thence results the hostility to the body which marks the extreme forms of asceticism, the morbid delight in self-torture, the attempt to wrest spiritual perfection from self-inflicted pains and repressions. Rare as systematic self-persecution has become nowadays, yet the germ of it lurks in the theory that the body is a prison, or a tomb, from which the soul must seek escape; that the flesh, or, generalised, "matter", is the principle of evil and imperfection, and that goodness can be attained only by emancipation from it. Asceticism is but a perversely logical attempt to practise this emancipation here and now. But death, above all, has been seized upon by the imagination of mankind as the release of the soul from the bondage of the flesh, as the gateway to a glorified existence. In "shuffling off this mortal coil", we terminate the ill-assorted *mariage de convenance* of body and soul. Yet, though death, viewed thus, should be welcomed as a blessing, it is often dreaded and generally accounted an evil—an inconsistency of which the Fool in *Twelfth Night* makes pretty play: "The more fool, Madonna, to mourn for your brother's soul being in heaven".[1]

At the same time, a moment's reflection shows that the discarnate or disembodied soul, which is held to survive the dissolution of its partnership with the body, whereas the body—"dust unto dust"—is dispersed into its elements, must be something very different from the embodied self as others know it, or even as it knows itself. On the question of the evidence for survival, we shall have something to say presently. For the moment, we are interested in these speculations concerning the destiny of the soul, chiefly from the angle of the light they throw on the nature of the

[1] Act I, scene 5.

self. In detail the survival-beliefs have been variously elaborated. McTaggart's contention that the soul's survival of bodily death ought not to be considered without weighing also the possibility of pre-existence before birth, has much plausibility. And if once we consider this present incarnation as an interlude in discarnate existence, we can hardly refuse to consider also the hypothesis of many such interludes, *i.e.*, the theory of successive incarnations, in higher or lower forms according to the moral merit of this present life in the body; with final emancipation from the need of incarnation as the reward for distinguished purity and saintliness. However, whether we take such beliefs seriously, or reckon them among the curiosities of religious mythology, it is not wholly beside the point to consider what consequences for the theory of the self they would involve, if they were true. The important consequences turn on the separability of body and soul. It implies that the normal theory of the self as consisting of body and soul somehow conjoined, has to be modified so as to identify the self essentially with the soul. And, this done, the problem becomes one partly of the identity of the soul in its incarnate and discarnate conditions of existence, and partly of the possibility of self-identification or recognition. Self-identification, we may say at once, requires memory. Survival without memory would, in effect, be survival as a different person; or, at least, in the absence of memory my relation to a previous existence of my own would be like my relation to the life of another person of whose very existence I am ignorant. Pathological cases of complete loss of memory, or of " alternating personality ", appear to show this clearly. The evidence for memory of previous incarnations is scarce, and its truth will, in general, be unverifiable.[1]

[1] I cannot pretend to an extensive acquaintance with the literature, and Fielding Hall's account of such memory occurring not infrequently among the Burmese is the only definite reference I can now recall

It does not really help us in this situation to claim, with Samuel Butler, that the automatic completeness and facility of many reflexes and instinctive actions are explicable only on the assumption, that we remember them so well from having practised them through untold previous existences; or to support this claim, again with Butler, by an appeal to Weismann's theory of the continuity of the germ-plasm. For the germ-plasm is a physical thing and its continuity, or deathlessness, assuming this to be conceded by biologists, is certainly not the same thing as what is meant in our present context by the immortality of the soul or the self. And, further, even if heredity be a case of memory, we are still far from the recollection of specific acts and incidents in historically discriminated previous existences, which would be required for explicit self-identification. Nor is it easy to see how identity could be conclusively established from the point of view of other persons. In cases of " alternating personality ", as in law-cases turning on claims to identity, it is in the main the identity of the body, as seen by others, which guides us. And the medical analysis of psychopathic cases hardly as yet makes it possible to decide conclusively between the two hypotheses of " dissociation " of one self and of a multiplicity of selves or souls, genuinely distinct, yet inhabiting the same body. On the former view —on the whole, the more plausible—we are dealing with split-off fragments of one self. On the latter, we are back at something like the old concept of " possession ". At any rate, the spectator's task of establishing the identity of a soul, in abstraction from the body, is one of no small difficulty, especially when there is no memory of self-identifica-

(*The Soul of a Nation*, Ch. xxii). Kipling's *The Finest Story in the World* (originally published in *Many Inventions*) is a good example of the literary exploitation of the possibility. The fact that memory is lacking is recognised by the provision in the myth of Er, according to which souls, prior to re-incarnation, drink of the river of Forgetfulness (Plato, *Republic*, Book X).

tion on the part of the self under observation to assist him.

It is also worth considering what a profound difference it would make to any one's experience of himself to be separated from his present body, or to be re-incarnated in another body, possibly not human at all. The change might well be so complete as, in fact, not only to destroy the possibility of self-identification, but identity itself. It is impossible, of course, to picture to oneself in imagination what disembodied existence, in terms of actual experience, would be like. The elimination of all the experiences which we refer to our bodies—and they are interwoven even with our most intellectual activities and our most spiritual moods—would hardly leave us, in any intelligible sense, the same.[1]

It may, of course, be retorted by some, that whatever the evidence for pre-existence or re-incarnation may be, we do have empirical and conclusive evidence both for the fact of survival and for the manner of existence after death. Taking this contention at its best, *i.e.*, as referring to such evidence (communication through the trance-utterances or automatic scripts of mediums, materialisations, cross-correspondence experiments, *etc.*,) as the Societies for Psychical Research have collected and sifted, the claim to conclusiveness appears to overshoot the mark. It is certainly true that many sitters are fully convinced of the identity of the

---

[1] It is perhaps worth while to remark that the teaching of the Christian churches gives by no means unqualified support to the notion of survival as a disembodied soul. Religious tradition on the matter is, indeed, as confused as the popular thought which it has so largely helped to form. Most of the tortures of hell, as painted by the imagination even of a Dante, would have few terrors for a disembodied soul. More to the point, however, for our argument, is the fact that, side by side with the belief in discarnate survival, there is taught the resurrection of the body. Theologically, this is important because it admits the body which is the principle of evil, to " salvation ". Philosophically, it seems to concede that without the body the self is not complete.

departed spirits who claim to be communicating, with, or without, the mediation of a " control ". It is true also that many of the investigators are, like Sir Oliver Lodge, trained in the scientific management of experiments and cannot *a priori* be accused of unscientific credulity. But, on the other hand, it is also true that other investigators, no less careful in method, and perhaps more cautious in hypothesis, are far from convinced, and that the telepathy-hypothesis has not been finally disposed of, though it is certainly becoming strained. But here, again, the crucial point for the establishment of the " spirit "-hypothesis is the trustworthiness of the identification. Considering that among the communicating spirits are some who claim to be identical with such well-known men, recently deceased, as William James, or R. Hodgson, or F. W. H. Myers, it is perhaps surprising that it should be so difficult to establish identity beyond doubt. The mere assertion of the alleged spirit, of course, goes by itself for nothing. Its truth precisely is the thing to be tested and established. The verisimilitude of the communication (its being " in character ") is liable to be very differently estimated by different observers. Specific memories are either unverifiable, and therefore useless as evidence, or verifiable, and thus open to the alternative explanation of telepathy. In general, telepathy may cover many things which can be trustworthily shown not to have been in the medium's normal knowledge. Experiments such as the attempt to communicate after death the contents of a sealed message deposited before death, have hitherto failed completely.[1] If, however, spirit-communication is a fact, it seems plausible to allow full weight to the contention, often occurring in the communications, that the communicators are severely handicapped by the limitations of the instrument (the medium) through which they have to

---

[1] See Sir Oliver Lodge, *The Survival of Man*, Ch. viii, pp. 121 ff.

work.[1] All in all, it hardly seems safe to say more than (a) that a body of evidence has been collected which demands, and fully justifies, further investigation; (b) that its proper theoretical interpretation is still open, the investigator's inclination towards spirits or telepathy being in part determined by what he would prefer to believe or not to believe; and (c) that the evidence, even when taken as favouring the spirit-hypothesis, is of doubtful value either for religion or for the consolation of the sorrowing survivors. Opinions on this last point are bound to differ. But, at any rate, it seems clear that the lover who cherishes the belief that his beloved still lives, does not need, nor commonly seek, communications to sustain either his love or his assurance. And it may be doubted whether many men would really look forward to engaging in this kind of communication after their death, even were they convinced that it were possible. There is something in the view of a critic of one of Sir Oliver Lodge's books, who said that if Sir Oliver's theory were true, it would " add a new terror to death ".

It must be admitted that scientific and philosophical orthodoxies have alike looked askance at these investigations and the speculative hypotheses they suggest. This attitude it is not possible to justify, even though it must also be admitted that both the spirit- and the telepathy-hypotheses, if either of them were to be currently accepted, would require wide-reaching modifications in our present theories of the human self. Whilst leaving this possibility distinctly open, we shall presently find, in a return to the facts of self-consciousness from which, above, we started out on the examination of the body-soul theory, a way to a more em-

[1] In detail, the evidence is rich in opportunities for ingenious speculation, e.g., concerning the limitation of the spirit by the medium's imagery and vocabulary; or concerning the physical appearance of the spirit in materialisation. See the publications of the Psychical Research Societies.

pirical study of the self—a study based on normal introspection and observation of selves in the normal setting and activities of ordinary experience, hence free from the toils of the body-soul problem in its bearing on the existence of the self before, and after, its present embodiment.

But before we can do this, we must glance at the scientific arguments for the distinction between body and soul. Here we can be brief, for the situation demands little more than an application of the conclusions suggested in the preceding essay. If we have succeeded in purging our theories thoroughly of the Descartian dualism, we are, in principle, ready to deal also with the psycho-physiological dualism which is its modern successor. No doubt, the latter has changed with the fashions of thought sufficiently to discard the Descartian " substances ", and put in their place two series of " phenomena "—a series of psychical processes open only to introspection (its own?), and a series of physiological processes open to public observation like all other physical facts. Descartes, fantastically enough, had made his two substances interact through the pineal gland in the brain—the " seat of the soul ". Modern theory, acutely conscious of the difficulties of this scheme, has generally favoured the happy expedient of a psycho-physical, or, better, psycho-neural, parallelism in a theory according to which mental processes are correlated, one-to-one, with processes in the cerebrum. The main virtue of this theory, in the estimate of its defenders, has always been that it isolates the psychical and the physical series of phenomena completely from each other—subjects them to a theoretical quarantine, as it were, so that neither can infect the other. Each series is regarded as causally coherent in itself, neither as causally related to the other. They accompany each other by a blessed miracle, for, on the theory, it could not, and would not, make any difference to either if the other did not exist at all. This device suited the materialistic temper of XIXth century science, enabling it to undertake the study of the physical world (including living beings) without having to bother about any thing so troublesome as " consciousness ". It shelved consciousness very effectively, without exactly saying, " there is no such thing ". It left a place for psychology, at the price of condemning it to study minds as if, contrary to all the evidence, they were disembodied. In fact, the most plausible argument for psycho-physical parallelism is, perhaps, this that it is an ingenious device for enabling the physiologist to study the bodily machine without reference to feeling, thought, or will, and the psychologist to study psychical processes without considering brain, body, or physical environment. Such a plea for confessed abstractions might be conceded. For every science has the right to abstract according to its needs, and an abstraction, recognised and acknowledged as such, becomes theoretically innocuous. It can no longer be mistaken for absolute truth. It is appreciated for what it is—a convenient supposition or makeshift.

But the question, of course, is whether it is really so satisfactory a device as its defenders represent it to be. We have already noted, in another context, how little it agrees with the function assigned to mind by the theory of evolution, which furnishes the background to all modern natural science. And it is obvious how unworkable parallelism is as a basis for the study of behaviour, be it human or animal, be it from the moral, the legal, or the purely biological point of view. Indeed, the constant recrudescence of interaction theories in some form or other, even at the price of harking back to the soul-substance concept, is evidence that the artificiality and inadequacy of parallelism have

never wholly ceased to be felt and proclaimed. At the present day, dialectician and experimentalist join in their attacks
upon it and, beset from every quarter, parallelism is fast
losing its position as the orthodox scientific formulation of
the relation of body and soul.   But it is not interaction
which is destined to supplant it.   For interaction, even if it
provides for a much closer connection between body and
soul, still has to retain the dualistic distinction between
them.   It may avoid the word "substance", but it will
effectually retain the meaning, for else it cannot intelligibly
state its own position.   If there is anything in the argument
of the preceding essay, the future lies, not with any body-
soul dualism, be it sharp or be it blunted, but with an objective and functional theory of mind, towards which "behaviourism" is leading the way, especially when under the
pressure of its own ideal of a full description of "what the
creature is doing", it is steadily being driven, beyond physiological reflexes in response to immediate sensory stimuli,
to an unbiased study of the behaviour of the creature as
a whole.   The way in which E. B. Holt, more particularly,
is employing the point of view of the whole, and the theories to which it leads him, of the "recession of the stimulus"
and of the reference of behaviour, not only to isolated objects, but to complex situations, are most instructive.[1]   The
study of the self by way of self-consciousness, *i.e.*, of experiences the structure of which is characterised by the differentiation of self from not-self (or what-is-other-than-self),
calls, so we suggest, for a synthesis of the objective and
introspective methods.   Introspection, however, for the purposes of this programme, must be extended from the narrow
meaning, in which it refers to noticing things not ordinarily
attended to, like images or kinaesthetic sensations, to the
wider meaning which it originally bore and in which it is

[1] See, *e.g.*, *The Freudian Wish*, pp. 78.

co-extensive with self-consciousness. In effect, this is done
in James's analysis of the self to which we must now
turn.

James offers his analysis of the self as a study of the
" empirical self ", the " me " or " object-self ". But, it is
not difficult to see that, in effect, his analysis is a study of
the " I " or " subject-self " as well. It is, in fact, a study
of the latter through the former, or, to put bluntly the principle on which James, with sound instinct, proceeds without explicitly realising it:—self-consciousness means self-
identification and self-differentiation. If we refuse to work
with this principle, we are left with the empty tautology " I
am I ". But the truth is that, concretely, what I am is revealed, or expressed, for me as well as for others, in my attitudes and behaviour towards the world in which I exist.
Every such attitude or behaviour, considered now from the
point of view of self-consciousness, is seen to be an act of
identifying myself—yes, quite literally my " self "—with
something, or turning myself away from it. Obviously, this
principle covers the facts on which the body-and-soul theory
of the self relies. What my body does, I do; when it is
hurt, I am hurt; when it dies, I die. When my soul is
joyful, I am joyful; when my will is stubborn, I am stubborn; when my thoughts are clever, I am clever. But identification is meant to be taken here in a further and less
superficial-sense. *I am what I identify myself with,* in such
senses as what I am interested in, what I give myself to,
spend myself on, even sacrifice myself for, still feeling myself realised in the very giving. Spending myself, I may
spend my money, my time, my physical strength, my
thoughts, my knowledge—in short, to be a self is to lead
a life into the tissue of which the world enters in countless
different ways and degrees, becoming thus *my* world, and
making *me* what I am. In saying this, we are but pushing
a step further that dynamic concept of mind, or soul, sug-

gested in the preceding essay. A self, even more obviously than a mind, is a unique and individual focus or concentration of elements of the universe.

True, James does not explicitly frame his theory in just these words, but any one who, with this clue, will turn to James's text, will, we suggest, find this principle staring him everywhere in the face. Even the body's place in the self is "fluctuating." "Our bodies, themselves, are they simply ours, or are they *us?* Certainly men have been ready to disown their very bodies and to regard them as mere vestures, or even as prisons of clay from which they should some day be glad to escape." [1] Does not this throw a flood of light on the angle from which the facts, travestied in the two-substance theory, should be approached? That theory stereotypes one of the fluctuations in self-consciousness, and exaggerates it, first, into a standing antithesis of factors in the self, and, next, breaks the living self into two disparate metaphysical figments. "We are dealing with a fluctuating material, the same object being sometimes treated as a part of me, at other times as simply mine, and then again as if I had nothing to do with it at all. *In its widest possible sense,* however, *a man's self is the sum total of all that he can call his,* not only his body and his psychic powers, but his clothes and his house, his wife and children, his ancestors and friends, his reputation and works, his lands and horses, his yacht and bank-account." [2] And then follows the principle, as near as James in explicit statement comes to it: "All these things give him the same emotions. If they wax and prosper, he feels triumphant; if they dwindle and die away, he feels cast down." There is no need to recapitulate the details of an analysis, so well-known, so deservedly famous, carried through with such wealth of illustration and insight. One may not think the classifica-

---

[1] *Principles of Psychology,* vol. i, Ch. x, p. 291.
[2] *Ibidem.* James's italics.

tion of the " constituents " of the self as (a) the material
self, (b) the social self, (c) the spiritual self, (d) the pure
ego, very happy, the last rubric especially not being on a
level with the others, but it is impossible not to admire the
masterly handling of such topics as self-feelings; self-seeking
and self-love; the rivalry and conflict of Mes; the hierarchy
of Mes, *i.e.*, the need for some organisation or order among
the fluctuating constituents of the self according to their
worth.   It will suffice to set down a few passages, picked
almost at random, to show the principle everywhere at work
in James's analysis.

   " We so appropriate our clothes and identify ourselves
with them that there are few of us who, if asked to choose
between having a beautiful body clad in raiment perpetually
shabby and unclean, and having an ugly and blemished form
always spotlessly attired, would not hesitate a moment before making a decisive reply." [1]   " When they [our rela-
tives] die, a part of our very selves is gone.   If they do
anything wrong, it is our shame.   If they are insulted, our
anger flashes forth as readily as if we stood in their place ".[2]
" The parts of our wealth most intimately ours are those
which are saturated with our labour.   There are few men
who would not feel personally annihilated if a life-long con-
construction of their hands or brains—say an entomological
collection or an extensive work in manuscript—were sud-

----

[1] *Loc. cit.,* p. 292.
[2] *Ibidem.* During the campaign for the first liberty loan a Boston
newspaper published a whole page appeal from which I quote a few
phrases. "This is *your* war, *your* Congress has declared war upon
Germany. Wake up to that, Mr. Citizen. . . . *You* go home and think
over *your* relationship to *your* government. *You* will find that *you*
cannot separate *yourself* from the State. *You* will find that *you* and
your government are identical. When the government, which *you*
created, declares war, *you* declare war. And you are obligated to do
your part. . . ." (*Boston American,* June 11, 1917). This is sound
philosophy in a place where it is unusual to find any philosophy whatever.

denly swept away." [1] Loss of possessions brings "a sense of the shrinkage of our personality, a partial conversion of ourselves to nothingness." [2] "We do not show ourselves to our children as to our club-companions, to our customers as to the labourers we employ, to our own masters and employers as to our intimate friends." [3] Further on, under the heading of "self-love", we read: "To have a self that I can *care for,* nature must first present me with some *object* interesting enough to make me instinctively wish to appropriate it for its *own* sake, and out of it to manufacture one of those material, social, or spiritual selves, which we have already passed in review." [4] And, then, comes another attempt at the principle: "*The words* ME, *then, and* SELF, *so far as they arouse feeling and connote emotional worth, are* OBJECTIVE *designations, meaning* ALL THE THINGS *which have the power to produce in a stream of consciousness excitement of a certain peculiar sort.*" [5] A page or two further on James concludes that the self in "self-love" is never the pure ego, the abstract principle of conscious identity. It is "simply my total empirical self-hood again, my historic Me, a collection of objective facts." [6] Why, for example, do I claim respect and resent disdain? "It is not as being a bare *I* that claim it; it is as being an I who has always been treated with respect, who belongs to a certain family and "set", who has certain powers, possessions, and public functions, sensibilities, duties, and purposes, and merits and deserts." [7] In almost so many words, James finally declares that the self is co-extensive with the range of things in which it takes an interest, which elicit its feelings, determine its conduct. Nor ought we to forget in this brief survey the startling pages [8] in which James ex-

[1] *Loc. cit.,* p. 293.
[2] *Ibidem.*
[3] *Loc. cit.,* p. 294.
[4] *Loc. cit.,* p. 319; James's italics.
[5] *Loc. cit.,* p. 319; James's italics.

[6] *Loc. cit.,* p. 322.
[7] *Ibidem.*
[8] *Loc. cit.,* pp. 295-305.

plores the innermost "self of selves" and finds it to consist of "*a collection of* (feelings of) *motions in the head or
between the head and throat.*"[1] They are the relatively
permanent core or nucleus of what each is conscious of as his
self. This both assigns a central position in the self to the
body, and traverses all attempts to cut the self into body
and soul and identify it essentially with the latter, divorced,
or at least divorcible, from the former.

The principle, then, on which James's analysis explicitly
or implicitly rests, appears to be perfectly sound. Change
my world and you change me. Introduce fresh objects
into my experience and I become a being of new feelings,
thoughts, actions. Everything is, or becomes, a constituent
of me in which I am positively or negatively interested, so
that my feelings are coloured by it, my thoughts are occupied with it, my actions directed towards it—technically
put, so that all these are a function of it. Or, as we put it
above, each self is a unique focus or concentration of elements in the universe, entering into it, occupying it, making
it in varying degrees what it is. And as we found James
incidentally recognising, there is no giving any account
of the " I " apart from the " Me ". Vain is the attempt
to seize and inspect the subject-self as distinct from the
object-self. For " I " am what " my " interests make " me,"
every interest being an identification of " my self " with some
object in the world of my experience of which my body is
the centre. The identity of the subject-self, to borrow
James's apt phrase, is not substantial, but *functional*.

Recent philosophical literature appears to show only
one serious challenge to this analysis from the same basis
of introspection, or rather self-consciousness. This is to
be found in Professor John Laird's *Problems of the Self*.[2]

---

[1] *Loc. cit.*, p. 301; James's italics.
[2] See especially chs. ii, iii, xiii.

Laird tries to show that the body is not part of the self, that the self is essentially soul, and that the soul, being a " unity of experiences ", may be called a " psychical sub-stance ". The theory is built on the analysis of every experience into an object and a mental act, the latter term covering feeling, volition and cognition. If this be granted, the principle may be laid down that objects are *for* the self, experiences are *of* it. The " being ", as Laird likes to say, of all experiences is to refer to objects. This reference to objects is for him " the only common characteristic of that which is psychical." [1] It follows at once that the body, as object, is *for*, not *of*, the self; an argument which Laird supports by polemic against the James-Lange theory of emotion, on the ground that it mistakes bodily sensations, *i.e.*, the objective data to which the internal sense refers, for the apprehension of them. The latter alone is psychical and forms part of the self; the former are part of the body, which is the self's most constant object and, in a sense, also its instrument.

The argument, of course, collapses if the initial analysis of experience into object and act be denied, by which alone Laird is able to evade the full force of James's theory. Now this analysis has been, and reasonably can be, denied.[2] But it is even more instructive to notice how close, pressed by the logic of the facts, Laird comes to admitting James's analysis. " Are the men whose lives radiate out towards other things and other persons less really selves than those who try to shrink into some unapproachable crevice of private being? Surely the facts are otherwise. To understand the self it is best to go outside it and consider its influence and the range of things which it contemplates." [3]

[1] *Problems of the Self*, p. 33.
[2] It is denied, *e.g.*, by many American neo-realists, see preceeding essay, pp. 229-31.
[3] *Loc. cit.*, p. 94.

" The mind grows as the objects revealed to it grow. It is not more of a unity than what it knows, nor is it less of a unity. It does not overlap its object but is co-extensive with that object." [1] " An experience is a reference to an object . . . it varies as the object varies, and to define it or to think of it, without reference to its specific object is plainly impossible. . . . Our private experience shows itself in the things and events to which it refers. These things and events are not ourselves, though we would not be ourselves unless our experiences were directed to them." [2] In such passages as these Laird, almost against his will, becomes a witness to the necessity of the view which his explicit theory compels him to reject.

(2) From the constituents of the Self we must pass to the vexing problem of personal identity.

Here, again, James's masterly commonsense shines like a bright beacon-light through the fog of dialectics. We cannot do better than gain a starting-point for discussion by quoting him: " This consciousness of personal sameness may be treated either as a subjective phenomenon or as an objective deliverance, as a feeling, or as a truth. We may explain how one bit of thought can come to judge other bits to belong to the same Ego with itself; or we may criticise its judgment and decide how far it may tally with the nature of things." [3] This puts the problem fairly and squarely. The " fact " of identity is to be examined by tracing the judgment of self-identity to its grounds; by exhibiting the factors in experience on which it rests. James is right, too, when he goes on to declare that " There is nothing more remarkable in making a judgment of sameness in the first person than in the second or third," [4] and

[1] Loc. cit., p. 223.
[2] Loc. cit., p. 247.
[3] Principles of Psychology, vol. i, p. 331.
[4] Ibidem.

that, in fact, the judgment of self-identity is but a special case of the judgment of identity in general.

This gives us the clue for our argument. Like all judgments, identity-judgments may be true or false. With the truth or falsity of any particular judgment in a given case we are not concerned. But we are concerned with analysing in general the conditions under which true identity-judgments may be arrived at. There are two platitudes which commonly loom large in discussions of this problem, but which do not advance the argument at all. One tells us that the judgment, x is identical with y, is true when there exists a " fact ", the identity of x and y. But what we want is something more than to be told that a judgment is true if a corresponding fact exists, and false if the fact does not exist. We want to find out what the empirical evidence is on which in identity-judgments we rely, and what logical right we have to rely on it. We want to be shown how the identity of anything with anything else, *e.g.*, of my self of to-day with myself of yesterday, is actually experienced. The other platitude, with a reminder of the school-boy's knife which is still the " same " in spite of a new handle and new blades, tells us that identity is a wholly relative and arbitrary matter, that it " depends on the point of view ". But the answer here is that some points of view are much more fundamental than others, and that in an orderly universe certain types of identity are so prominent as to demand, and receive, universal recognition.

This leaves us with two questions to discuss. The first concerns the fundamental logical issue whether a judgment which affirms that two differents are identical can ever be true at all.[1] The second has to be answered by setting out

---

[1] *Cf.* the phrases used above, " identity of anything with anything else"; " identity of *x* and *y*."

the empirical factors which enter into judgments of identity, and more particularly of self-identity.

As it happens, there is an empirical fact through which we are all made familiar with our first, the logical, issue. This fact is the fact of change. For anything to change is for it to become different and yet to remain the same. " It " becomes other than it was, and yet is still " it ". The dialectics here possible have been explored almost from the dawn of philosophy—our bare allusion to them will suffice to recall them. But the difficulty cuts very deep. When we probe it to the bottom, we are brought up against nothing less than the question, whether judgments conforming to the standards of consistent thinking can be made concerning the empirical world at all—or whether there is a fundamental gap between the data of experience and the logical realm of pure reason. Can we, in short, discover in the empirical world a rational system or can we not?

Now when the problem is brought home to us through the experience of change, there is an undoubted temptation to cut the knot by saying that only the absolutely unchanging can be, and be judged to be, identical with itself. And when we follow up this notion, we are, by the same logic, driven on to the conclusion that nothing but the absolutely simple, homogeneous, unrelated, can satisfy this prescription. But when we try to apply this concept to empirical objects, there appears nothing in the whole " choir of heaven and furniture of the earth ", from our " selves " down to the grains of sand on the shore, which is thus simple, homogeneous, unrelated, unchanging. This is certainly true of the self. We have seen how its constituents are fluctuating. Stability, no doubt, it has, but it is a dynamic stability, a self-maintenance in change, responding differently to different situations. But this is precisely the concept which, on the principles of the identity-logic, we must at all costs eschew. Even on the body-and-soul theory no simple, self-identical kernel for the self can be found. Consider the body's mobility; its modifications from infancy to old age; its decomposition after death; its constant metabolism. There is nothing in it on which we can lay a finger and say, " Though all the rest change, this is now what it always was and ever will be." The same result, no less obviously, is yielded by an analysis of the stream of consciousness. Hume has settled that, once and for all. It avails nothing here to plead that surely it is possible to have the same thought twice. The answer is, the second thought is another thought,[1] similar perhaps to the first, but not the same. Repetition yields similars, not identities. By this logic, as Hume clearly saw, there is no justifying any empirical judgment for, in some way or another, they all assert an identity between differences. Yet for all that this logic tells us that no two experiences can possibly be more than similar, we identify them by saying that it is the " same " object we experience on both occasions, and the " same " self, too, which experiences. The issue is clear. On the logic of abstract identity, of the principle that identity is identity, and difference is difference, and never the twain shall meet, all the thinking embodied in judgments about empirical matters of fact, is fundamentally inconsistent and illogical. Every empirical judgment is a slap in the face of the law of contradiction, an offence against reason. Either this, or——?

Well, the alternative is another sort of logic. The consequences of the identity-logic are plainly devastating except, perhaps, in the field of pure mathematics. As measured by its standards, the whole body of natural sciences, consisting as it does of statements of empirical matters of fact, requires to be either condemned or re-interpreted out of all

[1] *Cf.* also W. James, *Principles of Psychology*, vol. i, p. 480.

recognition. Or, else, we must explore the possibility of framing a logical theory which starts from the hypothesis that scientific judgments are rational, and makes it its business to formulate the standards actually used, and recognisable in them. In other words, we must adopt a logic of identity in difference, or of concrete universals. This is the substance of Kant's reply to Hume. Its principle is to treat every judgment concerning empirical facts as a " synthesis " of different data. Synthesis means identification; and every identification rests on a universal (or " category "). In other words, it recognises, or acknowledges, an identity in difference.[1]   In detail, judgments may be mistaken. But the judgment-function as such cannot be mistaken. We have no basis outside of it from which to criticise it. We can but trust it, as we do, both in practical life and in science; and, in philosophy, too, which is capable of endorsing this confidence against sceptical doubts. On this logic, which is the logic on which throughout these essays we have taken our stand, judgments of identity, *i.e.*, judgments identifying *bonâ fide* differences as elements in some form of universal, cannot be challenged as a class. A given judgment may be a case of " mistaken identity ", but the recognition of identities in the multiplicity of empirical differences is of the very essence of that advance in knowledge, which reveals the universe progressively as an orderly and rational system.[2]   Physical " things " and " selves " are such identities, or universals, though they stand on different levels in the order of the universe, and differ in the way in which

[1] That Kant made the categories "subjective", by calling them "forms of the human understanding" was, no doubt, a mistake. They belong to the "objective" structure of the universe, acknowledged in judgments.
[2] William James's struggles with the logic of abstract identity, and his revolt against it, though it took him to Bergson rather than to Hegel, will always remain instructive for students of philosophy. *Cf. A Pluralistic Universe*, Lectures III, V, VI, VII.

they appear, and come to be recognised, in experience. But there is, on the identity-in-difference logic, nothing illogical or irrational in the judgments which, following empirical clues, identify " this " and " that " as the " same ". " I am I " must, in principle, admit into itself both " I am this " and " I am that ", provided a distinction is introduced which prevents " this " and " that " from conflicting with each other. I cannot be both well and ill at the same time, but I who am well to-day may be ill to-morrow, and truly judge that both conditions belong to " one and the same " Me.

So much for the principle. It remains to say a few words on the evidence, on the " experience " of identity. James's analysis makes identity a conclusion from " resemblance " and " continuity ".[1] This clearly will not do. Similarity is precisely not identity. We need two distinct things, two particulars, in order to have similarity. We need only one, though this one capable of existing in different contexts and of undergoing change, in order to have identity. One self may be called similar to another in so far as both are selves, *i.e.*, members of the class " self." But a self is not similar to itself, for it is not a class of similar members at all—Russell's attempt to uphold the contrary notwithstanding.[2] Again, continuity will not do any more than similarity, partly because it would only be available as evidence in the form of memory, and memory is both fragmentary and fallible, partly because, in any case, experience suffers recurrent interruptions in sleep, so that at best continuity would not supply evidence for identity during more than a single stretch of working hours. In what, then, does the experience of identity actually consist? What is the evidence on which the judgment of identity rests? " Just as the concept blue ",

[1] *Principles of Psychology*, vol. i, ch. x, p. 334.
[2] *Principles of Mathematics*, Appendix B, § 497, "a person is a class of psychical existents."

writes Professor De Witt Parker, " has been derived from blue experiences, and so must apply to the like, so the meaning of identity has been acquired as a reflex of personal identity experiences. It means, aboriginally, a certain feature of experience and so must be true of it." [1] The experience of identity, Professor Parker goes on to argue, is given by the recurrence of what is actually the same experience on successive occasions. This, as he clearly recognises, is possible only if we are prepared to abandon the prevailing Humian view that one and the same experience can never be repeated, that experiences are fugitive, and that so-called repetition must refer to a second, similar, experience.[2] Are there instances, then, of the same experiences recurring? Parker instances the use of the same concept on different occasions, the concept even being modified and enriched by the fresh cases to which it is applied; the persistence of the same interests in the individual's life; the carrying out of the same plan through varied activities extending, it may be, over a long period of time;[3] the recurrence of the same imagery. These illustrations, undoubtedly, supply the kind of identity which is wanted, but they hardly quite bear out Parker's programme of showing that the same " experiences " (as distinct from experiences of the same " objects ") recur. Perhaps our difficulty is merely verbal. But " experience ", especially when thus set over against " object ", suggests an act or event, and it is not easy to see how anything into which time enters so essentially as it does into acts and events, can be " one and the same " on diverse occasions. The clue to the correct analysis of iden-

---

[1] *The Self and Nature*, p. 43.

[2] The discussion of Personal Identity in Professor Parker's *Self and Nature* (Ch. ii) seems to me the best in current literature, and I am glad to acknowledge here how much I owe to it.

[3] *Cf.* my paper on *The Analysis of Volition* in *Proceedings of the Aristotelian Society*, vol. xii (1912-13), p. 156 ff., where the same point is made.

tity would seem to be suggested rather by some such passage as this: " The universal, as possessed by the mind, is essentially a system or habit of self-adjusting response or reaction, whether automatic or in thought, over a certain range of stimulation.   An acquired skill, such as that of a cricketer, is a good example." [1]   Considered as acts, the cricketer's strokes are merely similar, or of the same kind, for balls of the same kind, but his skill in dealing with each ball appropriately according to its kind is identical, as a system or motor-set for producing acts adjusted to their occasions.   It is a universal, and a concrete one; an existing and embodied individual system, not a mere class.   In the same way every habit secures identity, or, at a higher level, every principle of conduct or judgment which the self applies whenever occasion arises.   It is clear that Parker's examples, the concept, the interest, the plan, are identities in this sense.   They are not recurrent events; they are growing and modifiable systems of response, issuing in action on successive occasions.

From this point of view, too, we can interpret the doctrine that identity is a matter of degree—that a man is sometimes more himself, sometimes less; sometimes at his best, sometimes below it.   It depends how much of the organised self, considered as a complex system of responses, comes into play.   In this sense Parker can rightly say that the amount of identity is " great when a man puts all his emotional energy into some task which requires the use of his whole past experience, the total resources of his memory and learning; then, as we say, he is most himself; it is little when, in a light moment of gaiety, he forgets himself, feeding on new impressions.   It is great again in constancy and continuity of work and affection, and less in disloyalties and infidelities." [2]

[1] B. Bosanquet, *Principle of Individuality and Value*, p. 40, *note*.
[2] *Loc. cit.*, p. 50.

(3) Having tried to argue that the consciousness, and judgment, of self-identity, so far from excluding differences within the self, consist in their identification, or synthesis, we are free to bring our discussion of the self to a conclusion with a consideration of the way in which the fluctuations of the self are influenced by its relations to other selves.

How far is a contrast, varying from mere difference or otherness to hostility, between self and not-self a necessary condition of self-consciousness and, therefore, of self-knowledge?

It is worth observing, in the first place, that a man's self is, in the main, not of his own making, nor, for that matter, was it consciously planned, such as it is, by any other human being. A man's self, however much in detail it may have been deliberately shaped and moulded by his own will and purpose or that of others, is yet, in the main, a thing of natural growth—in origin and development quite literally the product of forces largely beyond our control, if not beyond our present comprehension. Even when a man can be said to have been deliberately begotten by his parents (which is hardly the rule), they certainly had no provision or intention that he should be just the person he turns out to be. Not even the sex of the child is under the control of the parents' will, nor how much of their qualities, physical or mental, he inherits. After birth, deliberate training does much to mould the self, but in its response to, and absorption of, educational and environmental influences, it still is always growing into a unique personality, the pattern of whose intellectual and moral character no general formula enables us wholly to forecast. In fact, every man has to learn, and discover by experience, what is the nature of his own self, just as his parents and fellows have got to discover it. It is a plain fact of everyday life that men are full of surprises and revelations, not only to others, but to themselves. Every man has to find out, largely by trial and error, what are his capacities, physical and intellectual, and what their limits; what is his temper, and how to control it; what is his strength and his weakness; to what temptations he had better not expose himself, and what tasks he may confidently attempt. Moreover, this kind of self-knowledge, acquired in familiar routine situations, is liable to be upset by exceptional crises which may, for good or evil, reveal hidden depths, astonishing or shocking, not only onlookers, but the agent himself. Great excitement may put a man " beside himself," and in this condition he may rise far above, or fall far below, his " normal " self. Thus the self is plastic within wide limits. It is made what it is in part by the influences which press upon it. It is also in part made by itself—made, one is tempted to say, by what it succeeds in making out of its given endowment and all the shaping forces of education and circumstance in response to which it grows to its stature. As always, we find the self double-edged—self-made and world-made.

The same conclusion may be confirmed by another line of reflection. One's experiences are one's own: on any view they are of the very tissue of the self. Yet, if calling them one's own means that one is somehow their source and author, that they are the product of one's activity, it soon appears that in this sense the self has very little claim to them. Of sense-experiences this is commonly acknowledged. They are given to us. They come unsought. They even force themselves upon us. To them we are passive, as compared with our activity in thinking. For our thoughts are, as commonly, considered to be of our own making, or at least under our control, obedient to our will. Yet is it not true that, fundamentally, thoughts *come* to us, are *given* to us, *happen* to us as much as sense-experiences or feelings?

In the striking German phrase, *Sie fallen uns ein*. If we did not reserve the term " inspirations " for exceptionally striking and novel thoughts, we might fairly apply it to all thoughts whatever. Indeed, it is in many ways easier to control one's sense-perceptions than one's thoughts. I can move out of hearing of a disturbing noise, but I cannot so easily shake off a haunting memory. In a familiar environment I can largely, by suitable movements, determine what I shall see, hear, feel, and taste, but thought is proverbially like the wind which bloweth where it listeth. Even voluntary thinking is no exception. I may set myself, as now, to meditate on the Self, but I cannot choose or determine beforehand what thoughts shall come to me, or whether they shall be of any value. Volition can do little more than set the stage, but the right actors may capriciously refuse to appear. I may in vain strive to recapture yesterday's brilliant idea. Any name but the one I want to recollect may occur to me. Nay, the very fact that my will is what it is, is ultimately not my doing, but an expression of my nature, such as it is, reacting on my world, such as I find it. Again, I (*i.e.*, all that I am and say and do) radiate effects in all directions, few of which I intend, of most of which I am unaware, and none of which I can follow beyond a short distance. Every self is inextricably interwoven with the tissue of its world in all its variations and fluctuations.

And so again the greater purposes and achievements of this world in which I interest myself and with which I identify myself, are not of my making or of that of any other single man. The things in which many minds, and many successive generations of minds, coöperate—states and churches; sciences, arts, philosophies—these grow in and through human minds, yet as by an impulsion of their own. Men's minds are the organs of growth for them—very literally " organs ", through which, we may boldly say, the

universe is working. The organ's " own " will and wisdom
count in the result only so far as they express, or are a
function of, the forces of the universe. It is, indeed, the
fashion to speak of these things as man-made. But if
" made " means designed by men just so, this way of speaking is hardly even a half-truth. And if it does not mean
this, what more does it mean than that they come about
through men and fill their lives with such value as they
have? We may speak of " building up " a science. But
neither its principles nor its details were foreseen. Rather
they were discovered, and came to their discoverers as
revelations. We give credit to the inventor for his inven-
tion, but to him it was an inspiration. In fact, " man-made "
is appropriate only when it is a question of the attribution
of authorship for social purposes. It has no bearing on any
deeper theory of man's relation to the world of which he
is a part. A man's thoughts and works are his property
which he may sell and for which his fellows may give him
credit and reputation, but these social rights and claims of
ownership do not alter the fact that the intellectual power
which makes one man a great artist, another a great scientist,
and so on, is to each of them a gift not of his own devising
or procuring. Apart from social claims, the experience of
artistic conception or scientific discovery is truly described,
not by saying " I am the maker of this thought ", but
rather, " This thought takes form, or shapes itself, in me ".
Am I active in this or passive? It is my activity, no doubt,
and not another man's, but as between me and the truth or
beauty which inspires me, it is *its* activity *in m*e. It is
characteristic that the thinkers of the Middle Ages were
wont to speak rather of being " passive " in thinking. Passivity expressed for them the sense of being instrumental to
something which, whilst making the thinker great among
men, yet is acknowledged by him to be greater than him-

self. "Not I, but God that worketh in me." What is here " self ", what " not-self "? If we are to use these terms at all, we shall have to say that the destiny of a self lies in "transcending itself ", *i.e.*, in surrendering itself to, and identifying itself with, the universe. This may be traced, *e.g.*, in such a common experience as choosing one's career. We may set it down to natural bent or interest on the one side, and circumstances and opportunity on the other. But " bent " or " interest " are but names for the fact that some aspect of my world lays hold of me and makes me its instrument. A man's choice of science as a career may be due, say, to the chance reading of a book which fascinated him by its line of thought and suggested a field of work to which his whole being responds. Does he choose or is he chosen? Does he select the problem or does the problem select him? The man will probably say that the problem " took hold " of him, that the thought " possesses " him. He is, and makes himself, its willing and devoted instrument for working itself out. The career he chooses is his " calling ". This applies no less to those lives which are devoted to distinctively social service or to social reform and reconstruction. The individual's mind and will is the medium through which the social world strives to perfect itself.

The philosophical interest in all this is that the individual self is once more seen to be double-edged. Tennyson's triumphant " For man is man, and master of his fate " gives one edge. The view that we are nothing but " God's puppets " gives the other. The whole truth is neatly summed up in Bergson's *Nous sommes du réel dans le réel.* From this principle flows the spiritual structure of all self-consciousness. It implies both identity and difference of " self " and " world ". As a part, the self is distinguishable, not from, but within, the whole, and the whole so far con-

fronts the self as an overwhelming, and in some moods as a
foreign or hostile, " Other ".   But the part also belongs to
the whole, and the life of the whole pulses in the part; and
this sense of being at one with, or at home in, the universe,
is the complementary oscillation in the experience of being a
self and, as such, an individual focus of the universe.

CHAPTER X

NOTHING is more striking in modern philosophy of religion than the shift of emphasis from proofs of the existence of God to the effort to understand and appreciate religion, not merely as a historical and institutional phenomenon, but as an essential, and indeed dominant, factor in a fully-developed " life of reason ".[1] The point may be put, with perhaps exaggerated sharpness, in the form of an antithesis. Religion may either be made dependent on the success of demonstrations of the existence of God, or the existence of God may be shown to be revealed and guaranteed by religion.

The former approach may seem, on the face of it, the more plausible. It would appeal to the spirit of an age which has become critical of traditional dogmas and suspicious of being the victim of superstition. It is easy to urge that, if religion is to be justified to reasonable men, they must be convinced first that God exists. Religion is man's relation to God, but what if there be no such thing as God? What if God be merely a figment of the imagination, a survival of infantile stages of human thought, when natural forces, as yet not understood nor controlled, were personified as higher powers, good or evil, and when human safety was thought to depend on conforming to their capricious will or escaping their incalculable wrath? Religious practices and religious beliefs, in fact, the whole ordering

---

[1] I borrow, as best expressing my meaning, the title of George Santayana's well-known series of books, without pretending that he would endorse my use of it.

of life with reference to God, hinge, from this point of view, on the possibility of first showing, beyond any reasonable chance of doubt, that God exists and may be ignored only at inescapable peril to human fortune. Not only to sceptic and atheist has it seemed plausible to argue thus, but even believers have, at times, yielded to the temptation to accept this demand as reasonable. And, thus, " proofs " have been constructed by way of communicating a conviction, which is communicable only on the basis of actual religion, to those who are without that basis or have lost their hold upon it. God as the designer of the best of all possible worlds, God as first cause and creator of the world, God as necessarily existing because his " essence " as all-perfect logically implies his " existence "—there is no need to rehearse again the familiar details of the physico-theological, cosmological, ontological proofs. Divorced from their basis in religion, through which alone the very word " God " has any vital meaning, they become ingenious pieces of dialectics, easily riddled by counter-dialectics, and enabling the critics of religion to argue that a scheme of faith and conduct built on foundations so flimsy has no claim upon the allegiance, or even the respect, of reasonable men.

Far otherwise is the result if we take our point of departure from religion itself, if we approach God through religion, instead of religion through an argument about the existence of God. The crucial importance of Hume's *Dialogues on Natural Religion* and Kant's *Critique of Pure Reason* in the development of the philosophy of religion is just this that, by exposing the weakness of the traditional proofs, they cleared the ground for that fresh philosophical appreciation of religion in which Hegel showed the way, and to which various modern schools of thought are contributing. Technically, this movement may be characterised in several different ways. We may fasten on Hegel's defence, or rather re-statement, of the ontological proof, which rests, at bottom, on the principle that religion has metaphysical value, that it not only helps to reveal the nature of the universe, adds to our insight into it, but that it embodies, like philosophy, the point of view of the whole. " The objects of philosophy are upon the whole the same as those of religion. In both the object is Truth, in that supreme sense in which God and God only is the Truth." [1] Or we may say that theology, as the theory of God, presupposes " acquaintance " with God, and that religion is this knowledge of God by acquaintance. As Mr. C. C. J. Webb puts it: " The great question for the thinker about religion is not *whether God exists,* but rather *what God is.*" [2] For " ultimately our only evidence of the existence of anything must be in our consciousness of it. . . . Thus the religious consciousness is sufficient evidence of the existence of its object. . . . So far as we mean by God no more than the object of the religious consciousness, the existence of God is not really doubtful at all." [3] What is doubted, what may, legitimately in a sense, be doubted, is not God's existence but God's nature. Doubt of God's existence " means the doubt whether what we have been accustomed to call God is God at all. In the last resort of all it means the doubt whether the ultimate nature of reality, if it were known as it really is, would continue to excite the religious sentiment of reverence and worship." [4] Another illustration of the characteristic point of view of modern philosophy

[1] From the opening sentences of Hegel's *Logik,* ch. i, § 1 (translation by William Wallace).

[2] *Problems in the Relation of God and Man,* p. 145. Mr. Webb's writings belong to the very finest work in present-day philosophy of religion.

[3] *Loc. cit.,* p. 141.

[4] *Loc. cit.,* p. 143. It will be noticed that Mr .Webb's position agrees with the doctrine of these essays, that doubting the existence of a thing is doubting the truth of a theory concerning the nature of that thing; see Ch. iv.

of religion may be found in Professor W. E. Hocking's *The Meaning of God in Human Experience,* which, by its very title, proclaims that reversal of approach to which we have been drawing attention. Instead of starting with a defined meaning of " God ", and then inquiring whether that meaning applies to any object met with in experience, the new method seeks to give a meaning to " God " by philosophical examination of *what* experience (which term, of course, in this context includes thought, or, in Hocking's language, " idea ", as well as " feeling ") reveals of the nature of the universe. This is to " know " God and be assured of his existence. This is to *realise,* and make a vital possession of, what the word " God " stands for. And by calling this examination "philosophical " we mean, as explained in the first essay, that it requires not merely a stock-taking, but an evaluation, guided by the immanent dialectic of experience—by that process of correction, completion, deepening interpretation, which takes place when diverse " appearances ", as systems of judgment or theories, are focused together and press for inclusion in a coherent system, standing, relatively to the systems absorbed into it, in the position of " the whole."

Not least has modern psychology of religion reinforced this whole movement, though it is to be confessed that some of our psychologists have made a study of religious experience " from within " unduly difficult for themselves by approaching it with naturalistic or biological categories—anything but examining it on its own ground, or analysing it in its own terms, which is, after all, the only way of understanding it on its merits. Yet the man who was *bahnbrechend* in this field is not open to this charge, and his example may well serve to point our moral. The last chapter of James's *Varieties of Religious Experience* shows how profoundly his study of the forms of the religious consciousness had impressed him with its metaphysical implications. One may feel misgivings about the direction which he gave to his speculations on the nature of reality as revealed through religion, but his general principle is sound. One may not share his sympathy with Fechner's concept of a world-soul, or his opinion that the mind-cures of Christian Science are of special significance for religion and metaphysics. But the truth of his final estimate of religion is independent of these things. " The logical understanding, working in abstraction from such specifically religious experiences, will always omit something, and fail to reach completely adequate conclusions. Death and failure, it will always say, *are* death and failure simply, and can nevermore be one with life; so religious experience, peculiarly so called, needs, in my opinion, to be carefully considered and interpreted by every one who aspires to reason out a more complete philosophy." [1] This, as will have been seen, is the position of these essays, too.

If the efforts of modern philosophy of religion to understand and appreciate religion are themselves to be justly appreciated, two things must be borne in mind.

(a) The first is that, whilst these thinkers care greatly about religion, they care, as a rule, little about the institutional forms of religion, and the special problems which these raise. They think of religions rather than of churches, denominations, sects. They may even be said to be thinking more of religion *as such* than of religions, or of the minutiae of creed and ritual which are so often all that divide religions from one another. In this neglect of church, as distinct from religion, there is probably loss as well as gain, but it is the outcome, at any rate, of an effort to penetrate behind the outward form and body to the spiritual life. Moreover, it

[1] *A Pluralistic Universe,* pp. 306-07.

corresponds to the facts in an age when much genuinely religious thought is driven out of the churches, or, at least, cannot find free development in their cramping atmosphere, and when the reluctance of the churches to abandon traditional forms of words which have become outworn, condemns them to fall ever further behind the best modern thought. If we are to seek the " meaning of God " in human experience, we cannot prejudice the success of our enterprise by starting out with a burden of traditional terms and prepossessions. Philosophers, theologians, and literary men agree in urging that we must re-think, and reformulate too, our concept of God, if we are to deal satisfactorily with the age-old problems in the light of modern knowledge. From Professor A. Seth Pringle-Pattison's *The Idea of God in the Light of Recent Philosophy*, to H. G. Well's *God the Invisible King* and *The Undying Fire*, these experiments, as varied as they are sincere, in re-thinking and reformulating are going on. But, with rare exceptions, the representatives of the churches are holding aloof, and continue to speak, if not to think, of God in terms which " may be not unfairly described as a fusion of the primitive monarchical ideal with Aristotle's conception of the Eternal Thinker ". [1] Here, too, we must look for the reason why philosophy of religion is, as a rule, little interested in interpreting specific dogmas, especially when these, like the doctrines of most Christian churches, are made up of propositions of very different orders, partly purely historical, partly miraculous, partly attributing spiritual significance to certain historical events, partly expressing directly moral or spiritual truths. Moreover, there is much of metaphor and symbolism in the religious language of tradition, the interpretation of which is apt to take the interpreter far away from the more or less literal meaning demanded by orthodoxy.

[1] Pringle-Pattison, *loc. cit.*, p. 407.

And, lastly, the consideration of religion organised in churches is bound to draw the student into problems which cease, in any specific sense, to be religious. They are the problems which we may conveniently sum up under " church-politics "—problems of church-government; problems of the mutual rivalries of churches in the mission-field and at home; problems of the relations of church to state; problems of the entanglement of churches, as property-holding bodies, with the social and economic issues of the time. From whatever point of view these may interest the philosopher, they are remote from those actualities of religious experience in which he seeks to find God. Even Royce is not wholly an exception to this statement. For, although his study of " loyalty " led him in his *Problem of Christianity* to emphasise the social form of experience,[1] and to claim that " the church, rather than the person of the founder, ought to be viewed as the central idea of Christianity ", it is easy to see that Royce's " blessed community " bears the lineaments rather of the ideal " communion of saints " than of any historical organisation enmeshed in the toils of legal, economic, and political relationships. Or, at least, it is only after these meshes and encrustations have been torn off, that it can be made to appear how little the individual can do for his salvation, apart from that spiritual union with others through which alone the evil he does can be atoned. And even then it does not follow that the church of his fathers can be to a given man his blessed community. Royce's plea is a plea for a religious community *as such*. It is not a plea that existing churches, as they stand, are capable of rendering the spiritual services which he values.[2]

[1] See Royce's *The Philosophy of Loyalty* and, for its relation to the *Problem of Christianity*, the preface of the latter book (vol. i, p. vii ff.).
[2] The development of Royce's philosophy of religion would be an interesting subject of study. He would seem to have passed from

(b) Having, so far, considered what we are not to expect from modern philosophy of religion, we must now turn to our second point: what are we to expect?

In answer to this question we may at once crystallise what we have said so far into the affirmation that the student of religion, if he is not to miss the heart of his subject, must himself be religious.[1] To be religious, to know religion from within or by acquaintance, to know what it is to be religious by being it—these are ways of describing the prerequisite without which we may bluntly say that the student will not know what he is talking about. Without it, his thinking will not be, in Royce's phrase, " from the life ". Without it, his knowledge will be an outsider's knowledge— knowledge *about* religion, not knowledge *of* it. Without it, he will be a helpless prey to the danger which besets all reflection—the danger of over-detachment from its subject in the very effort to get a good look at it.

Further, being religious, his " criticism " of religion, *i.e.*, his effort to understand it, will be sympathetic and appreciative. His aim will be a theodicy, or, rather, as we must say, a justification of religion, an exhibition of its value. His theme will be the " truth " of religion, in the sense of its essence, its meaning, which, in turn, cannot be adequately appreciated except through a study of what religion truly is. For this purpose he must, of course, study it where it is at its best, where its true character is most fully manifest. So studied, he will find it to be a response to, or acknowledgment of, that character of, or in, the world for which we have the words " God " or " divine ". Religion is the consciousness of this character. The presence of this character

a concept of God in which Aristotelian were blended with Berkeleian motives, via the concept of Absolute Experience, to the concept of the Blessed Community.

[1] It is hardly necessary to repeat that "being religious ", here, does not mean being a member of a particular church, or accepting some set of " orthodox " dogmas in their orthodox interpretation.

is by it revealed. The sentiment of worship, reverence, awe, is our response to it in terms of feeling. The judgment of perfection [1] is our response to it in terms of thought.

This does not exhaust, as we shall see presently, the harvest of the philosopher of religion. But even at this point he has got beyond the estimate that the religious sentiment is a mere superstition or make-believe, a mere childish whim to be outgrown. It is not merely " subjective ", but charged with objectivity. A real character of the world is in it seized by us, brought home to us.

And what is this real character which religion is to be valued for revealing? It is that " the real world is infinitely charged with interest and value," [2] indeed that it is our weakness, or limitation, or self-will, our lack of power or understanding which brings moods when the world seems otherwise, and the above too hard a saying to accept.

For, certainly, this hard saying opens up further problems for the philosopher of religion. To acknowledge that *some* things in the universe are charged with interest and value is easy. To show that *all* things are, or rather that the *whole* is—for the value now in question is not to be taken distributively, as attaching to things in isolation, but as belonging to them through the whole of which they form part—this is a task not to be attempted by working with superficial impressions or shallow reflections. If we are to have a theory wrought from the life, then, as Dr. Bosanquet

---

[1] " Perfection ", in anything like its everyday sense, is, of course, an awkward term to use for what is here intended, though there is good authority, both philosophical and theological, for the use. Suffice it to say that 'the judgment of perfection includes such an experience as this: " In the spectacle of Death, in the endurance of intolerable pain, and in the irrevocableness of a vanished past, there is a sacredness, an overpowering awe, a feeling of the vastness, the depth, the inexhaustible mystery of existence, in which, as by some strange marriage of pain, the sufferer is bound to the world by bonds of sorrow." —B. Russell, *The Free Man's Worship* (*Philosophical Essays*, p. 67).
[2] W. E. Hocking, *The Meaning of God in Human Experience*, p. xiii.

puts it, we need not only the best of logic, but the best of life. Indeed, we cannot have the former in these questions of the central and fundamental values without the latter.

The full sting of this problem of the value of the world from the point of view of the whole is concentrated in the problem of evil, and in that solution of it which in the language of religious experience is variously described as salvation from sin, reconciliation or union with God, freedom or escape from bondage.[1] If the student would hold steadily to his path here, he must pass by the plausible despair of pessimism, the more tempting for many an eloquent utterance, and the even more plausible siren-song of meliorism, saying that the only problem of evil is how to do away with it, and calling to him to be its vanquisher. If he holds steadily on his path and learns to appreciate the spirit of religion at its best, he will find that it lifts him equally beyond despair at human impotence, and a too ready confidence in a victory to be achieved by human knowledge and power over a world inhuman and reckless of human ideals. He will find himself encouraged, indeed, to use his resources to the utmost—trust in God does not mean " moral holidays "—but he will be taught also that the roots of evil lie very deep and that his strength is weakness.[2]   Above all, he will be led to seek to understand, and form an estimate of, evil, not taken in the abstract, but in the context of what the best, *i.e.*, the bravest and most understanding, response can make of it.   And the reminder that Christianity is a religion of suffering, will help to teach him that he may miss happiness altogether, if he expects to get it on terms too cheap.

[1] *Cf.* the fourth and fifth books of Spinoza's Ethics, *de servitute,* and *de libertate humana.*

[2] " Sincerely to give up one's conceit or hope of being good in one's own right is the only door to the universe's deeper reaches."—W. James, *A Pluralistic Universe,* p. 305.

The problem of religion, in short, is a problem of confidence and trust in the universe—not the kind of confidence in which a man, hoping God is on the job, takes life easily himself, but the kind which is a source of power, and makes him an effective force for good. It is a confidence without which his heart may well fail him in the fight with evil, but which must be grounded so deep, that even defeats in that fight cannot unsettle it.

Such confidence is neither easily acquired nor easily maintained. It is liable to be assailed, even broken, by doubts, when greatly tried by pain, by sin, by the sense of meaningless effort against meaningless evil.

Such doubts have come to many during the soul-searching days of the war. " God and Christianity raised perplexities in the minds of simple lads desiring life and not death. They could not reconcile the Christian precepts of the chaplain with the bayoneting of Germans and the shambles of the battlefields. All this blood and mangled flesh in the fields of France and Flanders seemed to them—to many of them, I know—a certain proof that God did not exist, or if He did exist was not, as they were told, a God of Love, but a monster glad of the agonies of men. That at least was the thought expressed to me by some London lads who argued the matter with me one day before the German drive in March, and that was the thought which our army chaplains had to meet from men who would not be put off by conventional words. It was not good enough to tell them that the Germans were guilty of all this crime and that unless the Germans were beaten the world would lose its liberty and life. 'Yes, we know all that,' they said, 'but why did God allow the Germans and how is it that both sides pray to the same God for victory? There must be something wrong somewhere.' It was not often men talked like that, except to some chaplain who was a human, comradely soul, some

Catholic 'padre' who devoted himself fearlessly to their bodily and spiritual needs, risking his life with them or to some Presbyterian minister who brought them hot cocoa under shell-fire with a cheery word or two, as I once heard, of 'Keep your hearts up, my lads, and your heads down.' Most of the men became fatalists. . . ." [1]

Here we have the genuine voice of religious doubt. And let it be noted that it is a doubt not engendered by speculation about the miraculous features in traditional dogma, the virgin-birth, the resurrection, the ascension, and the rest; nor, again, by conflicts between the world of scientific theory and the world of religious imagination. The vital, devastating doubts about God's existence and goodness are born of the bitter experience of evil, of the overmastering sense of being engulfed in a world without sense or reason— a world without value.

Against such doubt, proofs of God's existence are powerless, and the best subtleties of theological speculation on the personality of God or his attributes little better than words borne on the wind. Such doubt cannot be overcome by argument, unless argument should 'succeed in mobilising again resources of confidence and appreciation of value which are, for the time being, eclipsed. Perhaps, as the author of the passage seems to imply, the best answer is to carry on, with steadfast courage, some unselfish action, revealing religious confidence more eloquently than words can do.

In any case, we have cited this example of doubt, in order to show that what matters, at bottom, when men believe in " God " or despair of him, is this sense of the pervading value, or worthwhileness, of the world.

The essence of religion is the claim that the world has this value and is, in that sense, divine. To be religious is to respond to, and appreciate, this value, not primarily by

[1] Quoted from an article by the war correspondent, Philip Gibbs.

dint of reflective theory, but in the simple straightforward spirit of one's living. But when life becomes dark and difficult, this sense of value may be lost and prove hard to recover. That it is not easy, nor in every one's power, when the test comes, to hold steadfastly to the attitude of confidence and worship, should not dismay us. *Omnia praeclara tam difficilia quam rara sunt.* A study of religion, above all in the lives of the men and women who have in an eminent sense been inspired by its power and courage, shows that no burden so heavy can be laid upon the human heart as to prevent " God from firing it with his presence."

INDEX

INDEX

Activity, mental, 229.
Adams, G. P., 191 *n.*
Alexander, S., 206, 219 ff., 228, 230.
Analogy, in knowledge of other minds, 207.
Animate, meaning of in biology, 155 *n.*
Animism, banished from science, 176 ff.; not based on analogy, 213 ff.
Antinomy, as a source of problems for philosophy, 15.
Appearances, saving the, ch. 5; 102, 111, 114.
Aristotelian, theory of mind, 203, 235, 237 ff.
Aristotle, 131, 142, 160, 242, 299.
Arrhenius, 198.
Augustine, St., 239 *n.*
Automatic sweetheart, 215 ff., 220.
Autonomy, of a science, 146, 176 ff.

Bacon, Francis, 142, *Novum Organum*, 28, 50, 60.
Bagot, R., *The Hyenas of Pirra*, 96 *n.*
Balfour, A. J., *The Foundations of Belief*, 64; *Humanism and Theism*, 66.
Behaviour, behaviourism, 203, 204, 225, 228, 232, 238 (B.= Aristotle's energeia), 242, 273.
Belief, instinctive, 124.
Bergson, Henri, 72, 96, 102 *n.*, 165 *n.*, 168, 175, *Note* to ch. 7 (pp. 196 ff.), 201, 241, 284 *n.*, 292.
Berkeley, 101, 117, 140 *n.*, 235 *n.*
Bernard, Claude, 146, 152.
Bethe, A., 148.
Boodin, J. E., 230 *n.*
Bosanquet, Bernard, 197, 332; *The Principle of Individuality and Value*, 27 *n.*, 48 *n.*, 185 *n.*, 287 *n.*; *The Distinction Between Mind and Its Objects*, 80 *n.*; *Logic*,

134 *n.*, 136 *n.*, 137, 188 *n.*, 190 *n.*, 192 *n.*, 248 *n.*
Bradley, F. H., 53, 232, 248, 254.
Broad, C. D., 140 *n.*; *Perception, Physics and Reality*, 103 *n.*, 121 ff.
Butler, Samuel, *Erewhon*, 161; *Luck or Cunning?* 201, 267.

Calkins, Mary Whitton, 102 *n.*
Cause, efficient *v.* final, 158 ff.
Chance, in origin of life, 199 ff.
Clifford, W. K., 102 *n.*
Cognitive Relation, 205 ff., *Note* to ch. 8 (244 ff.), 248 ff.
Comte, Auguste, 101.
Consciousness, how dealt with by science, 178; theories of, ch. 8; relation-1 theory of, 206, 230; existence of, 208; as cross-section, or as quality, 225 ff., 242 ff.; as stream, 235; Descartes' concept of, 241.

Dante, 268 *n.*
Darwin, F. S., *Descent of Man*, 68; *Voyage of the Beagle*, 93 *n.*
Data (see also Sense-data), of Philosophy, 14 ff.; Transition to non-data, 36; and interpretation, 77 ff.
Dead, how fitting into classification of living and non-living, 154 *n.*
Descartes, 28, 80, 81, 142, 203, 235, 239 ff., 240 *n.*, 241 ff., 271.
Descriptions, in the theory of unreal objects, 89 ff.
Determinism, 156, 187.
Dewey, John, theory of scientific method in philosophy, 38 ff.; *Democracy and Education*, 40.
Dreams, as unreal, 70, 74, 81, 96 ff.
Driesch, H., 142, 167, 175, 196.
Durée, or real time, 197.

For Product Safety Concerns and Information please contact our EU
representative GPSR@taylorandfrancis.com
Taylor & Francis Verlag GmbH, Kaufingerstraße 24, 80331 München, Germany